GENERAL OF GOD'S ARMY

Also by Henry Gariepy

Names and Titles of Jesus, 1974

Footsteps to Calvary, 1977

Study Guide—Footsteps to Calvary, 1977

The Advent of Jesus Christ, 1979

Study Guide—The Advent of Jesus Christ, 1979

100 Portraits of Christ, 1987

Portraits of Perseverance, 1989

Christianity in Action, 1990

Wisdom to Live By, 1991

★ ★ ★ ★ ★ ★ ★ ★ ★ ★ ★ ★ ★ ★

GENERAL OF GOD'S ARMY

The Authorized Biography of General Eva Burrows

BY HENRY GARIEPY

FOREWORD BY BILLY GRAHAM

★ ★ ★ ★ ★ ★ ★ ★ ★ ★ ★ ★ ★ ★

VICTOR BOOKS

A DIVISION OF SCRIPTURE PRESS PUBLICATIONS INC.
USA CANADA ENGLAND

Copyedited by: Carole Streeter and Barbara Williams
Cover Design: Joe DeLeon

Library of Congress Cataloging-in-Publication Data

Gariepy, Henry.
General of God's army: the authorized biography of General Eva Burrows / by
Henry Gariepy; foreword by Billy Graham.
p. cm.
Includes index.
ISBN 1-56476-044-8
1. Burrows, Eva, 1929-   . 2. Salvationists—Biography. 3. Salvation Army—
History—20th century. I. Title.
BX9743.B877G37   1993
287.9′6′092—dc20   93-7225
[B]   CIP

1   2   3   4   5   6   7   8   9   10   Printing/Year   97   96   95   94   93

DEDICATION

To Marjorie

CONTENTS

PART FOUR: THE WORLD HER PARISH

APPENDIXES:

ACKNOWLEDGMENTS

FOREWORD

General Eva Burrows is unquestionably one of the most respected and influential Christian leaders of our time. She is also an individual of great warmth, selfless compassion, unusual vision, and profound spiritual commitment.

Since her election in 1986 as General and world leader of The Salvation Army, Eva Burrows has broken new ground with her dynamic and able leadership. On one hand, she has reemphasized the spiritual roots of The Salvation Army, and has been responsible for revitalizing its commitment to evangelism as well as to practical social concern. She embodies the spiritual commitment and dedication that led to the founding of The Salvation Army by William and Catherine Booth over 100 years ago.

On the other hand, General Burrows has proven to be a forward-looking leader who constantly seeks new ways and new opportunities to serve others in the name of Christ. As a result, she has won the respect not only of those within The Salvation Army, but of religious and secular leaders around the world.

On one occasion my wife and I had the privilege of being with General Burrows in Scotland, where we were all guests of the Lord High Commissioner at Holyrood House. Again, we saw with what high esteem she is held by leaders in the United Kingdom. Yet at the same time, she is equally at home sitting in a squalid cardboard shack in the midst of an overcrowded slum or holding the hand of a dying AIDS victim in one of the Army's new urban clinics.

This inspiring biography by Colonel Henry Gariepy surveys the fascinating story of this remarkable woman, moving from General Burrows' early years in Australia to her dedicated service in Africa, Britain, Sri Lanka and elsewhere.

9

General Eva Burrows and Billy Graham in an informal discussion at the Army's National Advisory Organization Conference in Washington, D.C., 1992.

But this biography does much more than chronicle General Burrows' life. It also reveals the spiritual foundation upon which she has built her life, and which accounts for her single-minded dedication and service. It will cause every reader to reexamine his or her commitment to Christ, and will challenge us all to demonstrate Christ's love more fully through practical service to others.

Billy Graham

PREFACE

For The Salvation Army, the seven-year tenure of General Eva Burrows (1986–1993) is an era in itself. Under the vision and vigor of her leadership, epochal events took place in the international movement. One cannot come to the writing of such a biography without a sense of the historic significance of the project. Thomas Carlyle stated, "The history of the world is but the biography of great men." Emerson echoed this truth, "There is properly no history, only biography."

In these pages we will trace the providence of God in the making of a General for His Army. Our journey with Eva Burrows will take us from her humble beginnings in the small dusty towns of Australia to her worldwide travels as international leader of The Salvation Army. We will accompany her on a seventeen-year pilgrimage in Africa, and through successive appointments of leadership on four continents.

We will eavesdrop behind the closed doors and into her own mind and soul during the High Council that elected her General. Her influential voice will be heard in the corridors of power on moral issues and injustice. We will witness her virtuoso performances with the media. In her company we will be ushered into historic visits with heads of state as well as go into the "cardboard cities" and shantytowns of the world.

From her story we will also glean insights on the phenomenon of the worldwide Salvation Army. Few, if any, movements in history have matched The Salvation Army's century of giving expression to its motto of "heart to God and hand to man." The ethos and events of the Army during Burrows' generalship are intertwined with her story. One of the disciplines in writing this biography was to keep it a biography, not a history. The criterion set was to refer to the historical data only as it illumines the life and leadership of Eva Burrows. To another writer will be left the privilege of documenting the exciting and extraordinary developments in the international Army during this period.

A biographer is a heavy debtor to many persons and sources. Acknowledgments are listed to those who have shared so generously from their experience and insights. To those who made substantive contributions without which the book could not have been written, I am inexpressibly grateful. Eva Burrows' sisters, Joyce Bugler and Margaret Southwell, and Margaret's husband, Dr. Bramwell Southwell, helped fill in the family background and early years and shared their intimate knowledge of the General. Lt. Colonel Jean Issitt, aide-de-camp to Eva Burrows during the General's seven-year tenure, gave invaluable help and coordination to the research.

Commissioner James Osborne, National Commander of The Salvation Army in the U.S.A., accorded official support to the author for this project. Victor Books blended professional leadership and Christian commitment for a quality production. And to that wonderful friend of the Army and God's anointed messenger to our age, Billy Graham, we are profoundly grateful for his gracious Foreword.

Eva Burrows has been magnanimous in her cooperation and contribution to the project, giving generously of her valued time and providing material and documents. The manuscript was shared with her to ascertain accuracy and avoid gaps of pertinent coverage, but there has been no editorial control over the contents of this book, with the exception of one deletion of a confidential datum. Characteristic of her straightforwardness, she stated that she wanted the biography to be nonadulatory, to "tell it like it is." In addition, she sent word up and down the line that her friends and colleagues should feel free to speak openly with me. No Salvation Army biographer has ever had more helpful and cooperative assistance.

Eva Burrows is authentic in her love for Christ and for people, and is an extraordinary leader. She earns the admiration and respect of all who know her or who would study her life. But Eva Burrows is no plaster saint. The chinks in her armor are not spared, thus presenting her as all the more an authentic model of Christian grace and service.

When another writer was doing research for the biography of Barbara Bush, she was told, "If you look for dirt, you will only find lint." In my research I asked each interviewee and correspondent to identify weaknesses as well as strengths. The "lint" that has emerged will, I believe, not only help to portray "the real Eva Burrows," the person behind the image, but will further show how her extraordinary achievements are attributed to her faith and dependence upon God.

It has been my privilege to observe the life and leadership of Eva Burrows on four continents—in the most formal settings with presidents and ambassadors and famous people, and mingling with the homeless, the down-and-out and people of all ages and walks of life. I have been with the General when she has been the speaker and leader in over 300 meetings, both in the U.S.A. and abroad, and have reported on her leadership and taken over 2,000 photos of her. It has been my honor to accompany her for Congresses in Japan, Korea, and Africa, the latter including a visit to a refugee camp and audiences with two heads of state. I have had opportunity to sit in on her administrative work in her office, visit in her home, and to see her on rare social and informal occasions. I have tested her legendary prowess in Scrabble and found it to be true.

A period of a year was devoted to gleaning core material from interviewees, correspondents, documents, archival records, videotapes, and cassettes. At the outset we established a worldwide network of over 100 persons who could contribute from their knowledge and association with Eva Burrows. This included family, friends, four housekeeping companions who had lived with her, staff who worked intimately with her in the day-to-day routine of her office, those who had been her students in Africa, and former and current associates in her work. These sources provided golden grist for the biographer's mill.

A number of trips were made to International Headquarters for interviews with General Burrows and others in the network. The London venue included the able and unfailingly helpful executive and support staff working with the General, and active and retired persons who had association with her in the countries where she has served. Each person contributed valued facets to this "portrait" of Eva Burrows. Interviews with her former students in Zimbabwe were also productive.

Documents and materials made available by General Burrows and the archival records of the International Heritage Center in London were extremely helpful. A primary source has been the over six years of weekly issues of the Army's international and U.K. publication, *Salvationist,* that faithfully covered her travels, pronouncements, and the major events during her term of office. *The War Cry,* the national publication of The Salvation Army in the United States, provided fruitful gleanings. Wendy Green, who wrote the earlier biographical profile on Eva Burrows, *Getting Things Done,* made available her interview tapes. Photos that help "enflesh" this work were generously shared from the international photo files as well as from private and official sources around the world. The cover photo and several others in the book are by the Army's well-known international photographer, Robin Bryant.

In response to the publisher, the manuscript for this book is scheduled for release three months before the retirement of Eva Burrows as General. She acknowledges that her final months in office will be mostly a consolidation of the initiatives already taken. But being the kind of person she is, there may very well be some noteworthy postscripts for any future editions of this work.

Burrows' unfulfilled dream as she nears retirement is to see the Army return to China. A contact with a high ranking Hong Kong businessman, who is a good friend of the Army, has resulted in a tentative visit to China within a few months of her retirement, to discuss the possible return of the Army to that vast country which hosts one-fourth of the world's population.

Needless to say, this project has been a daunting task, done in addition to the heavy demands of my duties as editor in chief (Army's national publications in the U.S.A.) and busy round of engagements. John Ruskin wrote that the greatest reward of our toil is what we become from it. The writing of this book has been an immeasurably enriching experience. Also, the stern admonition of Milton has loomed over every page, "To serve therewith my Maker, and present my true account, lest He, returning, chide."

My wife, Marjorie, to whom the book is dedicated, bore my absorption with this task with uncomplaining grace and encouragement, and gave her astute editing help. I have prayed daily for the guidance and inspiration of the Holy Spirit and have been grateful for the prayer partners who have supported this project.

This book goes forth with the prayer that it may be something more than an informational work or historic document. May it make a compelling statement, not of what one woman can do for God, but what God can do through one woman. That is the way Eva Burrows would want it.

Henry Gariepy

PART ONE

★ ★ ★ ★ ★ ★ ★ ★ ★ ★ ★ ★ ★

THE EARLY LIFE

1

★ ★ ★ ★ ★ ★ ★ ★ ★ ★ ★ ★ ★ ★ ★ ★ ★ ★ ★

THE PEOPLE'S GENERAL

"A true man of God!"

"Eva Burrows elected General of The Salvation Army." This announcement was disseminated around the world on May 2, 1986. The event catapulted Australian-born Burrows to the highest ecclesiastical leadership position held by a woman. In that office she would lead the world's foremost combined evangelical and social service movement in ninety-seven, or more than half, of the world's 186 countries.

Appended to Salvation Army communiques was the dictum, "God bless the General." In 1977 a similar transmission had an amusing twist. Members and friends of the Army had eagerly awaited the outcome of the High Council's selection. Upon the election of Arnold Brown as General, a terse message was sent to Army territorial headquarters around the world, "Brown elected. God bless the General." In one of those inexplicable slips that pass through the type, the message received was, "Brown elected God. Bless the General."

There was no doubt about the outcome of the 1986 election. It provided a field day for the press as the new General was launched on the international scene with dramatic impact. The media was captivated by her charisma, striking appearance, and poise in interviews. A full-page feature with photos appeared in prestigious *Time* magazine.

Her elevation to the helm of the 121-year-old worldwide movement has generated much interest in a day when women still struggle to hold leadership in the church. Since its inception, one of the hallmarks of The Salvation Army has been its full ordination and opportunity of ministry for women. It is the only major Christian denomination that has more ordained women than men.

Commissioner James Osborne, National Commander for The Salvation Army in the U.S.A. during more than half of Burrows' term as General, stated while introducing her to a public gathering, "Since the election of Eva Burrows as General, The Salvation Army has never been the same." As international leader she would lead her Army to new initiatives and expanded frontiers of conquest for God.

A humorous incident occurred upon Burrows' appointment as territorial commander in Australia in 1982. A woman who heard her preach at a meeting came up to her afterward and said, "When I first learned you were coming as Territorial Commander, my instant reaction was, 'A woman leader—how terrible!' But, having heard you speak today, I can say, 'Now there is a true man of God!' " Quoting the story, a bold news headline read, "High Council Chooses 'A Man of God.' "

General Eva Burrows was elected the spiritual and administrative leader for an international constituency of over 2 million members, 27,000 officers and cadets, and 15,000 corps, in addition to over 4,000 institutions, schools, and hospitals in a vast worldwide network of evangelism and social services. Her Army preaches the Gospel in 116 languages. It has been among the final nominees for the Nobel Peace Prize, and recognized and honored by world leaders and heads of state.

Burrows brought impressive credentials to this high office. Her service on four continents included seventeen years of outstanding missionary service in Africa. She had proved herself to be an inspiring spiritual leader, an able administrator and highly effective communicator. Feminine charm and a compelling presence were further assets in her portfolio of leadership qualities.

But her most dominant characteristic is her legendary rapport with people. She mingles with equal ease among royalty and the "down and out." She epitomizes Kipling's model of one who can "walk with kings—nor lose the common touch." Wherever she goes she gives herself, not to the crowd alone but to individuals in all walks of life. As Tennyson was known as "the Poet of the People," so Eva Burrows became known in the Army as "the People's General."

2

★ ★ ★ ★ ★ ★ ★ ★ ★ ★ ★ ★ ★ ★ ★ ★ ★ ★ ★ ★

FAMILY BACKGROUND

"God saw us all through."

In the crucible of the hardships and sacrificial dedication of Eva's parents, Robert and Ella Burrows, God was forging a future General.

Eva's maternal great-great-grandfather, Henry John Dutton, was a Baptist missionary who in 1839 sailed from England to Jamaica. The old stone church where he preached, built in Clarksville in 1831, still stands. Her great-grandfather, John Robert Chappell, came with his parents in 1848 to Australia as a boy of ten from England. A success in business, he owned 40,000 acres of land with 16,000 sheep and lambs, and built an impressive mansion where the rich and famous were entertained and where Ella spent holidays with Eva's grandmother.

When Eva's grandmother, Maria Frances Chappell, eloped with Adam Watson, a volatile sheepshearer whose parents had come from Ireland, she was disinherited. Following Adam's conversion he became active in The Salvation Army. His fiery disposition made him "an out and out Blood and Fire Salvationist" whose religion on occasion prompted him to jump over the seats shouting "Glory!" Such was Eva Burrows' spiritual heritage from the maternal side of the family.

Love at First Sight

Eva Burrows was not to be the first general in the family lineage. Robert Burrows' grandfather had been a general in the Indian Army. Robert's father was killed by hoodlums on the streets of London, leaving him fatherless at the age of seven. In London Robert joined with those who had thrown rotten eggs and rubbish into Salvation Army meetings. He came to Australia from London at the age of l9 as an irreligious rebel.

Robert arrived in Murwillumbah, New South Wales, with a friend who had migrated with him. On their way to a tavern they strolled past an Army open-air meeting. His eyes fell on Ella Watson, a beauty with black curly hair, brown eyes, and fair complexion. He announced to his mate, "See that girl there? I'm going to marry her."

Some weeks later his mate, sleeping off yet another drunken spree beside the Tweed River, rolled down the bank and drowned. Robert was devastated. He tried to escape his sorrow in alcohol, but to no avail. Once again he was attracted by the band and preaching at the Army's open-air meeting. Pausing to hear a testimony from a young man (who turned out to be his future brother-in-law), he saw that the answer to his need was not alcohol, but Christ.

There in that open-air meeting he knelt in prayer and accepted Christ as his Savior. Little could he, or those in that ring, know the worldwide blessings that would flow from that life-changing decision on a street in a remote corner of the world. The Lord, who had His advent in nondescript Bethlehem and who chose unlettered fishermen for His coworkers, seems to delight in using the obscure and seemingly insignificant to accomplish His purposes.

Robert Burrows became an enthusiastic Salvationist and married the girl he had fallen in love with at first sight. By coincidence they had both been born in towns named Dundee—Robert in Dundee, Scotland and Ella in Dundee, Australia. As a young Christian eager to learn the Scriptures, he memorized Bible verses as well as the Army doctrines while on his job driving a horse-drawn delivery cart. Such was Eva Burrows' spiritual heritage from the paternal side of the family.

The Nomadic Life

Robert and Ella felt a compelling call to full-time ministry in the Army and responded to the challenge. They sold all they owned and with their three children entered the Army's training school in Sydney in 1921. Theirs was the first session that accepted married Cadets with children. Dorothy, the oldest daughter, stayed with her maternal grandparents, and Beverly and Joyce were placed in a Salvation Army children's home during the four-month training period.

On the one free afternoon a week, Mrs. Cadet Burrows hastened to the home to spend a few precious hours with her children.

Robert and Ella Burrows were commissioned as Salvation Army officers, and the nomadic life and hardships of the family are revealed in Robert Burrows' diary entries. "We were stationed at Haberfield for just five months and proceeded to Dee Why. This was another hard corps. The wherewithal to carry on was hard. Finance was very poor. . . . It was a heartbreak. Tired and hungry. To reflect on our early experiences has a dampening effect." Of another five-month appointment in a nearby coal mining community, he wrote, "We held meetings in the Portland Cement Hall used on Saturday nights for dances and on Sunday we had to clear it out to hold meetings. It was usually left filthy with beer bottles and cigarette ends."

With a new baby arriving about every eighteen months, living quarters for the growing Burrows family were cramped and always substandard. Burrows on one occasion wrote to the Chief Secretary to make him aware of the condition of the quarters, which with decrepit furniture was bereft of comforts and necessities. The Chief Secretary replied that he remembered it being "quite nice there with beautiful fruit trees." Burrows wrote back telling him you could not live or sleep on fruit trees. Shortly thereafter they farewelled and went on to Gulgong.

The Gold Miners' Drama

Robert Burrows recorded an incident which further reveals the soil of dedication and faith in which Eva was nurtured. Of Gulgong he wrote, "Being sick and with very little money coming in we were in a bad way. Mother and I prayed that God would help us. The children had what was there in the house for lunch but there was nothing for tea.

"After prayer I went up to the main street. A watchmaker by the name of Mr Brigdon called me over and said he would like to speak to me. He said that there were about fifteen old gold miners out in the reserve about three miles away. He had heard that some of them were very sick and had asked the ministers of the town to go out and let him know the condition of these men. So far, he said, none had condescended to go out, and he asked asked if I would go.

"Immediately I said yes and turned to go home and harness the horse up and drive out. He stopped me and said, 'Here, I was going to give this to the first minister who would go.' It was a ten shilling note. I thanked him and went home and told mother her prayers were answered and gave her the ten shillings.

"I went out to the camp and saw a sight which would have surprised the townsfolk had they seen these poor old men—some in a filthy condition, having laid in their bunks without any attention. I went back to town to get as much clean linen as possible. I think we got some hens to cook. I took out old kerosene tins, old pajamas, etc., boiled the water and washed and changed these men. Mother was with me and helped.

"Then I reported to Mr. Brigdon what we had done. He was amazed and, in the following morning's paper, gave an account of it. The townspeople were wonderful and came forward with every assistance. We no longer wanted for anything in the way of food. We read the Word and prayed with them. One, an old German who had been prospecting all his life, was not long for this world. We talked to him of the love of God and we believe he gave his heart to the Lord. On the Saturday before we left Gulgong, he died and we buried him."

The Long Road to Tighes Hill
Because there was no suitable living arrangement for the family in Gulgong, they were transferred after just seven weeks to Lithgow to work among "hardworking soldiers and coal miners." In this town, 3,000 feet above sea level, winters are severe. The Burrows family was most grateful for the donation of coal from miners who were among the corps soldiers, to keep their fire burning during winter months.

Robert Burrows went to great lengths, or rather "great depths" to understand and minister to the miners. "One night I got dressed in old clothes and a cap with a miner's lamp in front and went down the mine with Alex Lind. My first experience in a coal mine. It was of great depths. . . . I must confess I was afraid and, having spent the eight hour shift there, I was glad to get to the top again. I have since always admired the men who earn their living down in a mine."

From the extreme cold at Lithgow the Burrows family was transferred to the oppressive heat at Broken Hill, where "the dust storms were at times frightening. They could be seen coming from a long distance away, like balls of fire in the sky. To prevent the house from becoming full of dust, the windows and doors would be stuffed with old rags, anything we could find. Even then it could not be kept out. . . . The blight in the children's eyes was a very trying ordeal. The eyes had to be forced open and bathed. A very painful treatment."

Ella Burrows did all the heavy domestic work, including nursing the children through their illnesses and traumas, in addition to her active ministry as a Salvation Army officer in her own right. She faithfully visited the poor and sick, handled problems of corps members, comforted the bereaved, oversaw women's programs, and had an active visitation ministry. She took her turn in the pulpit, managing somehow to prepare sermons amid the bustling activity of a houseful of children endowed with high energy.

Early explorers of Australia often named places in response to the terrain they encountered, such as Mount Difficult, Mount Victory. The appointments for the Burrows bore some of these intriguing names: *Dee Why, Broken Hill, Wallsend, Tighes Hill* and *Fortitude Valley*. Eva's older sister Joyce writes of Fortitude Valley, "Everyone said it took fortitude to stay there because often the people were difficult to manage and finance was hard. Many burdens fell on my mother with a household of eleven." At Fortitude Valley the Burrows were met and encouraged by stalwart Salvationists who enabled them to overcome the otherwise difficult circumstances.

Travel in those days was hard and without comfort or convenience. Shortly before Eva's birth, the family traveled across a vast stretch of Australia from Broken Hill to their next appointment at Wallsend, going by motor lorry for days across a very hot, dry desert. They stayed at a tumbledown inn where during the night the local goats attacked their meager luggage and ate all the food which Mrs. Burrows had carefully prepared.

From Wallsend, Captain Burrows was transferred to Tighes Hill. He recalled, "We spent two years at this corps (an unusual length of stay for the Burrows family)—not an easy corps to manage. . . . We had a good band and stood forty strong in the open air. We labored hard and many souls were saved."

Although not recorded in his diary, a birth—an event of historic proportions for the worldwide Salvation Army—would occur at Tighes Hill.

3

★ ★

A CHILD OF THE DEPRESSION

"We lived a very spartan life."

Eva Burrows, the eighth of nine children, issued her first call for the world's attention on Sunday, September 15, 1929 in the front bedroom of the family quarters in Tighes Hill, a small mining community in eastern Australia. Joyce, ten years old and the oldest sister at home, was her "mother's right arm." Already helping with five younger ones in her care within their cramped quarters, upon hearing the lusty cry of the newborn baby, Joyce exclaimed, "Oh, no! Not another baby! We have enough!"

The midwife hurried to break the news to the father who was conducting a 7 A.M. prayer meeting in the corps building next door. He responded, "I'll attend to it all when I've finished here." Joyce took her little charges out of the house and around the block "to get away from the trauma." Thus the inauspicious entry of Eva Burrows into the world.

Following the prayer meeting, Captain Burrows returned home, held the newborn baby aloft and declared, "I dedicate this child to the glory of God and the salvation of the world." "It was a rather tall order for a little baby," says General Eva Burrows with a grin. Little did the father realize how seriously God would take those words of dedication.

Ella Burrows was thirty-eight when Eva was born. The Burrows' eighth child was named Eva Evelyn, after an aunt named Evelyn and the famous daughter of the Founder and fourth General of The Salvation Army, Evangeline Booth. The birth of Eva and the arrival of Margaret two years later completed the Burrows family with

Dorothy, Joyce, Beverly, Walter, Robert, Bramwell, Elizabeth, Eva, and Margaret.

The year of Eva's birth, 1929, was also the year of the first election of a General of The Salvation Army following the generalship of the Army's Founder, William Booth and his son and successor, Bramwell Booth. Little could that first High Council have guessed during its stormy session, that in the year they were conducting the first election for the Army's third General, its thirteenth General had made her debut into the world.

A Child of the Depression

The year of Eva's birth was also the year of the Wall Street crash. The Great Depression quickly spread to Australia. The fact that Captain Burrows was not able to draw a regular salary, and had scarcely enough to feed, clothe, and provide for his family of ten, did not deter his dedication. Members of the various corps would bring gifts in kind, such as vegetables, fruit, and whatever they could spare. Eva recalls, "We lived a very spartan life. Those days were difficult, but we were quite content and happy."

The living quarters were crowded, with up to ten persons under one roof. At one point their beds consisted of double-spring mattresses on top of six apple cases for the eight children at home. The country houses tended to have verandas and often three would sleep in a double bed on the veranda.

Joyce reminisces, "We had no washing machine, no electric iron, no refrigerator—just ice boxes. Clothes were washed in copper tubs over open fires. At the time we didn't consider these as hardships. We were poor, but oh so happy. We owe so much to a wonderful mother."

Shoes for nine children was a major budget item for which often there were no funds. During the Depression, the soles of their shoes were worn away. Mrs. Burrows made the need a special matter of prayer. One night, while closing the doors of the corps hall following an evening service, in the darkness she felt a hand reach through the opening and place in her palm an envelope. Written on it were the words, "Money for shoes."

The giving of thanks at a family meal would often follow a knock on the door. The family remembers "an angel of mercy" who descended on their front veranda each Saturday with a bag over his shoulder. The children with excited glee would spill out the contents that included a huge cabbage, a leg of mutton, potatoes, greens, and little goodies. The family thanked God for this ministering angel.

They could not afford to buy new clothes but, through the mother's industry and ingenuity, the children were always adequately dressed. Mrs. Burrows made clothing for her brood from hand-me-downs that she would wash, iron, and recut. She would sew into the early hours of the morning. Ella Burrows drew on unseen resources, with her favorite Scripture verse being, "I will lift my eyes unto the hills from whence cometh my help. My help cometh from the Lord."

From this unpromising beginning, in a land known for its harsh, isolated environment, God would bring forth a leader for His Army.

4

★ ★ ★ ★ ★ ★ ★ ★ ★ ★ ★ ★ ★ ★ ★ ★ ★ ★ ★ ★

THE EARLY YEARS

*"From our early days we thought of ourselves
as itinerants for God."*

A dangerous incident occurred when Eva was three years old and the Burrows were stationed at Nundah. Mrs. Burrows, with baby Margaret in her arms and accompanied by Joyce and Eva, went shopping in a large department store. Eva looked charming with her big brown eyes and wearing a cute red hat and a coat with fur collar and cuffs her mother had made for her. At a counter, Joyce let go of Eva's hand to look at something their mother was buying. Then Joyce turned around. "Oh, no! No! Eva!" Eva had vanished. Mother and Joyce were in shock.

Joyce raced through the store. When she reached the large entrance she looked down the road. There was her precious charge, being pulled by a strange woman. Joyce flew through the crowd, caught up with them and grabbed Eva's arm as forcefully as she could. The would-be child thief quickly released her prey and hurried off, never saying one word or looking around.

When Eva was four years old, Commissioner William McKenzie visited Maryborough, where Captain Burrows was stationed, and stayed in the Burrows' home. He was known as "Fighting Mac" for his distinguished service as a chaplain in the First World War, and had been awarded The Salvation Army's highest honor—the *Order of the Founder*.

As the father was introducing each member of the family to his famous guest, he said, "This is Eva." The Commissioner, a man with a huge frame, placed his large hand on Eva's head and said, "Captain and Mrs. Burrows, one day we will have another 'Evangeline' in this little girl. Another Eva." His reference was to the renowned Evangeline Booth, who was then the General. That impromptu prophecy would follow Eva throughout her life, for from that time on she would often hear herself referred to as "another Eva."

Eva made her public speaking debut at the age of four at the local eisteddfod—an annual program for recitations and performances. She stood in an embroidered mauve frock and with unusual poise took first prize for reciting "A Purple Pussycat." Little did her audience imagine that a worldwide speaking career had been launched before them in that modest setting.

Eva's siblings had the normal family spats—and sometimes with gusto. Eva recalls, "We had some great arguments, but as soon as it was over, it was over. We never held grudges or let flareups smolder."

When Eva was about six years old, her family traveled the few hundred miles to Brisbane to hear General Evangeline Booth. Her remembrance of the famous personality is meager except to recall that her father had the duty of looking after the General's personal flag that always accompanied her, with its special gold tassels on top. Years later, Eva would have her own silk flag with its unique gold tassels, a gift from America, as was Evangeline Booth's.

Eva tells of an experience as a young child that illustrates the love and spiritual training she received from her parents. She had taken a penny that did not belong to her. Her father, not knowing this, invited her to sit on his knee. "He held me in his arms and was talking to me when all of a sudden he said, 'What is that sticking in my leg?' I knew I had been discovered and began to cry, saying, 'It is a penny.' 'Where did you get it?' 'I took it from the shopping money.' My father did not scold or beat me. He said, 'That is wrong, isn't it? And Jesus wouldn't be pleased about that, would He?' And then he said, 'Why don't we pray?' And there at the very chair where I sat on his lap, Father and I knelt down and prayed that Jesus would forgive me and help me so I wouldn't do it anymore. Then he hugged me and all was well."

Order in the Home

"My parents moved a great deal," Eva recalls, "so from our early days we thought of ourselves as itinerants for God. We identified with our parents' commitment and were always excited when a transfer would come." Most of the children went to at least ten schools, Eva to eight.

28

With a growing family of nine children there needed to be organization and control. Father Burrows, a strict disciplinarian, ruled his household with military precision. He kept a strap hanging on a hook and one look from him was warning enough. Although strict, Robert Burrows is also remembered as contributing to the laughter and happiness in the home.

Eva says of her parents, "My father carried the discipline and my mother carried the mercy. My father was the head and mother was the heart of the home." Robert Burrows became less rigid in his older years and, after he had retired, he told Eva that if he had his life to live over again, he would have been more flexible.

Domestic duties were well ordered. A roster was posted on the kitchen wall with details for each one: "Dorothy, do ironing. Joy, do washing up. Beverly, polish silver. Walter, rake yard. Robert, run messages." Obedience was the order of the day in the Burrows household. By the time Eva came along there were so many to help that she escaped the domestic routines and spent the time reading.

Officers' living quarters are owned by The Salvation Army. It was customary for inspections to be made on occasion of the work of the Army in that community and of the residences as well. One day Commissioner Charles Duncan came to do an inspection of the Burrows' home and the corps. In a public meeting associated with his visit he remarked, "I have never been in such a well-ordered home. Everything is systematic. How Captain and Mrs Burrows achieve it, especially with all the corps work, I'll never know."

Respect and love forged the family of eleven into a happy and efficient household.

A Bit of "Army Barmy"

The Burrows children took a very active part in corps life and were expected to be examples to all the young people of the corps. There were no vans, buses, or a family car in those early days, so the children would walk to the corps for the various programs on Sunday and during the week. The father required that they attend all the Army meetings. They sat on the front seats during the meetings and if they became sleepy, there was a mat on the floor for them to lie on. Eva remembers enjoying the Army music, playing the tambourine, and even going to the open-air meetings. She wore a navy skirt as uniform and says of those childhood days, "I definitely was a soldier involved with my parents."

Eva at age eight.

Sundays at the corps started with an early morning "knee drill" (prayer meeting). When old enough, the children accompanied their father to these prayer meetings which began at 7 A.M. Then all returned home for breakfast, the "recruits" busy with assigned chores, then back to the Army hall for morning Sunday School at 10 A.M. Each would also be in place for the morning Holiness meeting (worship service) that followed.

Then it was home to dinner, which had been fully prepared on Saturday and simply had to be heated up. It often consisted of stew or soup, then a pudding or pumpkin or grammar pie—a family favorite of dried apples and milk topped with cream. After dinner the family returned to the corps for afternoon programs and a praise meeting. Then home again for tea, occasionally with the popular scones and a jam tart.

Following family tea it was back to the hall by 6 P.M. for the open-air meeting. The full Sunday of meetings came to a climax with the evening Salvation Meeting. Family members took part by reading Scripture, praying, singing solos, testifying. The Burrows had a family band and often took their musical ministry to jail services as well as to Army programs. Their father played the violin, their mother and Joyce played guitars, Beverly played the piano accordion, Walter a saxophone and Eva the tambourine.

From about age ten, each of the Burrows children took their place in the corps band, timbrels, songsters, and open-air meetings. They distributed Sunday School tickets, *War Cry,* and *Young Soldier* magazines. Later they joined the activity of Corps Cadets (Bible study), Girl Guards, Scouts, Sunbeams, Chums, Bible Class. There were also midweek open-airs and meetings. Amid all this activity, school homework somehow had to be done.

Robert Burrows frequently quoted the phrase "Army barmy" which meant a lifestyle totally absorbed in The Salvation Army. "My father was a bit Army barmy," Eva says. "He loved the Army, lived for the Army. His whole life was the Army."

Spiritual nurture went along with bodily nourishment with prayer and Bible reading accompanying the family mealtime. "Around the table," Eva recalls, "we took turns in reading the Bible and praying, and we knew that God was with us in the family." During these growing years Eva and her siblings committed to memory a good repertoire of Bible promises. "The greatest treasure in our family," she says, "was the love we had for each other with Jesus Christ at the center.

"Our home was often filled with the needy," recalls Eva, "drunks, prostitutes, anybody who was in need. As crowded as the household was, there always seemed to be room for everyone. Somehow our meal could include one more person mother had picked up in the streets.

"I remember a woman called Ethel who lived next to the corps. I didn't understand then, but I know now that she must have been a prostitute. Men were always coming and going to her house. She was untidy and unattractive, but my mother loved her. She often took some food to her home and spoke to her over the fence. What a surprise one Sunday morning when into the meeting with my father and mother came Ethel. She had a new dress and was tidied up. Everyone sat in stunned silence as Ethel came in, looking like a brand new person. But it really wasn't the Ethel they had known. She had come to know Christ and her life was changed. With that kind of example in our parents, it is no wonder that we learned to love people and to put God and others before ourselves."

Eva was developing into an assertive child with a strong will, vibrant personality, and zest for life. She was studious, energetic, and always wanted to excel in her studies and in sports. Even during her growing years she was developing what would become known as "a masterful persuasion." She impressed all who met her, and the family watched as she developed her talents and strengths, wondering where she would channel her extraordinary enthusiasm and gifts.

5

★ ★ ★ ★ ★ ★ ★ ★ ★ ★ ★ ★ ★ ★ ★ ★ ★ ★ ★ ★

REBELLION

*"I had no commitment to the Christian faith.
I just let it lapse."*

On September 3, 1939, Australia entered the Second World War.
The Burrows household was not immune to the social and psychic
dislocations of the global conflict. Ella Burrows wept in anticipation
that her sons would have to go to war. The close-knit family soon
became fragmented and life became more unpredictable than it had
been in the safe and sheltered corps environment in which the family
had been nurtured.

The four sons having put their ages forward by one year (unbe-
knownst to the parents), left home to serve king and country. They
gave distinguished service, with Beverly a Major in the Armored
Tank Division, Robert and Walter serving in the New Guinea war
zone, and Bramwell at seventeen years of age in the Air Force flying
sorties in the Pacific War Zone. At home Ella guided the girls in
faithfully sending the boys cakes, biscuits, knitted jumpers and bala-
clavas. The sons all returned, but the emotional scars of war would
remain with them.

Robert Burrows, now a Major, was appointed to serve in the Red
Shield, a program of service to Australian armed forces personnel
away from home. The greater freedom for family members gave
opportunity to make individual choices about life and to experience
the consequences of those choices. Individual personalities emerged
with strong, assertive qualities that would endow a staying power in
time of hardship. The Australians have a name for toughness in a
person who makes good in spite of a hostile environment—"the
Aussie battler." During this time, teenage Eva was coming into her

The Burrows family, circa 1941. The three brothers had joined the military and their mother wanted a family photo before the boys went to war. Robert Burrows is wearing his uniform for service to the military.
Eva, Bramwell, Robert, Walter, Beverly, Elizabeth, Joyce, father, Margaret, mother, Dorothy.

own. Her tenacious and resolute Aussie quality, blended with Christian grace, would become intrinsic to her life and leadership.

During the war The Salvation Army rented a home for the family in the suburb of Windsor at two pounds a week. It was a typical Queensland house with a surrounding veranda, offering more space and amenities, including solid antique furniture, a piano, and a rear garden. The neighboring school was set in ten acres with playing fields that included tennis courts and a swimming pool, which Eva regularly used.

Eva and Margaret traveled by train on Sunday afternoons with their mother to assist in the evening service conducted by their father for the soldiers. The solos Eva sang during the service were especially popular.

Halcyon Days

Eva careened through her teen years at full throttle. Life was full with school, outings, Shakespearean plays, dramas, youth camps, and corps activities. She was described during these years as "an attractive, confident, happy teenager with a vivacious personality."

Qualities were emerging that presaged the leadership she would someday give to a worldwide movement. "As far back as I can remember," Eva says, "I was organizing a group and telling people what to do. The way I related to people at that time was as important to me as how well I did in my studies."

Australia has one of the highest per-capita literacy levels in the world, and Eva developed an early addiction to reading. At night, her sisters would awake to find that Eva was not in bed, but in their father's study with the light on, often fast asleep with a book in her hands. In secondary school her teachers introduced her to the expanded world of literature and she energetically delved into works of poetry, fiction, plays, and novels. Books fascinated her inquiring mind and exposed her to worlds beyond the remote land "down under." She spent so many hours in the school library that she was appointed the librarian.

Eva's final years at home were spent in Brisbane, capital city of the state of Queensland. At this stage, her life revolved around herself and her personal success, with little concern for the heavy load of her mother and other family members. In the last year at school, students were selected by teachers to become prefects. One of the prefects was then appointed Head Boy or Girl. Eva graduated from Brisbane State High School with the honor of having been selected a prefect and the Head Girl, serving as spokesperson for the students and as liaison with the staff. From there she went to Brisbane University at the age of seventeen.

Eva's World Expands

Although the Burrows children aspired to higher education and professional careers, with nine children in the family during the long Depression years, this was not possible. Robert Burrows regarded college as an extravagance their family could not afford and each in turn, from Dorothy down to Bramwell, had to leave school and take a job to help support the family. Eva had shown unusual potential with her diligent study and academic performance and her mother declared, "Eva is going to the university if I have to go to wash clothes to get her there." Robert did not share her enthusiasm and felt Eva should do as the others. The rest of the family was determined that Eva's talents should not be wasted. Joyce recalls, "Mum would have her way and in this she triumphed."

Eva had attended high school on a scholarship and, at the time of her graduation, there were limited scholarships for the university, based on low income and top grades. Eva's diligence in study qualified her for a meager scholarship, and by living at home she could now realize her dream and go on to the university. She turned her scholarship money over to her mother, and unknown to her, Ella put the money in a safe place to be ready for the next door of opportunity that would open.

Eva describes the university as "a whole new experience, like an entirely new world." Previously her family and the Army had been her whole life. Now she moved in expanded circles of friends and culture, and the insularity of being in remote Australia started to break down.

As a university student in Brisbane, Eva spent what for her was a large sum of money to attend her first concert and hear Elizabeth Schwarzkopf as the soloist in the *Messiah*. That experience introduced her to the world of classical music, one that would enrich her life for years to come. Later, on the mission field in Africa, Handel's *Water Music* or Mozart concertos were heard wafting across the compound from albums she played over and over again.

Rebellion

Sport has always been a great obsession for Australians. During her secondary school years Eva became keen on sports. She was a 100-yard sprinter and her athletic skills and enthusiasm led her to be voted captain of the tennis and netball teams.

In these high school and university days Eva Burrows went through a rebellious teenage period. She refused to attend Army meetings, complaining that they were boring. Sports and studies dominated her life and her rebellious attitude became a source of anxiety to her parents.

Her father was serving in the Red Shield with the troops during the war, and his stern paternal discipline was absent. The Burrows belonged to a corps nearby to which Eva went only occasionally. Her mother did not insist that she attend the meetings and Eva stopped wearing the uniform.

There was keen competition to escort this popular young lady to the cinema or school dances. Her popularity with the boys at school social activities took over her life. She recalls, "I rebelled against the family's involvements in The Salvation Army. I thought it too disciplined and binding, and I said I'd never wear a Salvation Army bonnet like my mother. I wanted to make my own plans in life. For a while I wanted to be a teacher or a doctor. Probably because of my father's strict ways, I had no sense of commitment to the Christian faith. I just let it lapse.

"In our childhood," Eva reflects, "we were made to understand that it was God first, The Salvation Army second, and ourselves last. Perhaps my rebellion in part was because we always had to give up what we wanted to do for the good of other people. In my new self-awareness I wanted to do some things for myself."

It has been suggested that "a little rebellion can be a good thing." Later, as General, Eva Burrows looked back on this time as being used of God to better understand the youth of the world, saying, "God used even my rebellion for His purpose and work in my life."

She was a teenage rebel, not to the extent of wild living, but in her rejection of the discipline of the Army and her lack of commitment. It was for her a striking out for independence. But her Damascus Road was just around the bend.

6

★ ★

THE LIFE-CHANGING DECISION

"That moment was the most crucial moment of my life."

A cloud, no larger than a man's hand, came over her horizon—a small forecast of what lay in store—when a student friend invited Eva to go with him to the Christian Union, the InterVarsity Fellowship at the University. In that setting she saw older and intelligent students who impressed her with their serious and enjoyable study of the Bible.

She soon attended a student camp where Marcus Loane, later to become the Primate of Australia, was giving a Bible study on Romans. Her mind was opened to the Scriptures in a new way and she felt the sharp thrust of the sword of the Word into her personal life. "I came to an awareness of disobedience to God. I realized my sinfulness and my need to find grace through Jesus Christ. I thought, 'What must I do to get my life right?' "

In the meantime her father had returned from his service with the Red Shield and was stationed at Fortitude Valley. From that city all nine children had "grown and flown" and Major and Mrs. Burrows continued their nomadic pilgrimage as Salvation Army officers. The Salvation Army Youth Councils was being held and Eva, joined by her sister Margaret, decided to attend. Eva Burrows was about to cross her Rubicon and life would never again be the same.

She says of her experience at those Councils, "I went forward in a Salvation Army meeting and knelt at the mercy seat. That was really the crossroads of my life, a very significant decision, although in a way, at the university I was being brought to this point. I was going back to my childhood, where the mercy seat was the place of sacred decision-making. I went forward and knelt there.

"I remember I wept much. I was seeking forgiveness for those years when I had been downright disobedient to God and pushed Him right out of my life. A woman came to speak with me and she helped me see that it wasn't only that I was coming to be changed and converted, because in my own ways as a child I had given God my life. I was really coming to give it back to Him. As she gently probed and questioned me, I realized that I must give my whole self to God for the ministry, to give the whole of my life to Him.

"It was salvation in its fullest context, total consecration of all of myself. That moment was the most crucial of my life. After we prayed, I felt a great sense of release and peace, thoroughly glad to have given God everything.

"At that point I was almost surprised to find that my decision meant that I would stay in The Salvation Army and not join one of the churches of my university friends. God led me back to The Salvation Army and my call to service occurred at the same time. Because I am a very enthusiastic person, I do things wholeheartedly, and when I offered my life to God it was a total commitment. I gave Him my life, my future, everything."

Her sister Margaret, although she had not been through the same rebellion as Eva, also made her commitment to Christ during the Youth Councils. Margaret recalls, "I remember clearly the change which occurred in Eva's life at that time. Although she remained a strong, happy personality, everything about her seemed transformed. Eva became much more caring and concerned for the welfare of others in the family. Her strength was tempered by gentleness, love, and warmth."

When Eva and Margaret arrived home late from the Councils, their parents were already asleep. But they awakened and eagerly heard the testimonies of their two daughters who had returned with the radiant joy of their life-changing surrender to Christ. "From that point on," says Eva, "my life was right with God and I knew that I had to be a Salvation Army officer."

Did she ever have second thoughts when she realized the long-term implications, the cost of the giving of her total self? She says, "I was so overjoyed with my Christian faith that I just wanted to please God and do what He wanted, whatever it might cost. I was prepared because in my childhood I had seen that service to God had led us to a very spartan existence. I just wanted God to have everything. It

Eva Burrows as Brides-
maid at her sister Betty's
wedding in 1948.

didn't really worry me what it would cost."

In her rebellion, she had rejected the traditions of the Army. However, she was not able to escape the example of her parents and the
wooing of the Holy Spirit that led her to commit her total life to
God and the Army. Eva donned the uniform and became a fully
active soldier once more.

Relationships

Eva's attractive appearance and vivacious personality did not escape
the attention of some young men who attended the Christian Union
at the university. Several who dated her expressed an interest for her
hand in marriage. She admits to "a serious interest in a couple of
friends, but did not allow it to progress so the relationship would
take me out of what I knew was God's will."

She further reflects, "Once I became a Christian I had this awareness that it was a total dedication of my life to God and therefore I
could not allow any involvement which would deflect me from what
God wanted for my life. It was God first in every relationship. When
I planned to become a Salvation Army officer I left my future to

God, whatever it was going to be. Although I was attracted to a few men in my life outside of officership, I really didn't want it to go too far because I was committed to officership."

A Soldier in God's Army

Shortly after their dedication to the Lord, Eva and sixteen-year-old Margaret were enrolled by their father as senior soldiers. The ceremony concluded, as it often does in the Army, with both daughters being asked to give their testimonies. Eva likened her experience to that of Jonah, who had been disobedient to God. God pursued her too, until she turned and allowed God to use her life.

She and Margaret sang duets in the Army meetings, visited Boothville Hospital for unmarried mothers, and helped with entertainment programs for the women there. During this period Eva took instruction in the art of speech and drama and was often chosen for the leading role in plays and dramas. Margaret felt a sense of pride in Eva who helped her to blossom as a person, and who became for her a model.

Robert Burrows suffered chronic bouts with asthma. In his early officership he had taken a short leave to try to bring his condition under control. When he was the corps officer at Fortitude Valley, he once suffered a severe attack during the morning worship service just before he was to preach. As Major Burrows left with his wife, he turned to Eva, then nineteen years old, and said, "You finish the service."

The people in the service that morning were simple folk and many would have been too nervous to have taken over in such circumstances. Eva had just been to a Bible camp and had done a series of studies on the Children of Israel leaving Egypt. She stood up and preached her first sermon—an impromptu message on the Passover in Egypt. She discoursed on how the Israelites received freedom by the sprinkling of the blood on the doorpost and how the blood of Christ gives liberty from sin. Following the meeting she even went to the door and shook hands with the people. An old Salvationist chap said to her as he left, "Thank you, and Eva, always preach the Blood, preach the Blood."

Eva Meets the General

Eva received her Bachelor of Arts Degree the day after Mother's Day 1950, having majored in English and history. At the time of her graduation from the University, General Albert Orsborn, one of the Army's great leaders, came for a visit to Australia. Eva had been selected to be the youth speaker to welcome him to Brisbane. Later she would read in the Australian *War Cry* that the General had lauded her speech.

General Orsborn was to speak at a large open-air meeting in the square, in front of the town hall in Brisbane. It was the very day on which Eva's graduation was held in the town hall. Her parents in Salvation Army uniform and Eva in her graduate's gown came direct from the town hall to the square as the public meeting outside was finishing. The divisional commander stopped them and said, "Please wait because I am sure the General would like to meet you." General Orsborn came and greeted them, congratulated Eva and there, right in the courtyard of the town hall, offered a prayer for her, asking that the Lord would use her talent and training for His glory.

Manifest Destiny
Marie Chalk and Eva, both students at the University of Queensland, became close friends through their common interest in the Evangelical Union. Marie describes Eva in those days as "a bright personality, happy, easy to love, caring, and genuine. At the vacation Bible camps with Eva there were always plenty of laughs, but also a serious application to the Bible study.

"I was aware that Eve's parents were Salvation Army leaders in Fortitude Valley, not the most salubrious part of the city. Only in later years did she tell me that she hadn't realized what an advantage it had been for many of her peers to have grown up in homes filled with a wide variety of reading material. But her grounding in Scriptures provided not only the literary wealth of the Bible, but also the motivating force for the whole of her life."

Marie and Eva kept in touch during the ensuing years and on vacations Eva would visit Marie and her family. Marie shares, "I remember how readily she fitted into my home with my husband and three young children. The encounter with my family that stands out most was when she visited with us after my husband's sudden death in 1979. She seemed to gather us under her wing as she prayed with me and my three children. Her absolute sincerity and trust in God made a profound impression on me and my family."

Much later Marie would reflect on her vivacious university friend who had risen to such a high position of leadership. "In a world

*Eva Burrows as
undergraduate 1948.*

where so many women seem to be struggling to find their identity and fulfillment, Eva has walked tall. She has found herself by losing herself in a life of service for God and others. She provides an excellent role model today for girls who aspire to be women of achievement. Looking back over the years I would say that Eva was destined to be a leader among women and men."

As a daughter of Australia, Eva Burrows, reflected the vigor and vitality of the land that nurtured her. In its arts, sport, flora and fauna, landscape and people, Australia is a country like no other. Perhaps she was born with some of the Australian outback in her — a deep interior where thoughts blow free and the soul searches for far horizons in an otherworldly territory. Eva Burrows, even in these early halcyon years, bore upon her the mark of distinction.

She was now to discover the other world that awaited her, a world of wide vistas, far beyond the remoteness and insularity of the land where she had been nurtured to this point.

7

★ ★

LONDON–DOORWAY TO THE WORLD

"I felt a great sense of privilege to share the Gospel."

From Fortitude Valley, Margaret, youngest of the nine children, left for Melbourne to train for nursing in preparation for missionary work in India. Later she and her husband, Dr. Bramwell Southwell, would serve there as lay Salvationists for three years. From Fortitude Valley, Eva also embarked on a journey that launched her on a lifetime pilgrimage, ultimately taking her to the far corners of the earth.

A Vision for World Youth

The internationalism of The Salvation Army, its bond of unity and fellowship in Christ, is nothing less than a miracle wrought by God. But the outbreak of hostilities in the Second World War among its member nations had cruelly transformed this crown of glory into a crown of thorns. Following the war General Albert Orsborn had a vision of a youth congress that would bring together Salvationist youth from all over the world in a great demonstration and reinforcement of the international unity of The Salvation Army.

An International Youth Congress was scheduled for August 10 to 23, 1950 in London. The agenda called for the voice of youth to be heard in open forums and in the meetings. News of the Congress circulated to the eighty-four countries and territories of The Salvation Army. Upwards of 1,200 delegates under thirty years of age came from all five continents with the slogan, "Christ is the way for youth today." Bramwell Tillsley, a teenager from Canada who would one day be Chief of the Staff, (second in command for the Army world), Andrew S. Miller later to be the U.S.A. national command-

44

er, and a twenty-year-old university student from the continent "down under," were among those attracted to the historic event.

When Eva learned of the Congress, it became a great dream of hers to go. But the cost, even with the cheapest accommodation of six to a cabin, was beyond the meager means of the Burrows family. Sensing her daughter's dream, her mother said, "You're going." "But Mum," Eva protested, "we haven't enough money; we can't afford it." It was then that her mother revealed that she had saved the funds Eva had turned over from her scholarship while living at home.

From that moment Eva spent every spare hour working to make up the difference. As in prior school vacations, she worked in the soap factory, a pineapple canning factory, and anywhere else she could to earn money. Army friends helped raise funds for her fare, and her sisters and friends spent long hours sewing clothes for her to take.

In July 1950 a group of forty young Salvationists boarded the old passenger liner *Otranto*. Through the efforts of all involved, enough money had been saved for Eva to go to London. As her family wept for joy to see her realize her dream, none could know that she would not return, except for rare visits.

In later years one observer recalled, "I remember being in the lounge room of the boat and Eva was not very far from me. I didn't know who she was, I just knew this was a very striking girl. It was uncommon in Australia in those days for a soldier to wear a two-piece uniform, so that stood out to me—this girl in a two-piece rather than the usual dress-style uniform, with dark hair, and very striking in appearance."

The sea voyage took six weeks, taking them through the Red Sea, Suez Canal, and the Mediterranean en route to London. During the journey the forty delegates met for Bible study each day, with other passengers joining them. The timbrelists rehearsed daily for their coming performance at the Congress. To economize, they traveled six to a cabin. When the heat became oppressive as they traveled through the Suez Canal, they slept on the deck.

For Eva Burrows and the other delegates from Australia, to come to London in 1950 after the long war "was an absolutely exciting thing." As the ship neared port and the lights of England came into view, the elated delegates ran to the rail to get their first glimpse of the country that had brought them from half a world away. "When we got there," recalls Burrows, "it was really mind-blowing—as they say in modern terms."

Australian delegates on the deck of the boat that will take them to London for the International Youth Congress, and will launch Eva Burrows (center) on a worldwide journey far beyond anything she could have imagined.

International Youth Congress

The Youth Congress was a microcosm of the Army world. Delegates of all colors, languages, and continents experienced a common bond of fellowship in Christ that transcended national differences. The Congress was led by General Albert Orsborn, the Poet-General of the Army, whose platform eloquence captivated young Eva.

The Congress was an exhilarating experience as delegates shared in Bible study, and also marched through London to Hyde Park where they had a great outdoor meeting. The Australian timbrelists, presenting three drills in the Royal Albert Hall, took the Congress by storm with their exciting choreography of swirling arms and flying ribbons. These modern Miriams modeled a mode of playing the tambourine that spread around the Army world. The Aussie timbrelists, including the young Eva Burrows, gave the Army's traditional tambourine a new respect and status.

Eva Burrows at the International Youth Congress, on a London street is caught by a roving photographer as she adjusts the uniform headdress of a delegate from Pakistan.

An historic event occurred just before the Congress. Evangeline Booth, daughter of the Founder, and the fourth General, died in her retirement in America. In Army terms, she was "Promoted To Glory." A memorial service was to be held the night of the arrival of the Australian delegates who, although traveling the farthest to attend the Congress, arrived early because of the boat schedule.

Hearing of the memorial service, they wanted to attend and asked for directions. The route by London underground to Regent Hall Corps was more complex than they expected and they arrived late, during the first song. As usual, the front seats were empty and the Australian delegates were ushered right up to the front.

It was Eva's first Salvation Army meeting in London. She was captivated by the sight on the platform of the General and an array of Army Commissioners. In Australia she had never seen more than one Commissioner at a time. The characteristic fervor and zeal of the Australian Salvationists present could not be restrained in such a stirring meeting. During the closing song one of the Australian delegates took the Army flag and commenced a march around the hall, a practice in the Army known as "A Hallelujah Windup." The sight of the Australian Salvationists marching around the hall with the flag was thought significant enough to be recorded in the Army's publications.

At the conclusion of the worship service on the Sunday of the Congress, General Orsborn gave an invitation to the altar for dedication. Eva Burrows was among the many who went forward to kneel at the Army's mercy seat and renew her commitment to Christ. Kneeling next to her in prayer was retired Commissioner Allister Smith, O.F., an aged saint of God who had been invited to the Congress by the General. He had been a pioneer in the Army's work among the Zulus in Africa, and was well known in the missionary history of the Army.

Eva did not know the saintly warrior had knelt next to her until after she had become General. Mrs. Commissioner Doris Davis, also a delegate at the Congress, described as one of her fondest memories seeing Eva come to the mercy seat at the end of the Youth Congress and Commissioner Smith kneeling next to her. She recalled that General Orsborn leading the meeting, said, "Now, what a sight! Here is a young person and here is an old saint of God. There is always room at the place of prayer for the young and for the old." Eva Burrows was very moved when she heard that story.

Setting the Course

While Eva was still in Brisbane she had mentioned to one of her professors that she wanted to teach in Africa. He suggested that she go to London University, where they had a special study program in that field. She brought with her a nest egg of 200 pounds from the money her mother had saved. Arrangements were made for a place to stay in London for a year following the Youth Congress, to do post graduate work at London University before returning to Australia to enter the Training College for officers.

However, the farsighted principal of the training school in London, Commissioner John Bladin, suggested that she first go to the Training College in London and then do her study at the University. Quite a decision for a young woman from Australia to make on her own. She prayed about the matter, then cabled her parents informing them of her decision.

In 1950, Eva Burrows entered The Salvation Army's International Training College in London for what was at that time a nine-month course. The curriculum, as in all Salvation Army training colleges, included doctrine, Bible study, Salvation Army history and regulations, homiletics, finance, and practical training for Army leadership and service.

In addition to theology, the course included "scrubology"—the cleaning and dusting and sweeping of the college. Cadet Burrows, along with some 200 other cadets, had housekeeping assignments not only for her own area, but the entire college. Her first duty was in the assembly hall, where united services were held. On Friday mornings her work detail was to clean the brass on the windows and the door handles. She had never had brass to clean in Australia and went about her task enthusiastically, only to be called back during her free time by the sergeant in charge and told that her work was not done properly. Distressed, she discovered that in going about her work so enthusiastically, she had spilled little drops of the cleaning fluid on the floor.

A Persian proverb says, "If you have two loaves of bread, sell one and buy a hyacinth for your soul." Eva did not then know the proverb but she knew the experience. During free time she often walked down to Camberwell where there was a flowerseller on the street and bought a bunch of mimosa, bright yellow flowers that reminded her of Australia.

Two of Eva's close friendships were formed during her cadet days,

Cadet Eva Burrows
1950.

with Miriam Vinti from Italy and Ingrid Lindberg of Sweden. Lindberg had been a teacher and was also interested in teaching on the mission field. Later, for a period of ten years Eva and Ingrid served as colleagues in the teacher training program at Howard Institute in Africa. Their paths again crossed near the end of their careers. Lindberg, as a Commissioner and Territorial Commander, attended many of the high level international conferences over which Burrows presided as General. Near the end of Eva's tenure as General, Lindberg would come out of retirement to help her General with a dramatic development of the Army world.

Lindberg reminisces on their cadet days, "Eva Burrows considered it a privilege to prepare for her future service as an officer. Spiritual days with General Albert Orsborn made lasting impressions on us. There was great sincerity in her heart. She was also a very keen student and was the top cadet in academic attainments. She approached the Covenant Day with a sense of awe, for here was a lifetime commitment which could not be broken. What was given to God was given for life, with great joy to the Master she loved."

First Appointment

In May 1951, Cadet Burrows was commissioned by General Albert Orsborn in the Royal Albert Hall as a Lieutenant and appointed to assist at Portsmouth Citadel Corps, on the south coast of England. She recalls that the only sadness was that her parents could not afford to be present.

Portsmouth Citadel was a large Salvation Army corps where Eva Burrows now put theory into practice. One of the two single women officers had become ill and Lieutenant Burrows was sent there until she would enter the University, as a support for the officer in charge, Major Lilian Glase. At Portsmouth, the new Lieutenant was challenged by a good congregation and a busy parish.

She took her turn preaching on Sunday mornings and evenings. Major Glase, herself an eloquent platform person, reflecting on the first time she heard her new Lieutenant preach, said, "My, I had better pull up my socks!"

Lieutenant Burrows accompanied Major Glase on her rounds as they visited members of the corps. She went into the homes, prayed and encouraged those she visited, as well as spent an afternoon each week knocking on doors to contact new people. She looks back on these five months on the British field as a valued training experience at the beginning of her officership. General Burrows would later say of Major Glase, "She was a walking epitome of what a Salvation Army officer should be."

London University

In October of that year, Eva farewelled to take up studies in the Institute of Education at London University, where she billeted in The Salvation Army Women's residence. She had made known her interest to go to Rhodesia, where the Army had a major education program, and her courses at the university were designed to prepare her for service in Africa. Other students in the courses were preparing to go to Africa and India.

Studies were done in a tutorial fashion. Her tutor, Mrs. Baggott, who had been a missionary in Nigeria, was very helpful in preparing Eva Burrows for the interpretation of the Gospel in Africa. Lieutenant Burrows was eager to learn how to make the Gospel relevant in a non-Christian environment and did her major paper on the presentation of the Gospel in Central Africa. Studies included anthropology, colonial policy and history, cross-cultural subjects, and teacher training.

Australians and other English speaking peoples have sometimes accused each other of speaking different English languages. Eva's tutor pointed out that she had too heavy an Australian accent and that her voice was pitched too high. Later, Eva's audiences would be captivated by her clarity of voice and mastery of inflection when illustrating a conversation or a third person dialogue.

Eva practiced teaching history and religious education at a secondary school in Bethnal Green, East London, near where William Booth started the Army. There she taught students who had little knowledge of religion and the Bible.

In her studies she came to a fundamental concept that would clarify her whole approach to sharing the Gospel in Africa. She read of two methods for presenting the Gospel to non-Christian cultures. She recalls, "One was to present it as a new revelation. Some theologians, such as Emil Brunner, said, 'There's no point of contact.' The other approach was the sublimation theory. That is, what the people have been believing is but a groping for the truth. The latter was relevant to me because then I studied the belief of the Bantu people who were monotheists and believed God came to them through the spirits of the ancestors."

She took advantage of the opportunity to hear some of the great men in the London pulpits. There was Dr. William Sangster at Westminster Central Hall, Dr. D. Martin Lloyd Jones at Buckingham Gate, Dr. Leslie Weatherhead at City Temple, and a young John R.W. Stott who was making an impact on university students. Her ecumenical experience was further broadened by joining the Christian Union (InterVarsity) at London University where she was invited to serve as the women's representative on the executive committee.

While at the university she attended The Salvation Army Regent Hall Corps. She joined the Songsters and shared in Bible study and practical training which involved conducting open-air meetings and preaching on the streets of London.

The year at London University was a valuable preparation for what was to be a long ministry in the heart of Africa. In May of 1952 she finished her studies and received a post graduate certificate in education.

Eva Burrows reflects on an aspect of the cost of her commitment, "As soon as I entered The Salvation Army I realized that I might be called to a celibate life. I didn't rebel against it. I know that marriage is a beautiful thing, but the gift of singleness is beautiful too. God gives more than enough back to you when you give up something for Him.

"I think all along I felt a great sense of privilege to share the Gospel and that God had chosen me. That may sound naive to some people, but to me it was like a flowering of my life and the beauty of the flower is for Christ."

PART TWO

★ ★ ★ ★ ★ ★ ★ ★ ★ ★ ★ ★ ★ ★

AFRICA TO AUSTRALIA

8

★ ★ ★ ★ ★ ★ ★ ★ ★ ★ ★ ★ ★ ★ ★ ★ ★ ★ ★

TO THE HEART OF AFRICA

"My aim was to open the minds of African people to education and their hearts to the Christian faith."

In November 1952, Lieutenant Eva Burrows set sail to enter both the geographical heart of Africa as well as the hearts of its people. Her destination was the Army's mission compound at Howard Institute in Southern Rhodesia, now Zimbabwe. This landlocked country in south central Africa, then under British rule, bore the indelible footprints of the famed missionary explorer, David Livingstone, and is home of the magnificent Victoria Falls which he had named after his monarch.

Eva had completed her University studies in June and was not to arrive in Africa until November. She longed to visit parents and family before leaving for what was then a seven-year term. The policy of the Army, however, allowed only her cost of travel to Africa. The fare to Australia was far beyond her means. But even at that age, when Eva Burrows wanted to get something done, she was undaunted.

Through arrangement made by a friend in The Salvation Army's immigration office, she was able to earn free passage to Australia by taking a job on board ship. With another young woman, she looked after twelve orphan children — ten boys and two girls aged six to fourteen. Each morning Eva and her partner would conduct singing and competitions. Other passengers with children saw the lively activity and soon the two young ladies had all the children on board coming to their program.

In Australia, the days were spent with her parents and in visits with family members. Her parents had never expressed any concerns

Captain Eva Burrows with parents — Major and Mrs. Robert Burrows in cabin of the ship as she leaves for second term in Africa, January 1959.

Captain Eva Burrows in Africa, wearing the African style uniform she herself made.

about Eva going to Africa, but gave full encouragement to all her plans and preparation. Those months at home were used to further prepare her mind and heart for the challenging tasks ahead. After years of preparation and the days at home, the time came for a farewell to family, friends, and country, as she set sail for the faraway land and people to whom God had called her.

Howard Institute

Howard Institute was a compound that hosted a primary boarding school of six classes with about 200 students, a teachers training college for 60 students, a nurses training program for 30 students, the territorial training college for officers, a hospital, and a farm. Also on the grounds was the primary school for 600 children who lived in the village and walked three or four miles each day to school. Some 300 persons lived at Howard, with the compound serving a total population of over 1,000 people. The Institute was situated on an 100-acre tract that had been donated to the Army, with an additional l00 acres of forest. Its motto, "Godliness and Good Learning," expressed its ethos and set the standard for its people and program.

The area was picturesque with its huge protruding rocks along the landscape. Elephants and lions and other exotic fauna of Africa roamed the undeveloped regions beyond Howard. Parasites infested the streams and pools, causing a debilitating disease among many of the native people. Most Africans outside the Army compound lived in round huts with mud walls and grass roofs.

At that time 90 percent of the education in Rhodesia was operated by missionary societies. Eva Burrows was paid a salary by the Rhodesian government, an amount in excess of the modest allowance provided by the Army. The excess, which also came to other qualified staff, was all turned over to the Institute and helped to support the school.

Howard had earned an excellent reputation in the education field. Government inspectors highly regarded the program and would say, "We can always recognize a Howard-trained teacher when we go into a classroom." The Institute attracted the "cream" of students. To come as far as the teachers training college meant they were among the top students in Africa.

Following the long journey by boat, Eva took the train to the capital city of Salisbury [now Harare] and there was picked up by the van from Howard Institute. When the young, vibrant, and confident Lieutenant Eva Burrows stepped out of the minibus, the head-master of the school, Captain Caughey Gauntlett thought, "Wow! What have we here?" He and Mrs. Gauntlett became like an elder brother and sister to Eva, with their five children adopting her as "Auntie Eve."

The next morning Gauntlett introduced the new Lieutenant to her assigned class and then returned to his own. Shortly he and other staff were surprised to hear the sound of vigorous chorus-singing penetrating the quiet corridors of the school. That was but the beginning of the dramatic impact Eva Burrows would make at Howard Institute. Gauntlett acknowledges that "at times this vibrant personality proved to be rather too much for some of her colleagues yet there was the tacit awareness that she was transparently good, keen in her calling, and highly outgoing by nature."

Over four decades later, at her public welcome meeting as General in Westminster Central Hall in London, she would be presented by Commissioner Caughey Gauntlett, her first Chief of the Staff and second in command. In her response, she quipped, "He used to be my boss; now I'm his!"

In a letter to her family she shared her love at first sight, or rather sound, for the Africans' joyful worship and native singing. "It is wonderful to see them marching around the school on Sundays in their school uniforms, with the Army flag. And you should see their faces glow as they sing with a heartiness that I have never heard before in my life. Their voices are so fresh and alive, so rich and full. It is interesting to hear how they change the rhythm of well-known hymns to suit their own particular style of singing. Their harmonies are so unusual to our ears and I wonder just where they come from. All this adaptation I feel to be right, for we want to make them African Christians, not unnatural copies of a Europeanized form of Christianity."

Eva felt right at home from the start. She shared a small quarters with Lieutenant Helen Prosser, an American girl. Being the youngest staff, they lived in the oldest house which had a leaky iron roof and ants nesting in the cracks of the floor. A letter in her second month at Howard shares, "I am happily settled in my new home. Quite a nice little house except when it rains, which is all the time during this rainy season of the year. It hasn't let up for days and as every room except my bedroom leaks a bit, it's a case of floods within and floods without."

Lieutenants Eva Burrows and Helen Prosser on Burrows' first Sunday at Howard Institute. Huts are boys' dormitories.

When her companion complained about the sieve-like condition of the leaky roof and having to set the basins to catch the drips, Eva responded, "Well, look now, what are you complaining about? Don't you remember that Dr. Livingstone came all through this area and he didn't even have a roof over his head?" Helen retorted, "What makes you think we do?"

A letter from Eva when she had been at Howard just seven weeks, tells of some of her early work and impressions. "I have been doing a lot of preparation work, including the drafting of a complete new syllabus for religious instruction throughout the school, as well as quite a bit of language study. The work has quite captured my imagination, for I can see most wonderful possibilities in it, both spiritually and educationally. I had a couple of weeks before the school broke up, meeting the young people in quite informal lessons and having a taste of the glories of a Howard Sunday. I am to work in the central primary school. The students are much older than Australian children at that stage of their schooling. At home they would be about thirteen, but here they are seventeen to twenty, though as more Africans are becoming educated the age is lowering."

In her letter she spoke of a sadness in her initial experience and an awareness of how vital was the education Howard was offering. "It has been very sad this year to see many boys turned away because we have not the buildings or the staff. It is tragic to see them plead for a place which cannot be given them. It is just heartbreaking to have to refuse an old man who wants a Christian education for his eldest son, or to say, 'Sorry, lad,' to a boy who asks, 'But what am I to do?' Education means everything to these people."

Looking back on these years, General Burrows recalls, "We lived a very simple and frugal life, but I just felt a sense of privilege in being there. I had become, as my parents had been for years, the servant of all. To serve was a great joy. To enter into the life of the Africans was a rich experience. The singing and exuberance of the African people is unique. The Bantu people with whom we lived have this great expression of joy. The Salvation Army suits them well with our drum and tambourine and lively songs. I never worried if they sang a note different from the way we sang in England, for I loved their singing and tried to sing like them. Some people who are set in concrete might not like that style, but I find it exhilarating."

The young Lieutenant from Australia was intrigued by the names of her African students. Upon the birth of a child, a name would be given that had to do with the situation in the family. One of her students was named *Takawira* meaning "we fell down" – the mother had fallen when pregnant. One student was named *Kufa* meaning "death." Sitting next to him was *Muvengi* meaning "enemy." Some had amusing names such as *Tapera* meaning "we're finished" (having children) and *Mariyapera* which meant "our money is all finished." She even had one student with the sad name *Hamundide* meaning "you don't love me." Many had chosen a Bible name in addition to their African name. In her class she would have *Moses, Jeremiah, Isaiah,* and a good representation of the disciples.

Happiness and Hilarity

Eva was always a night owl. Sometimes the single women would work at the Teacher Training School until after 11 P.M., then cycle home, say good night, and go to their quarters. Captain Frances Tomlinson would be in bed, just dropping off to sleep, when she would hear a tap on her window, and a voice saying, "I'm not tired yet, Rusty. Let's play Scrabble."

Tomlinson, who served eight years with Burrows at Howard and three years at Usher Institute, recalls, "Eva Burrows loved every-one—the officers, the mission children, the students. No one ever felt left out of her great heart. She had no exclusive friendships. Anyone with a problem or a care or a sorrow would always find a listening ear."

Eva was always fascinated with speed. Nothing ever seemed to go quite fast enough for her. Speed limits were apt to be looked upon as options for slow drivers rather than legal restrictions. In 1958 Tomlinson bought a Lambretta 150 CC scooter and says, "I was the driver of it until I foolishly taught Eva to drive. From then on I spent more time as a backseat passenger. Believe me, we had some wild times, since we were fifty miles from town!

"In 1962 my scooter was replaced with a car, and again Eva wanted to learn to drive. She was so impatient to be up and at it. While still using her learner's permit, she was driving in a game park when we met a huge elephant with flapping ears. I told her to pull on the brake, put the car in neutral, and slowly slide out of the driver's seat while I crawled over behind her. She seemed more willing to accept that suggestion than many others I had made. I think the advancing, flapping ears convinced her."

"To Open Minds and Hearts"
"My aim," Burrows says, "was to open the minds of African people to education and the world, and their hearts to the Christian faith. I didn't see myself as bossing the Africans, nor did I have the white supremacy concept. I don't think I was paternalistic. I myself was learning from my relationships with African officers and leaders. I felt they had so much to teach me. I made a lot of mistakes like any young person does, but I never made the mistake of thinking I knew it all. I wanted to help the African strive for achievement because I felt that if they could get a good education, they had a better hope for the future. I remembered too that the parents, who were farmers and had very little money, had to pay boarding fees and sacrifice to send their children to school, and that they had such high hopes for them."

Lieutenant Burrows started her day about 5:30 in the morning, having her prayertime first and then a quick breakfast with her housemate. Next was united prayer with students and staff. School started at 7:30, continuing into the afternoon when she taught her students to play netball and to run track. She put her team captain experience from high school days to good use serving as coach for the Howard teams that competed against outside schools. Evening was devoted to study, with one night a week given for the Corps Cadet Bible study program.

Eva often walked to the villages and sat around the campfires with the Africans, shelling peanuts, listening to their stories, entering into their joys and sorrows. She learned to speak the Shona language, and further identified with the Africans by eating the native food.

At Howard her natural teaching gifts came into play. She quickly became absorbed in teaching her pupils, with thirty-five to forty students in her class. She taught math, English, history, geography, nature study, health and hygiene, every subject except their mother tongue which was taught by an African teacher. She found that students often relied heavily on memorization, since much of the African culture is passed on by oral tradition.

Students who were very poor were keen to secure jobs in the gardens of the missionaries to earn money for their school fees. Eva and the others always had plenty of help around the house and garden. This gave extra hours for preparation and creative work in her teaching.

One of the projects for which she enlisted student help was a first at the Howard compound. Usually the native grass was just cut down. But she decided to have a lawn. She hired some of the male students and, working with them, dug up the whole lot and planted the grass. Her manicured lawn became a unique and attractive spot on the Howard campus.

Many of the students had little or no knowledge of the Christian faith. One of Eva's priorities was to lead them in the study of the Scriptures and encourage a personal decision for Christ.

And how would the young Eva Burrows bridge the gap between the religion of the Western world and that of the African who was steeped in spirit and ancestor worship? Her studies at London University had prepared her for interpreting the Bible in a way that could reach the African. She knew that the religion of the people was passed down by oral tradition. She said, "The Bantu religious background was one into which the Christian faith could come and find a strong link." She now put into practice the insight she gained that the Gospel could be presented as the culmination of the African's searching. She taught the Apostle Paul's declaration, "This God whom you inwardly worship, Him I declare unto you," and Jesus' pronouncement that He had not come to destroy the traditions of the past, but to fulfill them.

"In that part of Africa," she says, "there was belief in one god, Mwari. He was great and far away, without much contact with you and you came to him through the spirits of your ancestors. I felt that the Christian faith could say that Mwari is God and that he is not very far away. He loves you and you don't need the spirits of your ancestors to approach Him, but you go through Christ who is the one and only mediator."

The Family at Howard

Her family back home became a major part of her support team. They prayed daily for her safety and her ministry and eagerly awaited her regular letters. They wrote faithfully to her and generously sent their gifts of money, food, and clothing.

Those with whom she worked in Africa became Eva's new and extended family. "We shared and became like brothers and sisters. The rich fellowship and affection that developed in those days still continues. As a young missionary I was privileged for this support and strength of family life. We were not isolated or on our own out in a village. We would often go to the villages—and I loved to do that—but normally we were home at Howard at night. So it was like a family home."

A bond of affection developed between Eva and the African children and children of missionary families. She became an "auntie" to many of them. One of the children's favorite things was to go on picnics and hikes with "Auntie Eve" around the countryside. Brenda, daughter of the Cottrills on the officer staff, would follow Eva around and enjoyed riding on the back of Eva's bike. When she became old enough to join the Girl Guides program, Eva made a uniform for her.

Birthe Bjorndal, daughter of missionaries from Norway, was another of Eva's adopted nieces. She often helped Eva arrange the flowers for Sunday—wildflowers and pods that Eva had picked from the forest. One day Birthe's mother was arranging flowers at home and Birthe said, "Mommy, you're not doing it right." When her mother asked why, Birthe replied, "You shouldn't be using the scissors." Her mother said, "Why?" Birthe said, "No, it isn't right. Auntie Eve cuts them with her teeth."

Eva recognized that even with differences in temperament people can find areas of common interest and can work together. However, she acknowledges one situation she resented. An older missionary officer often took it upon herself to correct her, suggesting that she was becoming too Africanized, getting too close to the Africans. The older officer believed the missionaries should maintain a certain distance, physically and culturally, between themselves and the Africans. Such advice ran across the grain of Eva's conviction and commitment to identify with the African people.

Identification with the African

J.B. Matswetu, corps sergeant-major of the Harare Corps and leader of the Army's Territorial Songsters, was born and reared in the area of Howard Institute. He observes, "Upon arrival in Africa, Eva Burrows was thrust into a climate of great racial distrust and hatred fostered by more than half a century of agitation and struggle for independence by the black people of Zimbabwe. It would take a great amount of love and perseverance to win the trust and confidence of the people among whom she was to settle. Eva Burrows exhibited courage and understanding and, even more importantly, accepted and treated all people as equals regardless of race, color, or creed. Owing to her love and unceasing efforts to improve the spiritual and educational life of our people, she was able to transcend the barriers of racial distrust and hatred that then existed in Zimbabwe."

Commissioner Stan Cottrill (R), reflects, "She had a great rapport with African students because they saw her total dedication to them." A compliment was given by an African who, realizing to what extent she had loved his people remarked, "If I thought my prayer would be answered, I would pray for you to be black."

When she became General, Eva Burrows was asked what she thought of the African tendency to break into a dance in their meetings. She said, "I think our objection to dancing is in terms of the Western style that may open temptation to sexual aspects. In Africa we would also be against the dancing which was connected to spirit worship. But in the exuberance of African life, dancing was part of their folk style. I like the African dance. Especially at Easter time, they were so excited about Christ's resurrection that they would dance around the compound before worship and I would dance with them. Even now, when I sing in a meeting, after all these years, I very easily move with the songs. I think it goes back to those years I was in Africa."

Life and Work at Howard

Howard Institute had an outstanding staff of capable and dedicated officers from various parts of the English-speaking world. In that remote setting, there were four who would become Commissioners, and one who would become General. Stan Cottrill, Caughey Gauntlett, and Ron Cox each became a Chief of the Staff—second in command in the Army world, and Ingrid Lindberg became a Commissioner and Territorial Commander. Appointments often overlapped because in those days the officers had long stays, often over ten years.

Ingrid Lindberg, Eva's close friend since Cadet days, was appointed to the teacher training program at Howard in 1957. For the next ten years they shared their daily work and later their living quarters. Lindberg writes, "What a joy it was during those years at Howard. It was indeed a place full of life and optimism. There was joy among the students for the opportunity of learning and joy among the teachers for the privilege of preparing Africans for the future. Many of the young men and women we trained now hold responsible positions in government, education, industry, and as leaders in The Salvation Army. Very early during our service at Howard Institute, we were well aware of Eva Burrows' leadership qualities. She is a born leader."

When Eva moved into another house with an English missionary officer, Captain Ethel Carmody, her new companion had a "radiogram" (record player with a radio) and had bought the first record to play on it. Burrows says, "On one side was Handel's *Water Music* and on the other was Mozart's *Haffner Symphony*. We played that jolly record so many times I think that I could sing right through Mozart's Haffner."

She joined a record club and started her own collection just when the LP records were becoming popular. "Lyndon Taylor had piles and piles of old 78s which he played, and we used to go and listen to his records. From that time on I developed a great love for classical music." Every Easter and Christmas she would play her three records of *Messiah*. The single women officers, sometimes as many as ten on the staff, would come to listen to the music. Her taste in music is cosmopolitan and she came to know by memory the lyrics and tunes from such musicals as *My Fair Lady*. Colleagues remember well her own rendition of "Why can't a woman be more like a man?"

Eva Burrows' voracious appetite for books was satisfied by a mail order and mobile library from Salisbury. A catalog was available and one could borrow up to nine books that would come to Glendale, about twelve miles away, where the books would be picked up with the mail delivery. While working in the bush where she was shut off from normal converse and contact with the Western world, she subscribed to *Time* magazine to keep current on world news and events.

Life in the compound was both spartan and frugal. Clothes for the most part were handmade, including uniforms. Eva spent many hours stitching away on the hand-driven sewing machine shared by those in the compound. The missionaries ate simply, growing their own vegetables, and were able to secure chicken regularly.

At Howard Eva was known as a neat housekeeper, good gardener, and popular entertainer. Fresh flowers and her best glass and cutlery along with an appetizing menu graced these occasions. A large painting of Van Gogh's sunflowers was on her wall. There was no television, so when staff got together they made their own entertainment. Eva was a good photographer and often put on a slide show. "She was great fun and the life of the party," recalls Colonel Lyndon Taylor.

Taylor worked closely with Eva Burrows at Howard for eleven years. He had been a school teacher in England and entered training for Salvation Army officership at age thirty-three. As he and his wife arrived at Howard Institute in March 1955, Eva Burrows and other staff members warmly welcomed them. He found that Burrows was installed in the same office he was to use, along with another officer, Major Lavina Benson. That cramped space also was full of tools—hoes, rakes, axes, saws—all in regular use on the compound. Thus a constant stream of students would come in and out collecting the tools. Those who came to the office found a friendly rapport with the young Lieutenant Burrows who was always very open, quick to greet people, and easy to talk to. That cozy closeness continued for two-and-a-half years until the new teacher training block came into use.

Eva was described by Taylor as "a bouncy, lively junior officer with abounding vitality and energy. She was at home in any company and could relate to everybody. She was cheerful and outgoing and related extremely well to all the African teachers and students. There was a constant interchange with them in the classroom as she sought to bring her students up to the highest possible level."

Taylor, whose own faith had to be hammered out on the anvil of

Captain Eva Burrows and two young men with leprosy in Zimbabwe.

Coach Captain Eva Burrows with 1953 netball Champions at Howard Institute.

doubt and struggle, was intrigued with the uncomplicated faith of the young Lieutenant. "She had a great sense of God. She would often speak about God and was taken up with His greatness and majesty. She had this kind of brute sense of God. She often knelt in prayer at various meetings, renewing her consecration.

"She had a lovely voice," recalls Colonel Taylor, "powerful and expressive as a soloist. I especially remember her singing so often 'How Great Thou Art.' She put a tremendous feeling into it. She learned the Shona language and could speak to any of the Africans in their native tongue."

Her extraordinary gifts of teaching, good voice, acumen for learning, phenomenal memory, grasp of detail and administration, platform poise—all would give cause to be tempted to pride. With an increased awareness and use of her gifts came an increased need for the discipline of humility, not always easy for Eva Burrows.

Corps Officer
The impressionable young Eva Burrows had good role models at Howard. One was Lt. Colonel Philip Rive, the principal, a New Zealand officer who became her mentor. A noted linguist, he translated some of the Bible, songs, and books into the Citonga language. He virtually rebuilt Howard, supervising construction of new buildings and upgrading Howard's facilities. Burrows says of him, "He was an example of someone who devoted his life to the African people." Later, as General, she would posthumously admit him to the *Order of the Founder*.

Colonel Rive needed someone to serve as the corps officer (pastor) for the compound. In Eva he found just the right person to take on this added responsibility. She enthusiastically responded to his request and in this role was free to do her own thing in her own way. This was largely an organizational task, enlisting the missionaries to take their turns at preaching, and African teachers and students on the compound to take part. She recruited leadership from the compound and took upon herself the pastoral visitation in the homes of members.

Sunday at the corps under Eva Burrows was quite a full day, starting with prayer meeting, morning worship, service projects, and Sunday School. The students marched in front of their houses for an inspection in their uniforms and then paraded to the center of the compound, to be greeted by the principal and march to the hall.

Corps Officer, Captain Eva Burrows, with some of her new Salvation Army soldiers enrolled at Howard Institute.

Major Eva Burrows, later to be called the Army's "Top Tambourine" shows new tambourines to students and timbrelists at Howard Institute.

There would often be 500 in attendance. "By the time of the evening meeting," recalls Colonel Taylor, "many of the staff were relaxing in their homes, exhausted, but Eva Burrows was still going on."

Commissioner Ron Cox, who was also then on the staff at Howard and later became Eva's Chief of the Staff, similarly recalls, "In spite of the workload she carried of teaching, marking lessons, coaching, and all the school activities, she was tremendously devoted to giving herself fully to her calling and the people. In those early days her qualifications were considerable and she has added to them since. She has always sought the very highest level of service as a Salvation Army officer all through the years." He adds, after forty years of observation of Eva Burrows, "One of the remarkable things about her, notwithstanding the increasingly heavy burdens which have come to her in the way of Army leadership through the years, is that she has never lost that touch with people. She genuinely likes to be with people."

The Sunday evening Soldiers meetings, led by Lieutenant Burrows, were exciting and joyful. Lyndon Taylor, who played the piano for her, describes them as "always very lively, entertaining, with much singing and testimony and an interaction between the platform and congregation. She knew the names of everyone and would call upon them in the meeting. With her wonderful voice she led the singing with great verve."

Eva describes her captivation by the natural rhythm and beautiful resonance of African singing. "When a song is sung in Africa, it's slightly changed in tempo and rhythm. And even the notes can be changed. When I first went to Africa I'd hear them sing and say, 'Oh, that's a wonderful African song.' And then I'd discover that it was, say, 'The Ash Grove,' an old Welsh melody which we adopted in The Salvation Army. But when they sing it, they really liven it up. The Africans are so filled with music and song. We used to go down to the primary school to hear the kindergarten children singing parts. In the Western world you first learn to sing in unison, but the little African kids start by singing harmony. Music is in their blood. It's a part of everything they do—working in the fields, chopping wood. Being there in my formative years, I absorbed some of that."

Her Corps Cadet brigade of young people enrolled in Bible study became legendary. She had some 150 students and enlisted Captain Ingrid Lindberg, Mrs. Captain Taylor, and other staff to help with the teaching. Forty-five of its members attended Rhodesia's first

Left: Guide leader Eva Burrows.

Below: Captain Eva Burrows with Girl Guides of Howard Institute, in African alfresco setting.

Corps Cadet Congress and took the first and second prizes in competition.

Annual Congresses were major events in the lives of the people. There were no Holiday Inn accommodations and at one camp Eva and delegates slept out under the stars. The opening meeting on Friday night would be followed all day Saturday by competitions in music, cooking, knitting, and marching. When awarded prizes, winners became very excited and broke into song and dance. Sunday was devoted to worship and dedication, with all the meetings held outdoors.

Eva recruited Ingrid Lindberg to help with the Brownies. Together they taught the young girls skills, modeled the Christian faith, and took them on hikes and camping trips. At Howard, although the schedule was full, life was also simple and serene.

The corps life was thriving under Burrows. By her fifth year at Howard, before leaving for her first homeland furlough, she had enrolled 117 soldiers.

Polygamy and Spirit-Possession

Polygamy and possession by evil spirits were two issues that confronted Burrows in the villages of Africa. Before her arrival, she had read up on these issues and had discovered that many churches did not accept a convert who practiced polygamy. Her research revealed that the problem was not a new one to The Salvation Army. Years earlier, Bramwell Booth had ruled that a monogamous man could not take another wife after acceptance in the Army fellowship and that a polygamous man could be accepted as a soldier, provided he did not take any further wives. On the women's Home League register at Nyachuru, you might hear the roll being called, "Mrs. Albert I, Mrs. Albert II, Mrs. Albert III."

Eva found that the teaching of Christianity in the schools and villages vastly reduced the practice of polygamy. Converts who became soldiers of The Salvation Army were required to take a six-month study course that included training in Christian standards. With the growth of education, the school fees parents had to pay toward their children's schooling led them to have smaller families. For the young Eva Burrows Africa was indeed a school in a culture vastly different from that of Australia and the Western world.

On one occasion when Eva was out in the village with cadets on a campaign, a spirit-possessed woman torn in anguish by the spirits came to the mercy seat and threw herself violently around on the floor. Some of the men came to hold her down. She was quieted as Salvationists put the Bible on her head, singing and praying for her. Burrows noticed a woman Salvationist who was very attentive and compassionate during the exorcism. When the convert became quiet, this woman took her by the arm and looked after her. Burrows then discovered that the Salvationist and the new convert shared the same husband. She recalls, "In sisterly love instead of jealousy, here was a woman Salvationist able to show one of the other wives of her husband such beautiful love and compassion." Later, when the woman brought all her paraphernalia used in her spirit worship to be burnt on the fire, the Salvationist wife was there comforting and helping.

In Africa Eva experienced much for which the textbooks gave no preparation. She came in direct contact with the diabolical forces deeply rooted in indigenous tribal beliefs, practices of animism, augury, witchcraft, and idolatry.

There were times when she encountered demon possession in the villages. To combat this, the Salvationists asked those who were demon-possessed to bring their paraphernalia to be burned in the fires. Some of the possessed would become wild and violent. As the fires were set up, the Salvationists sang and prayed. Often Eva was asked to sing. The people would be torn by the evil spirits until they had thrown all the things they used in divination such as black cloth or bones into the fire. Then the Salvationist leader would command, "In the name of Jesus, come out." The evil spirits were cast out and the persons became calm and give a testimony to the cleansing and saving power of Christ. The power of Satan and evil forces was often real around the campfires of Africa where a young woman from Australia was taking an apprenticeship in service for God.

The Territory's Training College for Cadets was located at Howard, and on occasion Lieutenant Burrows accompanied Cadets on a campaign. They once went to a mining village where they encountered a wild and rough crowd that had been drinking heavily. Neither the leader nor the Cadets could quiet the rowdies. Then the leader said to the Lieutenant, "Sing them a song." Lieutenant Burrows stood up and started to sing a solo, unaccompanied, in their Shona language. Suddenly the crowd became hushed.

A Trainer of Teachers

After two years Eva moved from teaching primary school into the teachers college to train teachers. Her students practiced teaching for

*Captain Eva Burrows
on her first homeland
furlough, 1958.*

several weeks at a time in the villages. When she traveled to the villages to inspect their teaching, she sat in the back of the class to assess their skills and style, critique whether enough visual aids were used, and evaluate the effectiveness of communication with the class.

"My greatest love in education was the training of African teachers," she says. "Howard Institute had a long tradition as an excellent teachers college. Although we were missionaries, we were also educators. We didn't see education as something just to make converts; nor did we use education as a bait to hook souls. We gave students the finest education possible and saw our Christian faith and our teaching as working together." However many of those trained were attracted to the Army and became Salvationists.

Burrows believes that teaching consists of two elements: identification and communication. She says, "I can put myself in their place, I never teach from a distance, but always alongside." The success rate with her students was so high that following one inspection from the African Education Department, the results were rechecked.

Religious education was not an elective but a part of the core curriculum at Howard. "We were not only training them intellectually; we were also training them to be good Christians. When they went out to teach they would be the most educated and respected people in the village. We wanted them to also be spiritual leaders and good Christian models."

First Return Home

In 1958 Eva came to the end of her first five years in Rhodesia and was eligible for a homeland furlough. At the time she had gone to Africa it was for a seven-year term, which since had been reduced to five. She eagerly looked forward to reunion with family, some relaxation from the rigorous schedule at Howard, and also to achieving a personal goal that would occupy a major portion of her furlough.

In later life Eva regretted that she had been so separated from her mother. On her furloughs, it was always to her parents she went, spending time with her mother and speaking at Salvation Army meetings. Her parents took great pride in hearing Eva speak from the Army platforms.

Eva's homeland furlough happily coincided with her sister Margaret's wedding in January of 1959. Eva was bridesmaid at the Salvation Army ceremony conducted by Commissioner John Bladin, Eva's former Training Principal in London. Margaret recalls, "It was a happy time and Eva's support was tremendous, doing ironing, packing, and helping with flower arrangements." Bramwell Southwell recalls that the bride, along with Eva and his sister Margaret, were "beautiful with floral headpieces and silver and golden sashes and bouquets. Ebullient Eva did her very best to make it the joyful occasion it was, in spite of the oppressively hot weather."

Education programs in Rhodesia were at a crossroads. Expanded opportunities were opening for the African, and schools and teachers who did not grow with the advancing system would be left behind. Eva Burrows was eager for herself and Howard Institute to keep pace with the rapid developments of education in the country. Her desire to upgrade her own credentials and expertise led her to apply for extra time on her furlough in Australia to return to the University. The request was approved for an extended leave of a year to earn a Master of Education Degree in Sydney, where her parents were then stationed.

Following her year at the University, now with the rank of Captain, she returned to Africa to start a second five-year term and to do her thesis on African teacher training methods. The thesis dealt with

Right: Captain Burrows on first homeland furlough from Africa.

Left: Captain Burrows with graduates of teacher training program at Howard Institute.

the type of training black teachers should have for self-development and creativity. Eva sought to show that it was not necessary for the African to rely on Western equipment or technology. She emphasized the African's own resources for opening their minds to ideas and concepts with practical applications. In 1959 she was awarded in absentia her Master of Education Degree from Sydney University.

A Quantum Leap Forward

Upon return to Howard, her new skills were quickly put to use. She was given the task of designing an advanced course that was a quantum leap for Howard's teacher training program. Up to that time teachers were trained in what was known as the PTL — Primary Teachers Lower Course, which equipped teachers to teach up to the fifth year in primary schools. Secondary schools were then developing throughout the country and the time was right for Howard to advance its program and move into what was known as PTH — Primary Teachers Higher Course, which would enable Howard graduates to teach the higher levels as well.

At the same time the Rhodesian Prime Minister opened a new teacher training block at Howard which doubled the number of pupils admitted to secondary education. During this period of rapid change, Eva Burrows was the architect for the advanced program that enabled Howard graduates to teach in three more levels. Colonel Taylor, head of the teacher training college, describes that step as "very satisfying and exhilarating."

The professional skills of Eva Burrows became widely recognized outside of Army circles. The Rhodesian government appointed her to a committee to devise a curriculum for teachers colleges. On the committee were also a Roman Catholic priest and a missionary educator from the London Missionary Society. This committee discussed and virtually designed curriculum for African education that became a national standard for use in the public schools. Later, Longmans Publishing House enlisted Burrows and the Howard teaching staff as consultants in testing their textbooks for African schools.

Eva undertook to research and prepare material on the history of teacher training in Africa, which was all done in mission schools. Soon thereafter, Captain Eva Burrows was made the head of the teacher training college at Howard.

Her leadership qualities were recognized and in June 1965 she was appointed vice-principal of Howard Institute, the first woman to hold the position. When Lyndon Taylor went on home furlough the following year Eva was asked to serve as acting principal during the six months of his absence. In June of 1966, she was promoted to the rank of Major.

Eva Burrows' days at Howard Institute were now numbered. She would soon take the next step in her pilgrimage of service and leadership.

9

★ ★ ★ ★ ★ ★ ★ ★ ★ ★ ★ ★ ★ ★ ★ ★ ★ ★ ★ ★

"A WHITE AFRICAN"

"I often call myself a white African."

After fourteen years at Howard Institute, on January 1, 1967 Eva Burrows was appointed principal of Usher Institute in Rhodesia, an educational center with an excellent reputation for its teachers college and secondary school for girls. Responsibility for the Institute, teachers, and administration of the school served to further develop Burrows' strong leadership skills.

Now she would organize, provide vision, implement policy, and make the final decisions. She no longer had to submit her ideas to someone else for approval, but could risk her own as they developed in her fertile imagination. It would be her first opportunity for unchallenged leadership. "Now I was in a position," she says, "to really have a go myself, and I found this quite exciting."

Brigadier Margaret Trefz, who served at Usher with Eva, recalls "a Saturday morning when I found the principal busy helping the girls clear out a drainage system on their compound. Another time she was among those who met the truck when it returned from a shopping trip to Bulawayo, helping to count heads of cabbage ordered for the menu, and while she was at it, posing with a cabbage in each hand and balancing another on her head."

In landlocked Rhodesia there were no safe places to swim because the pools and streams were infested with disease-carrying parasites. Eva had a swimming pool built at Usher to enhance the recreational opportunities for the students. There was excitement in the air on the day of its dedication.

Among the invited guests at its opening was David Stewart, Director of Education in Matabeleland. Funds were needed for its up-keep and Mr. Stewart looked at the principal in her smart cream color uniform and threw out a challenge, "I'll give a five pound donation (a fair sum at that time) if the principal jumps in the pool." A few seconds later Eva dove in fully clothed and swam across the pool. An amazed Director was five pounds poorer and the school fund five pounds richer. The girls cheered and Burrows had won the admiration of Mr. Stewart, who after the ceremony was heard to say, "She is no ordinary lady. She has so much to give to this school and the region."

The Impact of a Vision

Usher Institute quickly felt the impact of Burrows' vision and vigor. A development plan was initiated, curriculum and living conditions were upgraded, and soon new dormitories, a clinic, and other construction emerged on the compound. Lt. Colonel Almey Morris (R), who then served with her on the staff, recalls, "Her adaptability, enthusiasm, involvement, her ability to win support and lead by inspiration rather than by autocracy, made this period a time of growth. The school began to feel a sense of identity and worth. The girls saw a principal who had faith in them and was proud of them, and they responded, wanting to justify that faith. We had many gifted and skillful officers at the Institute and Eva was always ready to ask and learn from them."

Almey Morris conducted the teacher training for domestic science, which provided for practical needs of African families. Men wanted wives who knew how to run the home. Stories were told of wives who, unacquainted with some of the new home equipment, had actually started wood fires in ovens of electric stoves. Usher trained students in sewing, cooking, nutrition, and home management, help-ing to enhance African family and home life.

The math results Eva found among the girl students were "shock-ing." She strongly resisted the general opinion in Rhodesia that African girls did not have the acumen for math, and decided to prove that theory false. Rather than teaching her usual subjects of English or history, she took over the teaching of algebra, geometry, and related math subjects. She drilled mathematics into her students and gave them the confidence that they could learn it. The results were phenomenal. Her students took top honors in the country.

One day when walking through the compound at Usher she heard a student urgently call out, "Major, Major." Eva thought something serious had happened. Perhaps a bush fire had erupted, which would mean they would have to empty the school and go to beat the fire with sacks. Eva turned and asked, "What is it?" The girl replied, "I have just made up my own quadratic equation." Eva observes, "This was no simple feat. It is one thing to be given a quadratic equation and then to solve it. But what she had done was to make her own and then go back and solve it. The girls got excited about math and proved that they could do it as well as anyone else. It was just that they had been told that they couldn't. I showed them they could."

If an African girl violated what Burrows thought proper behavior, she would send for the parents, because parental authority was so strong for the African. One girl had stolen some food, a serious offense. Eva sent for the father and she dealt with the girl in his presence. Then she said, "Do you want to punish her?" He replied, "No, you have been right in the way you have dealt with her." The girl was forgiven. After she left the office, the man turned to Eva and said, "You are a real father to these girls."

Innovative ideas and programs resulted from Burrows' keen interest in making Usher the best possible education center. Discussions with staff members focused on such subjects as how to improve the meals for the students. This resulted in sending a young man to a Seventh Day Adventist mission to take a chef's course. He returned with a new repertoire of menus, adding some new tastes and more nourishment to the daily fare.

During her days in Africa extraordinary strengths of leadership were being developed in Eva. But also emerging were some of the weaknesses that would plague her through life. Even then she was identified as having certain insensitivities in her relationships. Officer wives sometimes resented that their husbands had a woman for a boss, and Eva's often dismissive demeanor toward the wives further fueled those feelings. And her own force of personality intimidated some who were less assertive and self-assured.

The Issue of Racism

Eva Burrows' sensitivities for the African carried over into the area of political discrimination. "I definitely felt for the African," she says. "Even in the church in those days the Africans were second-class citizens. You would rarely see an African in a white church. In those early days there was not the apartheid policy as such, but what was called 'partnership.' It was not equality, but more like junior and senior partners. I must say I was pro-black, and it hurt me that the white Rhodesians did not appreciate the capacities of the Africans."

As educator, Burrows reacted to psychological studies put forth to support apartheid, that showed Africans having less intelligence than Europeans. "You look at the studies and consider the types of questions. Many were linguistic, and an African thinks visually more than verbally. You can make tests to prove anything you want. Those things incensed me and I felt like standing up for Africans, speaking for them, articulating for them. If I'd been in the political arena, I'd certainly have shouted.

Later, as General she would say, "I have never changed my view that whatever color or race we are, there is this common humanity. Give an African the same opportunity as the Westerner and he will show the same capability to study and move ahead. As a missionary I must share blame for the fact that we changed the African life so much. The church has been very influential in changing Africa and we must take responsibility for some of the problems of the past and now help to direct change into ways of opportunity for Africans. In Zimbabwe today, with so many of the political leaders having had a good Christian education, I am positive and optimistic about the country.

"I also could not understand the white position that restricted Africans from certain trades. For example, an African boy could not become an apprentice to a bricklayer, or could not become a tradesman. It hurt me that an African who was good enough to hand up the cement to lay the bricks could not learn how to lay the bricks himself and become a qualified tradesman."

As principal at Usher Institute, Burrows initiated the construction of dormitories and a science laboratory. She had on her staff an experienced tradesman from New Zealand whom she recruited to train the Africans. Under his apprenticeship they learned to make large concrete blocks, acquired construction skills and put up buildings throughout the compound. Yet still, they could not become qualified for work opportunities outside.

It was during her time in Africa that Africans began to speak out about a new constitution to overcome the racial barriers of discrimination. The Unilateral Declaration of Independence (UDI) by Ian Smith in 1965 took Rhodesia out of the orbit of English colonialism, yet still maintained rigid discrimination against Africans. Burrows says, "I felt deep sorrow the day UDI was declared. I saw the inevitability of a clash and bloodshed if Africans were not given the opportunities and freedom they deserved. At an early stage there were enough moderate Africans who could have taken their place among whites in government and there would have been an evolution toward African leadership rather than the revolution that came about in the end. Although I'm against violence, I could see the logic in their having to fight in order to attain independence."

Back at Howard, Lyndon Taylor, as principal of the teachers training program, had launched an annual Salvation Army Students' Fellowship conference with Eva Burrows as his assistant. It was to be a conference with a revolutionary concept as some 300 delegates met in fully integrated programs. Africans and whites ate together, slept in the same dormitories, and studied and worshiped together. Out of that grew integrated Officers' Councils. It was an avant-garde program for racially segregated Rhodesia in the mid-1960s.

Her Mother's Death
Eva's parents had retired from officership in 1957 but kept involved with Army activity. Their letters had come faithfully to the daughter a half a world away, who had been serving the same Lord and Army to which they had given their lives.

On May 25, 1967, Eva's mother, at age seventy-six, suffered a stroke while walking in her garden. For six weeks her condition worsened until she was unable to move, see, or speak. Ella Burrows had been the heart and center of the family and was dearly loved by each member. Her pending departure from them was a time of unspeakable sadness.

Eva was about to leave by ship for London where she would shortly become a delegate to the International College for Officers. Her brother phoned her in Rhodesia, gave her the sad news, and said the family was paying her fare to fly home to Australia. Fervent prayer was offered by family members to spare their mother until Eva arrived.

Her father met her at the airport and drove her straight to the hospital. Sister Joyce describes the moment Eva walked into the hospital room to see her mother, who hadn't spoken since she had the stroke. "I shall never forget sitting by mother's bedside waiting. When Eva was about to walk into the room she paused, whilst I turned my mother's face toward the doorway. Joy, tears, and sorrow all welled up within me as I said, 'Darling, here's Eva.' Mother suddenly opened her eyes wide and with a beautiful look on her face, just said softly, 'Eva.' We knew God gave our mother that moment of recognition." Ella Burrows never spoke a word after that, remaining in her comatose condition. Robert Burrows sat at his wife's side day after day, and within a few weeks of Eva's arrival, she went to be with the Lord.

Mrs. Major Burrows had been greatly loved by people in the places where she and her husband had served. At her funeral the family was astounded at the large gathering of people who had come to pay their respects, many of whom the Burrows family had not seen for years. Family and friends joined in a spirit of reunion as they recounted happy memories of the departed loved one.

Eva shared in the task of sorting out her mother's belongings. In doing so she discovered that her mother had kept every letter she had sent from Africa, as well as news clippings about her. Eva thought back of her mother's early sacrifice that enabled her to go to the university and then to London, and about her unfailing encouragement through the years, and the pride she showed in Eva's work and achievements in Africa. In those moments she discovered how much she had meant to her mother, something that Ella had never seemed able to put in words.

Delegate to International College

Widened windows were about to open upon the world for Eva Burrows as she received her appointment as a delegate for the eight-week course at the International College For Officers (ICO) in London in the summer of 1967. She was scheduled to be in London following her furlough at home at the time of her mother's death. But she felt a responsibility to her father and asked to stay for a time to help him, even though he insisted that she go on to London. Eva was torn, but did stay with him some weeks, arriving in London late for the course.

Commissioner Olive Gattrall was the principal at the ICO. Eva remembers her as a woman of great spiritual sensitivity and gentleness, and having a fine mind. She observed that Commissioner Gattrall was very well read and through her influence Eva began to read classics of devotional literature she had not known before. A lifelong relationship developed between the principal and the delegate from Usher, with Commissioner Gattrall continuing to send letters of encouragement to her student, even after Eva had become General.

Commissioner Olive Gattrall, who in retirement married the widowed General Frederick Coutts, recalls, "Her delightful personality was at once evident, and it was no surprise to the staff when Major Eva Burrows was selected by her peers as session vice-president. She paid tribute to a new appreciation for meditation literature and the great European Christian classics which she introduced at morning prayers in the classroom. All the continents were represented by the session delegates, and presentiment developed that she would herself ere long be serving in countries other than Africa and Australia. Like many comrades, I saw her as a General-to-be."

A lecturer from the International Headquarters at that session was to have a profound influence on the life and career of Eva Burrows. Colonel Arnold Brown's keen perception took in the delegate from Africa, observing, "Though at that time serving in a missionary setting, she was certainly the most inquisitive of all, asking the most pertinent and probing questions of any delegate I had seen. I knew nothing about her personally, but I recognized that she already had a trained mind and was obviously an eager student. I was so impressed that I asked the principal about her. Her comments confirmed my impressions."

The positive impression Eva Burrows made on Colonel Arnold Brown in 1967 was indelible. When he later became Chief of the Staff and then General, he was increasingly linked administratively with her in the upward mobility of her appointments. He was impressed by her ability to adapt to whatever appointment she held. He noted that although the places she served were greatly diverse in culture, lifestyle, and ethos, Burrows "belonged" to Africa, to Scotland, and to Australia. Her adaptability and identification with the people led all three to "claim" her as their own.

General Brown further notes, "E.B.'s unusual abilities were recognized early in her career by the administration. When I was Chief of the Staff, General Erik Wickberg named her to me as one of the most promising of future women leaders and suggested that I should see that she had appointments which would provide her with the widest possible experience. She accepted every new appointment as a challenge and entered into every new command with eagerness. Our administrative relationship provided numerous opportunities for discussion which fairly frequently became debate. If an administrative decision was not of itself quite clear, then she requested elucidation and clarification, firmly but always courteously. She had enormous respect for those who carried major leadership in the Army."

Looking back, Burrows says of Brown, "He was my mentor. I learned much about leadership from him."

Her unusual leadership qualities observed at the International College led others to say to her, "Should you really be stuck out there in Africa?" For the first time the thought came to her that perhaps she would have expanded opportunities for leadership in the Army. But she was so happy in Africa that it never occurred to her to aspire to anything else. "I had great fulfillment in what I was doing and would have been happy to spend the rest of my life in Africa. Quite honestly, when I've been given appointments or promotions, they came almost like a surprise. They were never anything I'd been planning or maneuvering or working towards." When her territorial commander in Africa, Commissioner Ernest Fewster, called to tell her she was promoted to the rank of Major, earlier than the normal period, she said, "I couldn't believe it. I was amazed. And I had the same surprise when I was appointed to Usher as principal."

At the International College in London, Eva Burrows came to have a view of The Salvation Army that embraced a worldwide fellowship, with boundless and beckoning horizons.

Farewell to Her Adopted Land and People

General Frederick Coutts came to Rhodesia and in the course of his visit took note of the Australian Major with the extraordinary leadership qualities. The General was notorious for his taciturnity—he could spend several hours traveling with someone in a car and never say a word. But one day, upon return from Africa, he became uncharacteristically talkative, mentioning this splendid missionary officer he had met in Africa. He hinted in his well-known quasi-hesitant manner that although she seemed happy to continue indefinitely in her calling there, he felt that "perhaps one should . . . er . . . think of . . . er . . . bringing her to . . . the international center." When a General has such thoughts, they are usually translated into action.

After seventeen years in Africa, in 1969 farewell orders came for Eva Burrows to leave the land and the people to whom she had so fully devoted herself. She says of that change, "I accepted the fact that in God's purposes I was now ready for further responsibilities, but at the same time this immense wrench from Africa was like a bereavement."

When she came to make her farewell speech at Usher, no one could be heard due to the weeping, wailing, and moaning of the African girls who loved her and were traumatized by her leaving. Most of them would never again see Eva Burrows who had been to them as a mother.

Mother, father, teacher, model, encourager, counselor, minister, friend—Eva Burrows had been all of these to those entrusted to her care. But now Africa and its people were to be left behind as she took a giant step on a journey that ultimately would take her around the world for God and the Army.

Years later she reflected, "I love Africa for it has been very much a part of my life. My formative years were spent there, from age twenty-three to forty. For me Africa is not just something sentimental or nostalgic. It's really in my blood. I have a real feeling for the aspirations and hopes of the people. I often call myself a white African."

Many years earlier, another missionary had come to this part of Africa. David Livingstone left giant footprints upon the land as one who had a burning compassion and commitment to the African people. When his work was done, he was found by the natives dead in his tent in the jungle, in a posture of prayer. The Africans lovingly carried his body hundreds of miles through the jungle to the coastline so that his remains could be returned to his native land. Today he is buried in Westminster Abbey among the great. But the Africans, before they took his body away, cut out his heart and buried it in the soil of Africa because, they said, "His heart belongs in Africa among the people he loved and served."

Eva Burrows was now leaving Africa. But her heart would always remain with its people.

10

★ ★ ★ ★ ★ ★ ★ ★ ★ ★ ★ ★ ★ ★ ★ ★ ★ ★ ★

WINDOWS ON THE ARMY WORLD

"I discovered the international unity of The Salvation Army."

In November 1969 Eva Burrows left Africa, bound for Australia, to spend her five months' furlough with her family. She had heard that her father was ill, but the delay in receiving letters from home left her unaware of the gravity of his illness. Upon the ship's arrival at Perth, her sister-in-law, Ruth Burrows, who lived in a suburb of Perth, met her at the boat to say, "I'm sorry to tell you that Dad is very ill and we don't expect him to live." Robert Burrows was in the hospital with terminal cancer.

Instead of continuing the remainder of the way by ship, which would take another ten days to Sydney, Eva took the next plane home to Brisbane. She went straight to the hospital from the airport, as she had done years earlier for her mother.

Her father was comforted to see Eva—she was just the tonic he needed. He rallied enough for the doctor to allow him to go home if Eva would look after him. In her parents' small retirement cottage, Eva looked after all the needs of her father for two months. "Those last two months," she recounts, "were a great joy to me because after all those years of being away from my parents I could now be with my father. We knew he was going to die soon, and every day we would pray together and I would sing to him."

It is not unusual for those closest to God to often feel the most unworthy. During those days Robert Burrows went through a period when he wondered whether God would find him worthy when he met Him face to face. Eva helped him through that crisis, often singing one of his favorite songs of assurance:

I have no claim on grace; I have no right to plead;
  I stand before my Master's face condemned in word and deed.
But since there died a Lamb who guiltless, my guilt bore,
  I lay fast hold on Jesus' name, And sin is mine no more.

Eva cared for him up to the end, with her father returning to the hospital only two days before he died. "I was very privileged," she says, "to be with him during those months."

The family asked Eva to go through her parents' belongings and close their affairs. In so doing she came upon her father's diary consisting of scattered notes describing their corps appointments, tucked away among his books. Later she had them typed and compiled in a small volume.

While home on furlough, Eva also experienced the sorrow of the loss of her older sister Dorothy, who died with complications of diabetes. Eva spent as much time as she could with Dorothy, and spoke words of tribute and comfort at her funeral.

To the International College

During the remainder of her leave, she accepted many speaking engagements, describing the Army's work in Rhodesia. She had earlier been advised to report to the International Headquarters at the end of her furlough. On the day she left Australia, she learned that her new appointment was to be vice-principal at the Army's International College for Officers in London (ICO). She made the long journey to London via the United States where she visited former missionary colleagues. She stopped off to see Helen Prosser in Chicago, the young woman who shared her first house at Howard Institute. From there she went to Canada to visit retired Colonel Rive, her first principal at Howard.

In June 1970, at age forty, Brigadier Burrows reported to take up her new duties in London. The Salvation Army's International College for Officers provides in-service courses for twenty-four officers from around the world for eight-week sessions. The appointment was a decisive point of her career. Three years earlier as a delegate at ICO she had come to a new awareness of the internationalism of the Army. Now she would open those windows for others. She was happy that it was an international appointment. "Although I was in London, I was in the whole world."

Eva Burrows felt comfortable with the charm of the old world mansion that served as the central building and also her quarters at the ICO. Here she could meet and mingle with people of all races and continue to have contact with Third World people to whom she had a special devotion. She would often spend added time with these delegates to aid them in understanding lectures given with Australian, Yorkshire, Scottish, or American accents.

Commissioner Albert Mingay who had come as principal while Eva Burrows was assistant principal, recalls, "When I arrived to the Principalship of the ICO, I found Eva Burrows to be fully conversant with the organizational program. Indeed, she seemed to embody the ethos and the spirit of the College. She handled the domestic and curricular aspects with equal skill. Despite her competence, she never infringed on the principal's prerogatives, but showed appreciation for seniority and recognized the gifts of leadership and ministry."

Hitting the London Scene

If Eva had to be ready for London, conservative London also had to be prepared for irrepressible Eva Burrows, her openness springing from the rugged soil of Australia and blossoming in the warm culture of Africa. She reminisces, "I think sometimes they felt that I didn't observe all the rules of protocol, but I didn't know them and was just being myself." One observer at that time recalls, "She really hit the London scene with her flamboyant personality."

The uninhibited and spontaneous qualities of the brash Australian created some interesting ripples on the placid waters of the conservative Army in Britain. One observer says, "She strode right through the IHQ pecking order when she was vice-principal. She was unaware it existed and didn't kowtow to it."

At General Wickberg's public farewell meeting, the high ranking Commissioners sat in their order of rank and position, Commissioners in front and the lesser lights behind them. When Eva Burrows arrived, she noticed Commissioner Catherine Bramwell-Booth, legendary granddaughter of the Founder, sitting in the front. None of the Commissioners or others present presumed to go up to this distinguished personage. But Eva, seeing the famous Commissioner, strolled up to the front and greeted her familiarly like a long-lost auntie, having had her as a guest lecturer at the ICO. No one else present had so dared approach a Booth, but she did it spontaneously, oblivious of any of the restraints of tradition or protocol.

While vice-principal, she on occasion went with Major Jenty Fairbank during Holy Week to hear Bach's *St. Matthew Passion* at the Royal Festival Theater. Together they also enjoyed the theater, including a superb performance by the Royal Shakespeare Company of T.S. Eliot's *Murder in the Cathedral*.

During this period, silver threads started to appear in her jet black hair. Like her mother, Eva was to turn gray by her mid forties. Her hair became a trademark of her appearance. One young woman officer who met Eva after she became General, said, "That hair—I would give anything to have hair like that!"

A memorable event in her London life was a royal garden party at Buckingham Palace, to which several Army leaders had been invited. She was thrilled at this opportunity to meet royalty and thought nothing of going right up to the Archbishop of Canterbury to strike up a conversation. "If I'm going anywhere," she said later, "I just don't stand there as a single person by myself. I just naturally greet people and enter into interesting conversations."

Smartly dressed in her uniform and always a standout in the crowd, Eva was approached by one of the Queen's attendants who came to her and after brief conversation said, "I will introduce you to Her Majesty." In her elation she thought, "I must remember what the Queen says so I can report it to the delegates when I return." Eva Burrows was impressed with the appearance and charming manner of the Queen. Eva was introduced as one who had been in Zimbabwe and was now at the International College for Officers. The Queen made inquiry about the College and then asked, "How does this group get on when they come from so many national backgrounds and cultures?" Burrows replied that they were a very happy family. The Queen responded, "Well, The Salvation Army has certainly found the secret of happiness. I can see that."

At ICO, delegates were enthusiastic about her visit with the Queen and royalty's interest in the Army. Burrows acknowledged that it was her uniform that made the contact possible. "The uniform," she said, "is respected and gets you noticed."

The Teacher

When the principal, Commissioner Herbert Westcott, broke his leg, the responsibility for the day-to-day operation of the ICO fell to Brigadier Burrows. One delegate, Major Robert E. Thomson, upon return to the U.S.A., responded to the principal's request for a letter recording his impressions. He wrote, "I must pay tribute to Brigadier Burrows who carried a heavier than usual load most admirably, but who by her spirit and application of knowledge contributed much more than was evident in the classroom." Thomson, later a Commissioner and Territorial Commander, saved the handout material of memorable quotations Eva had shared with the delegates.

Colonel Lyndon Taylor, who observed her teaching skills in Rhodesia, says, "She is a wizard with the chalk." Those who sat under her teaching at ICO had demonstrations of her extraordinary skill in using the chalkboard as a teaching tool.

One of the delegates in her first session was Captain John Larsson, later to become a Commissioner and well-known Army leader. He recalls, "She won the hearts of all the delegates. We noted how much she went out of her way to look after the delegates from the Third World countries and to make them feel that they counted and were really important. Her experience came over in the classroom. When my attention wandered, as it must have done once or twice, I heard her say, 'And what do you think about that, Captain Larsson?' which made me attend from then on. And I thought, 'Well, that was cleverly done.'"

Period of Adjustments

ICO was a period of major adjustment for Eva Burrows. In Africa she had spoken simple English for her students. Now she would be speaking to Salvation Army leaders from around the world. In Africa she spoke with a deliberate slowness and with much emphasis. Now she had to learn to speak more quickly in the mode of conventional English.

After having scant resources in Africa, she was shocked by affluent Westerners engrossed with possessions and bigness. She had to learn to communicate with those who came from a world of consumerism, urbanization, and technology. At the same time cataclysmic events on the political and technological scenes were also reshaping her world.

In reflecting on this period of adjustment, she referred to Evelyn Underhill's analogy of the Holy Spirit working for change in our lives as though are dough. When dough is mixed with yeast, the texture changes and the bread that results is quite different from the dough. Dramatic and often uncomfortable changes were taking place in God's servant, Eva Burrows, to make her God's broken bread to a needy world.

At the ICO

*Right: Colonel Eva
Burrows lecturing as
a principal at the
International College
for Officers.*

*Below right: In ICO garden
with delegate from Japan
Below left: Attired as "General
Eva" by ICO delegates*

Life at ICO

During free time it was not unusual for Eva Burrows to take a group of delegates to a concert or to broaden their experience on a free Sunday by taking them to hear famous preachers of other denominations. "I realized," she says, "that they were mature students. I tried to ensure that I didn't treat them like Cadets. They were people of ability and leadership in their own spheres, so I think I found a balance between the role of leadership and that of companion or friend to these delegates."

Each session at the College has one night devoted to fun and fellowship. One group of delegates adorned Eva Burrows in the gold trimmings of a General and had her pose in front of the Army flag, similar to a famous photo of General Evangeline Booth. Some pondered whether that moment contained more foreshadowing than lighthearted entertainment.

Major Jenty Fairbank shares an incident when she herself was ready to leave for service in Africa in 1973. She had vacated her apartment and went back to it with her father, who was retired, to clean it up. There was no heat and the electricity had been turned off, so there was no hot water or means for making a warm drink. Suddenly they heard a knock on the door, and there was Eva, herself nursing a cold, with a flask of coffee and refreshments. "She brought them to help keep us going," says Fairbank, "and to give us a bit of encouragement. That was a nice touch."

At the ICO there were young women from Switzerland, Denmark, Sweden, and France who came to do the housework for the opportunity to learn English. These girls grew to have a special fondness for Eva. Between sessions she would take them on trips to further their education. One girl remembered her often running up the stairs whistling. She said of Eva, "She was not like some of the people who came to ICO. Whereas some of the other high-up officers ignored us, she would talk to us as people."

With her full schedule and extracurricular activities, Eva Burrows did not give much attention to domestic duties. She also disliked washing and setting her own hair, and each week, as a personal luxury, would go to the hairdresser.

In the rain and fog of London, Eva missed the warmth of the African sunshine. She booked a December holiday for a week in Majorca, an island 140 miles from the Spanish mainland in the Mediterranean Sea, with scenic highlands and fertile lowlands. There she basked in the warm sunshine and felt a touch of Africa with the thatched open-sided huts along the golden beach.

After twenty-one months as vice-principal, Eva Burrows was promoted to principal of the International College, and at age forty-four to the rank of Colonel, making her the youngest Colonel in The Salvation Army world. It soon became common for leaders and discerning observers of her ascending star to whisper their wonderings, "Could the Colonel, later Commissioner, perhaps . . . one day become . . . the Army's second woman General?"

The ICO has aptly been referred to as "the house on the hill with a world view." Lt. Colonel Lucille Turfrey recalls her impression as a delegate, "Colonel Burrows knew how to open the shutters on parochial minds. Her ability to be at one with East and West, to encourage a sense of 'world family,' was unforgettable. Her broad understanding of national traits and cultures enabled the weaving of the fabric of our experience at ICO to be strong and colorful."

Becoming an Internationalist

Burrows remembers one woman delegate from Kenya, saying at the end of the course, "This has been like a very deep well of pure water, and God has given me a long rope to draw up this water to nourish me and satisfy my own soul." To Burrows' delight, this Major became the first woman Territorial Social Service Secretary for the Army in East Africa.

More than any other appointment could have done, ICO gave Eva contacts with Army leaders around the world, leaders with whom she had spent more than two months of intensive study and fellowship. She shares, "I discovered the international unity of The Salvation Army, a unity different from many other churches. I had not realized this in Africa. I suppose I concentrated so much on seeing the Africans receiving the Gospel, and on how The Salvation Army could be accepted as an indigenous movement. Before I came to ICO I never knew or understood Asians. For example, I expected Japanese Salvationists to be quiet and reserved, but at ICO I saw our comrades from Japan as enthusiastic evangelists. I came to realize that The Salvation Army is a subculture, merging our common characteristics with the national cultures of Salvationists around the world. We do not become a foreign entity, but are built into the fabric of their own national culture. ICO was for me a learning as well as a teaching experience."

Four hundred and ninety-six Salvation Army officers passed through the doors of the International College during the five years Eva Burrows served as vice-principal and principal. She found every group to have its own personality. The ICO experience provided an excellent laboratory for study in group dynamics, the delegates coming together from different backgrounds and possessing varied temperaments. She observed how "key personalities tended to color the group, without manipulation but by interpersonal osmosis." Many of them rose to top leadership positions around the Army world. Later, as General, when names would be proposed for leadership positions, she would remember them as delegates to the ICO and have a valuable assessment from that time of relationship.

The appointment at ICO, in the land of the Army's birth and association with International Headquarters, was a foundation experience in the making of a General.

11

★ ★ ★ ★ ★ ★ ★ ★ ★ ★ ★ ★ ★ ★ ★ ★ ★ ★ ★ ★

TO THE LOST AND LONELY

"In that post I got a feeling for the lost and lonely."

"The General wants to see you in his office," was the message that came to Eva Burrows. She had no idea what it was about, but knew it must be important to meet with General Clarence Wiseman and his Chief of the Staff.

"Colonel Burrows, you are the right person to take over the leadership of the Women's Social Services here in Great Britain," was the jolting announcement she heard. Eva, not one to be easily shocked, nevertheless was stunned. She remonstrated, "Well, General, I never in my life questioned an appointment, and if you are giving this appointment then I'll go. But I've never had any experience in this field. I don't think I'm the one to do it."

Eva Burrows had been in education throughout her career, and she wondered if she were really the one for this specialized work. General Wiseman stated that they had given the matter much thought and felt she was the person who should head that department.

Eva Burrows left the General's office "quite shocked, and sad at the thought of leaving the ICO." However, she accepted the appointment without further question. The Women's Social Services embraced a vast network of institutions and services to women in Great Britain and Ireland. At that time it was considered one of the top positions for a woman officer.

Meeting the Challenge
A new provision allowed an officer to have a six-week leave with their fare paid to go home, if they were far from their homeland and

had served in a Western country for five years. This enabled Eva to return to Australia for a vacation before taking up her new post. It also gave her time to ponder how she would meet the challenge of heading this section with all its unique programs and experienced personnel.

Her relentless drive to prepare herself for any assignment led her to contact an old friend in Australia, Brigadier Jean Geddes. A retired officer, Brigadier Geddes had been a close friend of Eva's parents and had known her since her teenage years. She was one of the Army's top experts in the field of social services where she had spent most of her career. No time, not even on vacation, was to be lost in preparation. Brigadier Geddes recalls Burrows' visit at that time. "She picked my brains. We visited all the institutions we could, even while driving here and there she was asking questions. She has a great capacity for learning and retaining."

Her appointment did not bring rejoicing to the Women's Social Services. Some actually resented this "outsider who had no experience in the field." There were others "in line" who had "paid their dues" by service in the department and were considered more qualified.

In November 1975 Colonel Eva Burrows assumed her appointment as leader of the Women's Social Services in Great Britain and Ireland. For the first time she would be responsible for a budget in the millions of dollars. Although she had no background in fiscal management, her intelligence and strong sense of accountability led her to monitor carefully the financial affairs and budgets of her administration. She was assured there was money to cover every expense; however, she did not follow the practice of building up reserves with funds contributed for the Army's work. She believes, "Money is functional. If you have a purpose for it, use it, don't just store it. When you use God's money for God's purposes, you get that money back."

Initially, her aggressive efforts to effect change only fueled the fire of resentment that smoldered within the Women's Social Services. As always, Eva Burrows refused to be satisfied with the status quo. But she soon realized she needed to respect the experience of veteran officers in the field and seek their consensus in the changes that needed to be made. A turning point came while conducting an officers' council. She acknowledged, "I have never been in this field of work, yet I have criticized and tried to change your whole approach that has been born of experience. I realize that I've been wrong."

A new spirit of teamwork and cooperation was generated. Resistance further mellowed when staff members observed how Burrows gave herself and how she really cared for the destitute people who comprise the parish of the Women's Social Services. It was now "full steam ahead" under her dynamic leadership. When she found areas still operating on outdated practices, she vigorously led the Services into new methods and programs. The Army's women's hostels, with their old-fashioned and Dickensian dormitories that offered no privacy, were ushered into the modern era with upgraded facilities and procedures. The needs of the day were met by converting homes for unmarried mothers into shelters for battered women.

Burrows did not have the problem that has beset many in religious work—an artificial polarization between social work and evangelism. She acknowledged that in the Army of Great Britain "there often seemed to be a gulf between the spiritual and the social work. Jesus did not say to the man filled with many devils, 'If you follow Me, I'll cure you.' Jesus just met the need. I have no problem that we are in social work to meet the needs of people, but the spiritual is one of their primary needs as well. I do not see any dichotomy in this area."

Traditionally the Army's social work in Great Britain had been divided into two sections—the Women's Social Work and the Men's Social Work. Eva discerned that it would be much more effective for these two Services to be combined, and she so recommended it in her farewell brief. Several years later the two Services merged, resulting in greater economy and efficiency. Now men and women are cared for in the same senior citizen centers, and integrated in most of the Army's social service programs.

Burrows was not one to confine her Social Services leadership to the office. She went out on the rounds to visit the homeless and destitute, to talk to them personally, and try to understand their problems. She made the startling discovery that many of the destitute did not want help. Even when she would go on the night rounds in the cold of winter and invite the homeless living on the streets to come in to a warm Army shelter, they would not do it. "They want to live that way," she observed. "They don't want to live with others. They want to do their own thing. It's a psychiatric problem. There are many people whose problems will not be solved by physical amenities and decent accommodations. That's why it is so difficult for the police and authorities to solve these problems.

"As I moved among the people, I wished I could live among them and help them more. But when you are in top leadership, you can't do that. But I could go and visit with them in the hostels where we were caring for them. I admired our staff who worked with the women of the street and the alcoholics all the time, bathing them when they came in filthy, doing the most menial tasks of love.

"You may change the location, but that doesn't change the person. You may improve the facilities, but that doesn't solve the problem. Really, the need for these people is to receive love and warmth in these most difficult of circumstances. These lonely and unhappy people need to know that somebody loves them. When you are dedicated to Christ, that love of God is shared through you. The Holy Spirit enables you to love the unlovely, to love where love is not returned, because you are bringing Christ to these people who hurt and are in need."

God's Creative Will

As she confronted these problems, and came in contact with some of the people who were lonely and hurting, she began to have a strong attachment to her new work. This post, she realized, filled a gap in her life. "I had been involved so much in education that I hadn't had the opportunity to understand these areas of human need. I came to see more fully the poverty, despair, and sadness in the Western world. I think something of my mother has come back to me—the way she had worked with the lonely and lost, the poor and the prostitutes. Now when I look back on her example I am grateful."

Eva Burrows was in the Social Services for only sixteen months, but in that short time she left her indelible mark on the program, and it left its mark on her. Looking back at the appointment she initially thought so inappropriate, she sees that "God's providential handling of one's life is amazing. His creative will can take whatever happens in your life and make it of value. Even if The Salvation Army puts you in a position or a job that you may not have chosen and may not even be in line with your temperament, God's creative will can make out of that something of value. Some people talk of God's permissive will, but I like to think of God's creative will."

When she received farewell orders, she felt she was just starting to come to grips with the work in that field. Of the change, she says, "I was sorry to leave and quite surprised that my time there would be so short, especially since I was told when I began that I was really the only person available in the whole world to do it."

In retrospect, it has been surmised that the reason for the quick change was to achieve more representation of women on the next High Council, and Eva Burrows was looked on as one of the most promising and capable woman leaders in the Army. Appointing her as a territorial commander made her eligible for the High Council, due to convene in May 1977 to elect a successor to General Wiseman.

After she became General, she said that one of her most important appointments had been as leader of the Women's Social Services. "My background had been such that I had not come close to such deprivation, sorrow, and despair among the wanderers of the world," she said. "In that post I got a feeling for the lost and lonely."

12

★ ★ ★ ★ ★ ★ ★ ★ ★ ★ ★ ★ ★ ★ ★ ★ ★ ★ ★

CHALLENGE IN SRI LANKA

"I preach Christ, not Christianity."

An Italian friar in the fourteenth century said that Sri Lanka was but forty miles from paradise. This fair and fragrant island, renowned for an extravagance of flora and fauna, is garlanded by pristine beaches shimmering under a tropical sun. Sri Lanka, a paradise in the Indian Ocean off the southern tip of India, means "resplendent island."

But the island's natural beauty is a stark contrast to the poverty and struggles of its people. Ethnic violence stalks and brutalizes them. Half the population lives in poverty. To this underdeveloped and politically unstable island republic Colonel Eva Burrows was assigned as Territorial Commander in January 1977.

Sri Lanka is a challenging and tough command, torn by political strife and also beset by problems endemic to its religious pluralism. Of its approximately 14 million people, 74 percent are Sinhalese who are Buddhists, and 18 percent are Tamil who are Hindus. Smaller numbers of Muslims, Burghers, Eurasians, Malays, and Europeans make up the remainder. An estimated 1 million are Christians with about 70 percent of those Catholics. English is spoken by only 10 percent of the population. More than three-fourths of the people live in rural areas. Into this melange came the Australian-born, African-seasoned, and British-experienced Eva Burrows.

The Army's Territory consists of some fifty corps and outposts, 5,000 Salvationists, 100 officers, and twelve social institutions. Many in that small country look to the Army as a major source of help for the critical needs of its people. The Salvation Army in Sri Lanka is well known and has an influence well beyond its small numbers.

104

Here was another enormous challenge for Eva Burrows: a different culture, unfamiliar language and the requirements of leadership in a strange country. Once again Eva was constrained to throw herself on the guidance and resources of God. But she knew well that inspiration must be wed to perspiration and that "we should pray as though everything depended upon God and work as though everything depended on us." She undertook to read every book she could find on Sri Lanka to understand its history, geography, people, problems, and culture. By the time she stepped off the plane, she already could identify by name every department head in her new headquarters. At her welcome meeting she surprised and delighted her audience by responding in a few words of Sinhalese.

Eva witnessed serious riots that broke out during her time there, striking very close to home. Next door to her was a Hindu family; all the others in the area were Sinhalese who were hostile to the Hindus. Each morning she could hear her Hindu neighbors singing their religious songs with the children. When a terrible riot broke out, Eva remembered the Hindu family. She went to their house and found them loading up their goods and preparing to flee. She spoke encouragingly to them, offering use of her car and other help. But they left on their own just before a mob smashed their home.

Colonel Eva Burrows knew that Christ offered the ultimate answer for the strife and violence around her, and she found it difficult to restrain her evangelistic enthusiasm. She would like to have said to the Buddhists, "Christ is the answer." She knew that for a person to become a Christian often meant a significant break with their families. "In Sri Lanka," she admits, "I learned a new tolerance for other faiths. I could never come to the point where I would say, 'All faiths are equal,' because of my firm belief in the preeminence of Christ. But I learned to respect other religions and the sincerity of their followers."

Ecumenical Fellowship

Having a strong commitment to ecumenical fellowship, Burrows took an active role in the Christian Council, an association of church leaders of Sri Lanka. The Anglican Bishop and president of the Council, Lakshman Wickamasingha, was a highly educated Christian leader with a strong sense of social justice who had earned Eva's admiration. When election time came for the Council, he said to her, "I would like you to be one of the vice-presidents." She replied,

"Bishop, I don't see myself doing that. I would like to help but I'm not Sinhalese and don't think it would be right." The Bishop assured, "Look, I'll be here and the other vice-president will be here and you won't have anything to worry about." The Bishop's charm and persuasive powers won the day and Eva became a vice-president.

Shortly thereafter the Bishop went to Britain on a study tour and the other vice-president left on an extended journey. Then a crisis arose in the Christian Council and the remaining vice-president had to deal with it. Burrows personally visited all involved in the dispute and piloted the Council through its stormy recriminatory passage to a reconciliation. A Sinhalese minister of the Anglican Church later said to her, "I think the fact that you were not Sinhalese or Tamil made it possible, under God's hand, to bring about a reconciliation in that situation."

A surge of love from the other churches was felt by Eva, in spite of her being a non-national. This was especially evident when she returned to Sri Lanka as General and was invited to preach in the cathedral on Christian Unity Sunday. All the church leaders were present to welcome her back as a sister in Christ, including the Roman Catholic Archbishop and his bishops.

Commissioner Eva Burrows with church leaders in Sri Lanka.

Tools to Get the Job Done

Eva found people in one village sitting on the floor for worship. She thought it would be good if they had chairs. No money was available but she went ahead in faith and ordered them. Shortly thereafter she received a letter from a man in Canada. He sent $100 and indicated he had heard about the Army's work in Sri Lanka and was going to send $100 a month. She wrote and thanked him and told him his initial gift would purchase the chairs. He replied saying, "Fancy putting chairs in the church for $100. It would cost $3,000 here."

In subsequent correspondence he shared his desire to become a Salvationist, but had not been able to meet the requirement to give up smoking. He said if he gave up smoking he would donate an additional $30 a month. Burrows had her staff and those using the new chairs pray for him. The man conquered his habit, became a Soldier, married a Salvationist and ultimately sold his business, sending one-tenth of the proceeds to Sri Lanka. He later became a Salvation Army officer.

Upon Burrows' arrival in Sri Lanka, she was greeted by the stern plaster walls of the old headquarters. One of her first acts was to brighten them with prints of classic art. Inexpensive reproductions they were, but selected with an eye for excellence. In property renovations and capital projects under her initiative throughout the territory it became clear that aesthetics and frugality need not be at odds.

Winston Churchill said during a critical stage of the Second World War, "Give us the tools and we will get the job done." Eva believed in Army workers having functional facilities to get their jobs done. The old headquarters and corps building in Colombo was a proud but dilapidated structure, and scarred by the lashing of innumerable monsoons. To fund a replacement was unthinkable in a territory with such scant resources. But Eva Burrows is a visionary and a pragmatist, and each time she went into the inadequate and obsolete building reinforced her conviction that the problem had to be solved.

She shared her vision of a new worship center and modern headquarters with her Advisory Board. Its forward-looking chairman, a businessman who admired the work of the Army, also had a temperament for getting things done. Together they launched a long-range planning project that identified the property and program needs. With a Sinhalese architect they drew plans for the new buildings, planning to launch the initial phase during the Army's centenary in Sri Lanka, four years in the future. By the time the plans came to fruition, Eva Burrows was no longer in Sri Lanka. However, through her vision and vigor, she had assessed the needs and laid plans for expanding and upgrading the Army facilities. She secured a substantial pledge from the Army in Canada and financial aid from Sweden toward the forthcoming centenary redevelopment scheme in Colombo. Before leaving she had a check in hand in the amount of $1.3 million for the first phase of the project for a new headquarters, social service center, young women's hostel, eventide home for thirty-two elderly women, and a new corps worship hall.

The 1977 High Council

During her appointment in Sri Lanka, Eva Burrows attended her first of three High Councils, called to elect a new general. In preparation she read the biographies of former Generals and noted their comments about them. She took note that General Orsborn had said, "At your first High Council, you just keep quiet a good deal of the time, and don't open your mouth too soon." Uncharacteristically, Eva Burrows did not speak much, but listened and observed.

At age forty-seven, she was the youngest member since Commissioner Catherine Bramwell-Booth attended the stormy session of 1929. As the junior member she sat at the end of the table. She recalls, "For me that first High Council was a precious and beautiful experience."

Certain offices in the Council are filled through election—president, vice-president, secretary, committee chairmen, recorder. The chaplain, who oversees the spiritual exercises, is appointed by the president. Eva Burrows was shocked when the president, Commissioner Bramwell Tripp, approached her and said, "I would like you to be our chaplain." She couldn't believe it and said, "I think you have made a mistake; after all, I'm the youngest one here." "No," he replied. "I believe it is important we show all are involved in this occasion, and I'd like you to accept this responsibility."

As chaplain she would be responsible for the daily devotions and prayers and times of worship. It was an intimidating assignment. Eva went to her room and prayed. She stayed up most of that first night preparing for the next day's devotions before these eminent leaders of the Army world.

She shared with them the surprise she had experienced as a young missionary officer in Africa when she discovered that the leaders had to vote for the General. "Surely," she thought, "in all these holy men coming together, the Holy Spirit will put the same name in each mind. Why do we have to vote?" Colonel Rive, then the principal at Howard, had shown her a verse from Proverbs which says that men cast the lots, but God assures the outcome (Proverbs 16:33). She told the Council that God would guide their votes to the right decision. To those gathered at that High Council it seemed that God assured the vote for Arnold Brown who was elected the eleventh General of The Salvation Army.

A Landmark Revelation

Back in Sri Lanka Eva Burrows was invited to give a series of Sunday morning radio meditations. She had never listened to the program because she had been out preaching on Sundays. Tape recordings were made so she could have an idea of the content. She discovered that the morning program consisted of a "Thought for the Day," not only from a Christian speaker, but also from Hindus, Buddhists, and Muslims, in five minute segments one after the other. It was an honor for a "foreigner" to be invited to do such a series.

She felt challenged to communicate the Christian message in a nation that was so strongly entrenched in Eastern religions. She wondered, "How can you be true to the preaching of the Gospel and not be offensive to the beliefs held by most of the Sri Lankans?" She noted in listening to the broadcasts that there were similarities in the code of conduct, the morality, and ethics of each religion.

As she pondered this challenge and asked the Lord for guidance, the illuminating thought came to her, "Preach Christ, not Christianity." She realized that too many have perceived Christ only through the accumulated refractions of lenses of various systems. But, she clearly saw, "Christ is the difference. The Buddhist presents a noble path, saying 'Walk in that path.' But in our Christian faith Christ says, 'I am the path.' He does not merely tell the way but He walks with us, supports and strengthens us, and is our living Savior. And so I spoke about Christ. If you merely teach Christianity and not Christ, then you are just one among the others."

This was a landmark revelation for Eva Burrows. Later she said, "Always after that experience in Sri Lanka, I have sought to lift up Christ in my preaching." She endeavored not to preach the system but the Savior, not creeds but Christ. Christology became the center and thrust of her theology. She knew that too often the preaching of the Gospel in non-Christian cultures is clouded with the trappings and encumbrances of denominationalism. She read and studied again the life and teachings of Christ and sought to present the beauty and majesty and love of Christ to her listening audience. Later, upon her election as General, she reiterated this principle of proclamation, declaring, "I preach Christ, not Christianity."

While in Sri Lanka the tragic news came of two young women staff members at Usher who were murdered by members of the Patriotic Liberation Front. Eva Burrows could imagine the horror and suffering back at Usher. It was for her a very sad moment. "I wish I could have shared with them during those difficult days," says Burrows. I wasn't there during the whole of the seven years war, but I remained interested, and prayed for them all that time."

The Cyclone Strikes

On November 23, 1978, a cyclone struck and ravaged Sri Lanka, leaving in its wake over 1,000 dead and 800,000 homeless. But Colonel Burrows did not wait for the storm to strike. As soon as warnings were received of approaching 100-mile-an-hour winds and 15-foot tidal waves, she assembled relief teams ready to move into action. Burrows, the leader "who leads from the front," went from group to group as they were packing the emergency supplies, often stopping to help bag sugar or flour, encouraging the relief workers by her personal interest and involvement.

The teams found that the storm had torn off almost every roof in its path, polluted every well, contaminated food supplies, and demolished countless dwellings. Transportation, power, and telecommunication services had collapsed. Emergency funds were released by International Headquarters and gifts came from other sources. Staff and volunteers loaded food, mats, blankets, clothing, and other essential items on two large lorries which set off on their mercy missions.

Burrows herself went into the stricken area and, while offering help and comfort, noticed some homeless people digging out a big tree trunk. Not being fluent in Sinhalese, she asked the officer with her what were they doing. These people, who had just had everything destroyed, were already working to make new canoes from the trees that had fallen, so they could start fishing again. She would later say of that experience, "No matter how devastated people can be, there is a tremendous resilience in human beings that allows them to get up and start over. I never felt we were just handing out things to people, for they were already showing they were trying to make the best of it and to rebuild their lives."

An elderly and highly respected Sri Lankan Salvation Army Brigadier died while serving the critical needs of the people. He was a district officer, well known by Burrows who used to enjoy hearing him play the violin. His son, one of five children, served as her private secretary.

Upon word of his death she immediately started out on the long journey, several hundred miles over terrible roads, to conduct his funeral. She had not thought about where she would sleep. She found everything in shambles. Many people were sleeping in their cars. She stayed in the damaged hut where the body of the officer lay. The roof had been blown away, the wind was still howling and the rains pouring, with the only shelter above them that of coconut leaves.

The funeral was a very sad affair. The rain never stopped. When they arrived at the cemetery the grave was filled with water which had to be scooped out. Standing next to the casket as she conducted the service, Eva could not hold back the tears. She entered into the sorrow of her people. Captain Jayaratnasingham later said, "That was the first time I had seen a Territorial Commander cry. She had always been so joyful, but that day she cried because of her compassion for this officer, his family, and the people."

By that act Burrows demonstrated her recognition of the worth of one person's life in service to God. The travel and exposure to rough weather left her exhausted. But hers was an act of compassionate leadership that Salvationists in Sri Lanka would never forget. Someone once described her as "speaking the language of love." Years later they would still speak of this act and their territorial leader who had an Australian accent but a heart that beat as one with theirs. A newspaper editorial in Sri Lanka later commented:

Miss Burrows was one of the first to go to the cyclone stricken areas. We were proud to publish her comments. We did so because she did not speak as a Christian missionary on the lookout for converts. She spoke as a human being, concerned and agitated about the human suffering caused by the cyclone. There was not one word of propaganda in her pronouncements. She was not recruiting for The Salvation Army. She spoke as one who loved Sri Lanka and its people.

Colonel Eva Burrows helps distribute goods to cyclone victims in Sri Lanka.

The Sleeping Watchman

Burrows found grist for her homiletical mill in her everyday experiences. She often told of how she lived in a dangerous neighborhood in Sri Lanka where gangs of robbers roamed. She, as her neighbors, hired a night watchman. He was given a table and chair at his post.

One night she returned from a meeting and her car lights shone on the watchman. His head was on the table, and he was fast asleep. He did not see the lights, nor hear the car. Burrows got out of the car, went up to him, and said, "Good evening, watchman!" The man startled out of his sleep, jumped up and said, "Madam, I am watching your house!" "No you're not," she responded. "You have betrayed the trust I put in you."

Driving home her point at an officers' council, she would challenge, "How do you care for your people entrusted to you by God? Are you keeping watch over them?"

"She Dreamed Big Dreams"

In June 1979, Eva Burrows was appointed Commissioner, the highest rank of The Salvation Army, except for the General, with about thirty holding this rank in the international movement.

Major and Mrs. Graeme Crowden, who served with Eva in Sri Lanka, observed, "She was a first-class leader, a hard taskmaster, but she never asked us to do anything that she herself was not willing to do. She delegated duties and then let the person get it done. At the same time her help was there for the asking.

"She was satisfied with nothing but the best, whether it applied to the quality of the stationery used in the office, uniform wearing, or the service rendered. Shoddy or lazy work could bring forth words of strong rebuke. She could be very impatient with those she felt were only offering second best.

"On the many building projects undertaken, she took a vital interest in every detail, even checking how much sand was used in the cement to assure the quality of workmanship. When visiting a center she would often inspect cupboards for cleanliness and tidiness, keeping all on their toes and at the same time giving the staff the feeling she did care about them."

Burrows is described as being thoughtful and generous to her staff. Her officers received her congratulations on birthdays and special occasions. On the day when a staff couple was promoted to the rank of Major, she came to their home before office hours to present a card congratulating them on attaining their 'majority' along with a lovely bouquet of flowers.

"Perhaps her most important accomplishment," say the Crowdens, "was the self-confidence and self-worth she built up in individuals. She encouraged all she met—whether the President, the Bishop of Colombo, a sheik, Army officer, paddy farmer, or a dirty little urchin in the street. All received that same smile, interest, and touch. She made women feel that they were important to God and the Army, and were to use the gifts God had given them. She drew out, or sometimes 'pulled out,' the potential that was within us. She was interested in people at every center visited, whether it was the manager, the cook, or an inmate. When she wanted to stop and talk to an elderly person, or play with a baby, she did, and everything else waited. She dreamed big dreams and was not afraid to set out after them, carrying others with her enthusiasm."

On a Christmas morning in Sri Lanka, over 500 homeless persons were fed by the Army. Burrows was not content to just put in an appearance when all was ready and tidy. She came early and helped organize the seating of the hungry, desperate people. Then she helped distribute the food, mingled with them, and spoke personally with as many as possible.

Indigenous leadership for Sri Lanka was a principal objective for Commissioner Burrows. She had strongly recommended that when she left Sri Lanka she be succeeded by a national officer, a Sinhalese. She groomed her second-in-command, Colonel P. William Perera, whom she considered worthy and capable of following her. He became the first Sri Lankan Territorial Commander and led his country through its centenary celebrations. Upon word of her pending farewell, she worked extraordinarily hard on his behalf to insure that money and plans were on hand for what needed to be done.

An Extracurricular Project

Burrows remembers that General Arnold Brown had always wanted to know the course of action for recommendations made. She recalls that he would often say, "If you really want this to happen, then get out your diary. When are you going to do it?" Always a quick learner as well as an inveterate activist, she observed that action could be lost by delay or stymied by the voluminous pages that ensued from conferences. Recommendations needed to be wedded to a plan of action.

In early 1979 Burrows attended a zonal conference in India, led by General Brown. On that occasion he said to the group, "I see that you have discussed a regional college for officers, but nothing has happened. Do you want one? Well, then you should have it." He pointed to Burrows and said, "Colonel, you were the principal of the International College for Officers. Would you design a course for the South Asia area and be the principal?" She replied, "Yes, I am quite prepared to help with the design, but I think the principal should be an Indian officer."

Then and there a committee was chosen, a date and place set for planning the regional college for South Asia. From that exchange came one of the most dynamic programs of the international movement.

Although under heavy work pressure at the time of her farewell from Sri Lanka, Burrows flew to Bombay to meet for several days in committee to design the course for the first Regional College for Officers, to be called SACO—South Asia College for Officers—to serve the Army territories in India, Pakistan, and Sri Lanka. The program would provide two-month training sessions to develop leadership and management skills. Burrows made an inestimable contribution with her training in education, Third World experience and sensitivities, and service as principal at the International College.

The success of SACO under her tutelage spawned a prodigy of Regional Conferences and a new vocabulary of acronyms for the Army's command in developing countries. Offspring would include colleges for officers for South Pacific and East Asia—SPEACO, Africa—AFCO, Latin America—LACO. These zonal colleges were designed for a homogeneous group with sessions for divisional commanders, training principals, public relations officers, and editorial staff.

The Approaching Shadow

During a period of great pressure in her official duties, Eva Burrows designed the pattern for regional colleges that would serve the worldwide Army for generations to come. But this project added to the demands on health and strength, for which she would soon have to pay a heavy cost.

Burrows traveled on most Sundays to conduct meetings in the Territory. There were no jet planes or trains or modern hotels along the route. The travel to the out-station corps in the heat of this tropical country was wearing, with miles of bone-jarring roads, followed by long walks across wet paddy fields when the road ended. The unexpected often greeted her upon arrival—some ceremony, function, grievance, or visit added to the already full agenda of scheduled meetings.

The intense tropical heat of Sri Lanka could exact an unforgiving cost to those who ignored its peril. Natives had learned to pace themselves with a midday siesta. But not Eva, the hyperactivist. Major Lyell M. Rader, Jr., who served concurrently with Burrows in Sri Lanka, describes her as "traveling the island without respite and maintaining a prodigious schedule."

She bore no resemblance to the long distance runner who conserves energy for the final laps. She had long-distance objectives but always went after them as a sprinter. Her open door policy at the office meant that she took home a good deal of her office work to do late at night. This unrelenting pace in the torrid climate of Sri Lanka, the pressure of her last few months, and having to abbreviate her vacation in Australia—all would exact a heavy toll.

In retrospect Eva acknowledges, "I wasn't as wise as I should have been about my health in that intense tropical heat. It is wise to take a siesta after lunch and I did not often do that. I felt I could keep up my usual pace. It wasn't sensible and I've learned from that experience."

"She Became a Sri Lankan"

On one of her visits to the training school she noted a young officer on the staff, Captain P. Jayaratnasingham, who showed high intelligence and potential. As General she appointed him to the staff of the International Secretary for South Asia. He says of that appointment, "I never expected I would come to this position here at International Headquarters. When I received the appointment it was a shock, but we felt that God wanted to do something through us for the Army in Sri Lanka and Southeast Asia. I am Tamil and my wife is Sinhalese, so we both can contribute something. I also know some parts of India, the people, language, and culture. So I think the General thought that a person from this part of the world could be helpful here." The Captain became the first Sri Lankan appointed to IHQ, as part of General Burrows' overall goal of the internationalization of the headquarters staff.

Captain Jayaratnasingham remembers Eva climbing up a muddy, slippery hill in the rain to visit her people. At other times she would walk through the wet rice paddies, taking off her shoes, to get to some of the corps made up of farmers. Today the Captain says of the General, "She was not only our leader, but she was a spiritual mother to every one of us."

The Captain further describes her as adapting herself to the Sri Lankan style of living, "She took her illustrations not from Europe or a foreign land, but from Sri Lanka itself, from the trees and seashore around us. She really became a Sri Lankan." Lyell M. Rader, Jr. says, "On the platform she had the teacher's aptitude to grasp the humbly familiar and to make it shine with serendipity. Her mental acuity is legendary. She mastered the convoluted Sinhala alphabet in a single weekend."

Eva further identified with the people by wearing a sari, as all Sri Lankan women, as part of their uniform. The sari is a broad and colorful cloth six yards long, pleated in front and wrapped around the waist with the balance thrown over the shoulder. Sri Lankan women wear a sari from their teen years, but it can be difficult for an adult to learn to walk in it if it is not draped correctly. Mr. Mallory Wijesinghe, who was on the Advisory Board in Sri Lanka, tells how, when she visited his home for Christmas, "Eva Burrows moved

Commissioner Eva Burrows in her Sri Lankan uniform.

around in the sari as though she wore it every day."

Major H. Ella, a Sri Lankan officer who served with her, recalls, "She followed our customs when she was with us. She wore our uniform sari even more beautifully and neatly than our national officers. She traveled the length and breadth of our country without any fear. I can never forget how she responded during the great flood that devastated our Eastern Province. When the roads were impassable, she risked taking a lorry loaded with food and clothes to the victims. When we were in sorrow she shared our sorrow, and when we were in joy she shared our joy. She visited every corps of our island and knew our soldiers by name. All the people loved and respected her. Years later, when she returned as General, she still remembered the names of our people. We are proud that she is our General."

Upon farewelling from this appointment, Burrows was quoted as saying that Sri Lanka had taught her many things. She benefited from living among a people deeply entrenched in four great religions of the world—Buddhism, Hinduism, Islam, and Christianity. Drawing as always her illustrations from life around her she said, "Living in Sri Lanka has taught me to love your trees, especially the coconut tree. It bears fruit always and serves as a good example for a fruitful life. The time has come to work and be useful citizens — not only to lie and wait for the fruits to fall into one's lap, but to dig the soil, plant the tree, and see it bear fruit."

Upon her departure, an editorial appeared in the September 12, 1979 issue of the *Ceylon Observer,* a leading newspaper of Sri Lanka.

Eva Burrows is a foreigner. She is a Christian, which by silly standards should cut her off from the people in our predominantly Buddhist country. She is not even black like the rest of us. She was head of The Salvation Army in Sri Lanka and leaves our shores shortly. A foreigner, a Christian of one of the lesser known sects, we ought not to think her departure worthy of editorial attention. . . , We say without fear of contradiction that people like Eva Burrows grace any country they serve in. . . . Sri Lanka will miss this woman, Eva Burrows.

13

★ ★ ★ ★ ★ ★ ★ ★ ★ ★ ★ ★ ★ ★ ★ ★ ★ ★ ★

SCOTLAND AND THE HEART ATTACK

"We have to do something."

In November 1979, Commissioner Burrows became the first woman to head Salvation Army forces in Scotland since two "hallelujah lassies" had pioneered the work there more than a century earlier.

She was thrilled to be in Scotland, among other reasons because that is where her father was born, in the city of Dundee. She said, "I'm sure my father would have thought it quite marvelous that I was now the commander in Scotland."

Heart Attack!

But Eva Burrows, the activist, for the first time in her life would be forced to come to a halt.

On January 11, 1980, Captain Sylvia Lane, Eva Burrows' new private secretary, arrived at Burrows' quarters in Glasgow to live there for a period, until they worked out a permanent arrangement. On January 12th, Eva awakened about 4 A.M. with crushing pains across her chest and shoulders.

The shadow of coronary disease had often been cast over the Burrows family. Two brothers had died suddenly of acute coronary occlusion, and other family members had suffered nonfatal heart disease and strokes.

Eva awakened Captain Lane and said, "I'm sure I'm having a heart attack. I feel this tightness and pain in my chest." She thought she might die. Having only recently come to Scotland, Eva had not registered with a doctor and did not know how to reach the hospital. Captain Lane phoned the people next door, who had extended kind-

119

ness while Eva was settling in, and they quickly gave the emergency number for the hospital.

Eva had come downstairs and was lying on the sofa awaiting the ambulance. In those moments she had the feeling of impending death. She breathed the prayer, "Well, Lord, if this is the end of my life, I just have to say how thankful I am. What a wonderful privilege it's been. But if it's Your will for me to live, I just give myself to You all the more, to live for You to the best of my strength."

An ambulance came quickly and minutes later Eva was in the Stobhill Hospital of Glasgow. When she finally regained consciousness, she saw a black nurse standing over her and for a moment thought she was back in Africa. The nurse said to Eva, "It's all right, Major. You're going to be all right." She identified herself as one of Eva's former students at Usher Institute in Rhodesia. Eva asked, "Where am I?" The nurse explained what had happened and said, "You did so much for us in Africa and looked after us there and now I'm going to look after you." Having finished nursing school in Zimbabwe, she had come to Scotland for a postgraduate course in nursing. "That was quite amazing," recalls Burrows, "and it seemed to me almost as if God were saying, 'You're going to get better.'"

Eva was kept in the intensive care unit. Lt. Colonel John Hounsell, her second in command, and his wife were accepted by the hospital as her next of kin and were the only ones allowed to visit for the first few days. They, with the rest of the Army in Scotland, were in a state of shock. He asked what she would like him to do. Eva told them, "Look, you'd better ring my sister Margaret. She's in Melbourne." She gave him the number and the news of Eva's heart attack traveled across the miles to her family back in Australia. Later Burrows was not able to remember any of the conversation from that first day. On the second day she was unable to talk or respond. The Hounsells left the hospital dismayed, feeling that the leader they had come to love would not be with them much longer.

The news of the heart attack of one of the Army's brightest stars and outstanding leaders stunned the Army world. Many who had speculated on her potential destiny realized the devastating impact this could well have.

Recovery

However, Eva's progress was so good that she was transferred from intensive care to the general ward after only a few days. The large ward did not have private service, not even for the "commander in chief" of Scotland. But this move was encouraging to her, signaling that recovery had begun.

When visiting restrictions were lifted, one of her staff, Lt. Colonel William Rivers and his wife, came to visit her. To their surprise they found her sitting up in bed wearing an attractive cape, her hair immaculately coiffured, and their leader almost smothered in an avalanche of flowers, including orchids from Sri Lanka. There was a large bouquet from the Lord Provost of Glasgow, and a giant basket of fruit from Lord Wallace of Campsie. Postcards and assurances of prayer poured in from Africa and Australia and around the world. Before leaving the hospital, she asked her divisional commander to pray with her, clasping his hand as he petitioned God for her strength and healing.

It was arranged for retired Brigadier Beth Groves to come to live with Burrows and take charge during her convalescence. Beth had served with Eva as an officer in the Women's Social Services. "There was no doubt that she had taken a battering," says Groves, "but although down, she was not out. The task of putting the brake on a person with such a strong personality was not an easy one. I was glad when her sister Margaret arrived from Australia, for then I had a good ally.

"Commissioner Burrows did not take easily to convalescence. Instructions to visitors not to talk about work were useless. It was not the visitors who brought up the subject. We walked daily, gently at first, but in a short time it was she who was taking the lead, measuring and timing her distance, and then continuing indoors to the detriment of the carpet. When word was received that she could start work again, there was no stopping her, no half measures, no part-time. It was full speed ahead."

A Hospital Diary

Although lacking private amenities, the large hospital ward had given Eva "a fine opportunity to see how people lived in that situation and shared their problems with each other." For the two weeks she remained in the hospital, her acute observation and keen humor led her to compose a diary which scintillates with insight and humor. The following are excerpts from her jottings, January 12–26, 1980. They reveal her spiritual sensitivities and how she was handling this experience.

Listening

Thank God for the inventor of the transistor—and especially the chap who added the earplug for personal listening in the hospital.

Seeing I've been told not to think about work and all the things that naturally crowd into my mind, I must fill the time somehow. As yet, reading takes too much concentration. So I enjoy listening to classical music on Radio 3. I've heard several of my old favorites: Mozart's 39th, Beethoven's 9th. But there's been something new—I've really been listening. Not just having them as background music to some task, but really listening, absorbed listening, concentrated listening. And what new delights I have discovered. New notes not previously heard, instrumental solos (sometimes only a few bars) not previously noticed. A whole new rich dimension to the music because of my single-minded listening.

May I do more listening of that quality to God's own voice. How rarely we listen to Him with single-mindedness. Our thoughts are racing at various mental levels—and the quality of our concentration on God suffers.

May I be an active listener to God.

Humor in the Hospital

Heard through the screen where a professor and students were around a neighboring patient's bed. The patient said, "Doctor, I wish I knew the meaning of those big words you are using." One student piped up. "Don't worry, so do we."

I heard today from one of the nurses of a famous surgeon of a nearby hospital. His name is Dr. Butcher. True. He is often assisted by another fine surgeon, Dr. Bones.

Quiet Authority

You don't have to shout to prove you're the boss, do you? My doctor's a perfect example of that. He's a consultant who comes every morning with his group of young doctors. Quiet, fatherly, elderly too, with large, grey, bushy eyebrows.

He never raises his voice, but everyone hangs on each word. His presence commands respect; he has about him a gentle power. We all recognize it—from the simplest patient to the cleverest doctor-student. And I, so often in the role of command myself, watch with a mixture of pleasure and awe. My esteem for him grows each day. And when he stands at the end of my bed saying, "And now, Miss Burrows . . ." I have complete confidence in him.

Many a day, after he's gone, I ponder on Him who spoke as One having authority—the quiet authority that inspired faith and fullest trust from all whose lives He touched.

Tennyson and Inner Resources

From the small room at the end of the ward there is a great view over the Campsie Hills. Today they're lightly snow-covered, but the land in the foreground, lit up by unexpected shafts of sunlight, has a green and brown field, and rows of winter trees. I was telling my elderly friend "the flower girl" how much I admired the treeshapes in winter, whereupon she began to quote at length a poem by Tennyson about brooks and trees. And that at eighty-six years of age! Like the brook, she babbled on and on. Poem after poem in her sweet, gentle voice. I was enchanted.

"When I feel lonely," she said, "I just recite some of my favorite poems. Then I'm not alone anymore." What a rich inner resource—those poems memorized over the years, and recalled to delight and sustain one in moments of need.

She knew the Bible—especially the Psalms—just as well. What an inner treasury to draw on. I've found myself doing the same, lying in my hospital bed quietly meditating and calling to mind songs from our Army Song Book as well as favorite passages of Scripture.

Such rich passages and poems committed to memory provide an unfailing resource within—and we can draw on that resource, like drawing water from a deep well when we need a draught.

A Special Sunday

The Springburn Band came into the ward, and conducted a beautiful twenty-minute service. Lovely old hymns, and a helpful reading from God's Word. A songster with a beautiful Scottish voice read one of Mrs Commissioner Larsson's "Just a moment, Lord" poems.

Everyone enjoyed the service and seemed that much brighter

and happier. "The Salvation Army always has such cheerful music," was the common comment. First time I've had the citadel come to my hospital ward, but I liked it. I liked it very much, and was grateful to have my worship time shared with so many others.

Don't Be Too Busy for Your Own Good
That was the heading of the front page article of the South African *War Cry* that came in today's post. Not a bad reminder, is it!

Running Feet
The quiet of the night was disturbed by the sound of running feet, a sound that aroused everyone, a sound that spoke its own message — "emergency." The half-lit ward was galvanized into action. I could hardly believe my eyes; before a few moments had passed there were almost twenty people and several machines all tensely engaged in saving Margaret's life.

These people seemed to appear from nowhere, by some mysterious inaudible instruction. The emergency team was in operational order, and before long, the patient breathing again, they quietly slipped out of the ward. I wondered if I'd seen it or dreamt it. It happened so swiftly.

Readiness — disciplined readiness, really. It must be so in any life-and-death business.

Eva had become a case for special interest by the doctor who treated her. He asked her to describe what happened when she had the coronary. She related the sense of peace that came over her when she thought she would die, she did not struggle against it, but accepted whatever would be the outcome. The doctor said that was a great help to her and that if she had been agitated or worried, the consequences might have been different.

Recovery
During her time of recovery she spent many hours reading and decided to use the time for prayer and a study of Christ. She went through the entire New Testament, marking every reference to Christ. "That was a lovely experience," she recalls, "because I really felt Christ's presence with me at that time."

She admits going through a stage of questioning, "Why should this have happened to me?" But in her questioning she sensed the Lord was saying to her, "You're pushing too hard. Let go, and let Me lead you and work through you."

General Arnold Brown added his words of caution along with an extraordinary comment. "If you go on as you have been doing, you may have a few more months to give the Lord and the Army. But if you pace yourself, you could give the Lord and the Army a good many years, and," he added cryptically, "you may one day be the leader." A silence followed, leaving Eva Burrows to ponder yet once again, a prophetic statement of destiny.

Determined to regain her strength, Eva obeyed the doctor implicitly, including a regimen of daily walks. Her brother-in-law, Dr. Bramwell Southwell in Australia, sent her literature about recovering from heart attacks. Her one indulgence was to answer the letters and cards she had received from all over the world.

She gained confidence, made a good recovery, and within three months resumed her work as Territorial Commander. The six-month checkup revealed she was doing so well that she did not require further medication. Soon she was energetic and vivacious as ever.

Did her heart attack cause her to restrain her efforts? She later said, "I never pulled myself back for fear lest I die. In fact I cleared that very much with the Lord in that I said, 'Lord, I'm going to give myself as I always did. I'm not going to be overprotective of myself and if I die I know it will be according to Your will and purpose. I will live in a sensible way, but I will not restrain from giving myself completely.' My temperament is given to God and I must live that way. Death has never been a fear to me."

The heart attack experience was not without its valuable lessons. Among them, "It made me more sympathetic to people with health problems. Probably in the past I was not understanding enough in this area. I would tend to say, 'Come on, you can get over this, you'll be all right.' Now I am much more understanding."

Later she was invited by Major Arthur Thompson, one of her divisional commanders, to speak to his officers on "Lessons Learnt from My Heart Attack." He reports, "She gave a masterly presentation, disclosing how a proud, independent person had been rendered helpless, had to ask service from others, and be content to accept limitations. She deeply inspired our officers with her witness of how the presence and peace of God sustained her."

The first meeting she attended after her recovery was at the Springburn Corps in Glasgow. Comrades at the corps were moved that Sunday morning when, during the prayer meeting, they looked up and saw their Territorial Commander kneeling at the mercy seat. It was her way of publicly saying, "Thank You, Lord, for sparing me. I commit myself afresh to You for the work You have yet for me to do."

"We Have to Do Something"

Commissioner Burrows was confronted with both desperate need and the opportunity to alleviate some of the social ills in Scotland. During one of the brutally cold winters, it was discovered that a woman had died in the rubbish chute of a high-rise building. Suddenly, there was great concern throughout the country for the homeless, known as "gutter people." These men and women were very often heavy drinkers and slept in the streets. There was an uproar as to why they weren't being cared for.

Eva announced, "We have to do something." So, in a Salvation Army hall and a small day care center, Salvationists provided breakfast and lunch for the "gutter people" who slept outdoors in that part of Glasgow and were not welcome elsewhere.

At The Salvation Army in the Lauriston area of Glasgow, destitute and homeless women were welcomed every night. The Army provided sheets and blankets. The women, many of them drunk and difficult to handle, would sleep in their clothes. The Army housed and fed them until the government was able to find other accommodations for them.

Many nights Burrows visited the women who slept outdoors. One of these was Jennie Kennedy, who often drank herself into a stupor. Like most of those women, she had formed a partnership with a male friend, so that they could help each other. Captain Arnott, who himself had been an alcoholic and was now in charge of helping these people, told Commissioner Burrows that Jennie's friend was very sick and in the hospital. He had some money, about 200 pounds, and told the hospital chaplain that he wanted to give it to Captain Arnott for Jennie. When he died, Captain Arnott told Jennie, "I've got your money—200 pounds, and I am going to look after it for you. When you need something, I'll see that you get it, but I'm not giving it to you so you can drink up the whole lot."

A couple of days later she came back and said, "I want my money."

There was a great discussion about it, but he couldn't withhold it from her. So a little time later she came and asked if she could borrow 25 pounds. Captain Arnott said, "No, I'm not going to give it to you. I already gave you your 200 pounds. What do you want 25 more for?"

She said, "I want to give my friend a nice gravestone. It was 225 pounds and if you can lend it to me, Captain, I will be able to give him a nice marker."

"I always remember people saying that Jennie was a woman who'd sunk into what some people would call 'the dregs of humanity.' But even in the lowest depths, there is a spark of goodness. Any other time she would have wasted all her money on drink, but now she wanted to do something for her friend, whom she really loved.

"It doesn't matter how low a person sinks, somewhere there is a touch that love can spark. There's a beautiful verse in our songbook which says,

Down in the human heart, crushed by the Tempter,
Feelings lie buried, that grace can restore.
Touched by a loving heart, wakened by kindness,
Chords that were broken will vibrate once more.

"I still believe that there is nobody sunk so low that there isn't hope. People sometimes say, 'Will you look after the people that nobody else wants to know? Will you look after the people that no one else wants to help? They're hopeless, aren't they?' But, we believe there is still hope for everybody."

A Street Fight

Some major scuffles and problems with marches in Scotland resulted in a proposed bill that would ban street marches and assemblies, including the Army's open-air evangelistic meetings. The way the bill was worded, The Salvation Army would have to apply for permission for every Sunday march and open-air meeting it conducted.

Commissioner Burrows did not mind requesting permission for a major march through Glasgow or Edinburgh, or a special one elsewhere. But she was not prepared for the Army to have to ask for permission for every march, every week, and in every town, throughout Scotland. She stated, "We had long ago won the right to stand on the street and hold our open-air services. Our history includes a time when our people were in prison because they spoke on the street, marched, and played in their bands. We had already won that right and I wasn't prepared to see it taken from us."

Now was the time for Eva to use the influence of the friends in high places she had made for the Army. Government leaders from Argyle, in conference with Burrows, helped work out amendments to the bill that would cover the Army. In the Commons the argument of the Army was put forward and their right to hold street meetings upheld.

Burrows, whose father had been converted in a Salvation Army street meeting, asserted, "I'm always ready to fight and fight hard for our right to go on the street. As long as we are not obstructing the traffic, we have the right to preach the Gospel there."

"Effervescent Eva"

An amusing incident occurred during the visit of Pope John Paul II in Scotland. Eva had gathered with other church leaders to welcome the Pope and upon his entrance greeted him with The Salvation Army salute (index finger of right hand held upright). The newspaper recorded her greeting with a photo and a caption that read, "Commissioner Burrows making a feminine point with His Holiness the Pope." A correction was printed a couple of days later.

Lords and ladies, and the ranks of the common people, all came under the spell of Eva Burrows. The provost of Glasgow gave her a nickname which caught on in Scotland, "Effervescent Eva." In January 1982, there appeared in the Commons Diary of the Arbroath *Herald* a comment by Peter Fraser, a member of Parliament, after meeting Eva Burrows. "Every now and again you meet someone you immediately know is out of the ordinary. I doubt if I shall meet anyone else in 1982 who will so powerfully impress me as Eva Burrows did."

On an official visit to Scotland, General Arnold Brown posed for a photo with Commissioner Burrows and Brigadier Beth Groves—the companion housekeeper for Burrows. Brown cryptically remarked, "One day, Beth, you may show this photo—you and the two Generals!"

14

★ ★

RETURN TO HOMELAND

"I must raise my voice for the poor, the disadvantaged."

Commissioner Burrows was appointed Territorial Commander for the Australia Southern Territory on October 1, 1982, thirty-two years after leaving her homeland. The first woman to lead a Salvation Army territory in Australia, she was the head of an otherwise all-male cabinet, chief executive of a headquarters staff totalling 160 persons and administrative and spiritual leader of almost 1,000 Salvation Army officers and more than 25,000 lay Salvationists. The territory covers the whole of the country, except for New South Wales and her home state of Queensland.

Eva's family received the news with elation and joyful anticipation. Her older sister Joyce and brother Robert flew to Melbourne for her installation as Territorial Commander.

Upon her arrival in Australia at age fifty-three, she was described as "a trim figure in navy uniform, with silver hair, looking younger than her age, attractive and bandbox smart, totally in control of the situation. She also gave the impression of tremendous vitality."

The macho male image in Australia has always been strong. "G'day Mate" has been the traditional greeting of its male-dominated society. Women as yet had not taken a prominent role in political leadership. And the idea of a woman commander was not without its covert doubters within the Army itself.

News of her appointment startled some of the hierarchy at the Melbourne Headquarters. With a new Chief Secretary also to be appointed, someone said, "She'll need a good strong man as Chief Secretary." The implication was that a woman might make a figurehead, but a man was needed to do the real work.

But Australians also have a strong sense of justice. If you "win your spurs" by your achievement, they're behind you. An astute observer writes, "Within a month of the Commissioner's arrival, it was clear that she was quite capable of running this or any other Territory. Indeed it soon became obvious that she could run the whole Army—and not long thereafter was elected to do so!"

Observers quickly noted that Burrows had a very effective platform ministry. She led a good meeting, with lively content and results. Australians were also greatly impressed that she came to know everyone so quickly. These qualities established a good rapport with the people.

The appointment was a major promotion. Scotland is a small command, but Australia Southern is one of the top Army commands in the world. Eva said, "They never had a female Territorial Commander in Australia and I realized that this was a very big task for a woman. As I was doing some Bible study, I came across Romans 4:21 about Abraham's faith and the promise to him, who was then 'convinced that what God had promised He was able to perform.' I said, 'Well, that's a promise for me, Lord. You promise that You are going to be with me when I go to this big job.'"

Her staff prepared a welcome for her first morning at the Melbourne Territorial Headquarters. They read from the Soldier's Guide, which has a brief daily devotional for each day of the year for Salvationists. Burrows remarks, "You won't believe what they read— 'being assured what God has promised, He is able to perform.'" The reading for that day was compiled in the late 1800s and yet there was the promise that God had given her. She accepted it as a confirmation, as God saying to her, "Yes, it is going to be all right. I am going to be with you."

On her first visit to Adelaide, the city where the Army in Australia commenced in 1880, she asked the divisional commander, Major John Clinch, to take her to the very spot under the gum tree in the Botanical Park where the first Army open-air meeting had been held. Upon arrival she knelt on the ground and had Major Clinch pray in thanksgiving for the past and in petition for the future.

When the Major finished his prayer, he noticed that Eva had gathered fallen leaves and twigs. That evening in the meeting she displayed those leaves as she described what an emotional experience it had been for her to visit the gum tree site and to thank God for all that had developed in Australia and in her life from that humble beginning. Burrows respectfully referred to the people of Adelaide as "a people always proud of their place in Army history."

Speaking "Real Ocker"

Eva was concerned about communicating well with Australians, since she had been out of the country for thirty years. So she prayed, "Lord, when I talk, am I going to be able to reach through to the Australians? Am I going to speak on their wave length?" To her surprise, within a fortnight, she found her Australian dialect had returned, words that she hadn't used for years, and she thanked the Lord. She said afterward that although she had been away for so many years, it took no more than two weeks for her to again feel "a fair dinkum Aussie."

Not long after her return, she went to speak at a men's hostel in Melbourne. The Sunday morning service was attended by men who had lost their way, many with serious drug and alcohol problems. They joined in hearty singing and worship. Eva related the story of the Prodigal Son, how he had come to himself and how we can come to ourselves. After the service one of the old chaps came up and said, "You know, Commissioner, you speak real ocker." Most people would not like to be told that they spoke real ocker, because it is slang, the common speech of the man in the street. Eva thought, "That's nice. For Jesus spoke in the language of the common people who heard Him gladly." In that moment Eva Burrows felt like a daughter of Australia once again. An Australian newspaper article would later describe her unique accent:

> The new General of the world's two million-strong Salvation Army, Australian Eva Burrows, has traces of Bantu, Singhalese and Scottish in her accent. But even after thirty years of spreading the Salvationists' message abroad, her Australian drawl still drowns the other acquired tones. She is very proud of her roots and of being introduced as "The Australian General" and is pleased to no end when people recognize her accent.

A Compassionate Leader

Upon her arrival in Australia she went to the hospital to visit Major Malcolm Bale who was seriously ill. They had met fifteen years earlier, and now he was editor-in-chief for her Territory. She greeted him as an old friend. "What are you doing here, mate? Where's your Army flag?" Her friendly, buoyant greeting that day was for her editor better than all the medicine and hospital treatment.

"As Territorial Commander she came as a breath of fresh air," says Bale. He adds, "The first time we met in executive officers' meetings, a topic came up for discussion which had been on the agenda for the past three years. We had talked about it incessantly and never came to a decision. Suddenly Commissioner Burrows stood up and said, 'Well, we all seem to be agreed about this. Let's do it!' No one had ever thought the matter would come to taking action."

Burrows' first Sunday meeting as Territorial Commander was at the small corps of Fitzroy. Over lunch she chatted with the people who found her warm and friendly. After the meal Envoy David Eldridge, the corps officer, and Major Frank Linsell, the divisional commander, took her to see the Army's homeless youth center where the Envoy served. It was then a shabby suburban home for ten homeless teenagers. The Commissioner was impressed by the dedication of the staff and the warm atmosphere, but shocked by the inadequacy of the facilities. She resolved that if it was the last thing she did in the Territory, she would open a new center for homeless youth at Fitzroy. But formidable obstacles frowned on such a vow — government restrictions, lack of funding, and local opposition.

"She led from the front," is the description of her by Major Barbara Bolton who served on her staff, adding, "She reminded me of the stage direction in *King Lear,* 'Enter Cordelia with drum and colors.'" Eva Burrows always entered with drum and colors, galvanizing the Territory into both prayer and action. She had a passionate commitment to both soul-saving and social justice.

On one occasion in Australia her Field Secretary for Personnel had been counseling an officer couple whose marriage was breaking up and their ministry at stake. Eva personally interviewed them and kept herself informed of the situation. The couple came for what turned out to be the last chance interview in the office of the Field Secretary. Eva waited several hours past her workday to hear the result. When Lt. Colonel John Clinch told her it was hopeless, she burst into tears, and went to the couple weeping with concern for them. Today Commissioner Clinch says, "I have seen tears in her eyes on several occasions, always for others and their failures."

Colonel Gordon Fischer, who served as one of her divisional commanders in Australia, recalls a Christmas Day with Commissioner

Eva Burrows. "I saw her with a deep measure of genuine compassion on many occasions, but two I readily recall. On Christmas morning 1985, it was arranged for her to meet the homeless men of The Gill Memorial Home at breakfast. She arrived early to have the opportunity to meet the men as they came down from the dormitories. It was more than the formal 'Merry Christmas' greeting she offered. It was an outstretched hand, a word of encouragement, and for some a warm hug. This was no public relations stunt. There were no cameras, no reporters. Hers was an expression of heart-feeling for some of Melbourne's most neglected.

"I shall never forget the heartrending interview, when an officer of some considerable success had need to appear at the Territorial Commander's office because of serious financial misdemeanor and deception. Eva Burrows was fairminded and generous in understanding, but still had to administer justice, ending the officer's cherished active officership. After she prayed with him at the end of the interview and he departed, Eva Burrows cried the tears of one who felt deeply about her officers. Such needful disciplinary action was not easy for her."

At a Saturday night fellowship program of Youth Councils in a dimly lit pavilion, Eva enjoyed mingling with the youth. She took the arm of a young man passing by. "Hello young man, what's your name? Where do you come from?" He responded, "Stephen Millar, Glenelg. What's your name and where do you come from?" "Eva Burrows, Commissioner, Melbourne," came the answer. Stephen's shocked response was, "O God!" Her instant reply, "No, just Eva Burrows." The lad was somewhat embarrassed, the Commissioner highly amused.

During the morning session of the same Youth Councils, a young man moved in and out of the meeting a number of times. Commissioner Burrows was not amused. Stepping into the car after the meeting, she spotted the offender. The instruction came, "Ernest, call that young man over here." She wound down the window of the car and said, "Young man, have you a problem?" The lad looking quite puzzled by the question answered, "No." "Well," said the Commissioner, "I thought you must have a bladder problem as you were in and out of that meeting so often, each time disturbing those who wanted to listen. Next session make up your mind if you want to be in or out." With a bright "cheerio" it was off to lunch. The lad stayed in for the rest of the meetings and came forward to the mercy seat at the end of the day.

Hands-On Leadership

During her time in Australia, a great catastrophe struck—the Ash Wednesday bush fires. People were burned to death in the holocaust. Three million dollars was received in contributions from the general public who were confident the Army would use it appropriately. Burrows set up a trust fund and took oversight of the work throughout that entire area. With her staff she visited the people whose homes had been burned down. Food, clothing, and bedding were provided, and such practical assistance as barbed wire for a farmer's fence and radios for people in rural areas to keep in touch with each other.

The total male staff with whom she worked found that she appreciated their views and encouraged them to put forward initiatives for which she would assure they would receive the credit. They didn't have any "stand-up fights," but disagreed on a number of things while maintaining mutual support. Her staff also saw that Commissioner Burrows was willing to change her mind if new information or a more effective rationale was forthcoming.

The staff noted that she always did her homework before a committee meeting or conference. Even board meetings crackled with a certain electric alacrity. She prepared herself thoroughly, but did not make up her mind concerning matters until she had input from others. A give-and-take discussion was common, with a respect shown for views differing from hers.

Her hands-on leadership style did not always result in smooth sailing. More than one staff member tells of "heated disagreements" with their Territorial Commander. She complained to a department head that he did not visit the executive suite to let her know what was going on, whereas others consulted with her frequently. One day in her office she pointed an aggressive finger at him, and calling him by his last name, charged, "You are a unilateralist! You want to run your department independent of the rest of the team." The staff member stood his ground. The next day she saw him in the office car park, took hold of his arm and said, "I still love you, you know." He replied, "And I still love you, but nothing has changed."

Eva Burrows was not endowed with a surplus of patience. A department head was known to be habitually late for board meetings. When he did not show up on time one day, Eva locked him out of the board room and went on with the meeting. The incident converted the man to punctuality.

When Eva left the Third World, she did not forget the needs of the people there. She used her leadership and resources to continue to address them. In Australia she sponsored a six-week leadership training program that brought together potential leaders from the Third World. The program has been an annual event ever since.

Speaking Out on Issues

"There are certain aspects of human life that the church should speak out on," stated Burrows. While maintaining the Army's nonpartisan posture, her strong statements became heard on such issues as the legalization of prostitution, opening gambling casinos, in vitro fertilization, and taxing of the poor.

She fired the Army's biggest guns against the legalization of prostitution, which would allow any house in any area to be legalized as a brothel, as long as it was not within a prescribed distance of a school. When application was made for a license for a house to be a brothel, Salvationist women would stand outside the door in protest. This attracted the press and gave the Army opportunity to point out the dangers of a brothel that children passed on their way to school. Concerned parents would then reinforce the Army's protest.

Burrows had the Army also take strong exception to the red-light district proposed for Melbourne. The Army was at that time picking up teenage girls who walked up and down the streets. Eva herself went down into the red-light district to see the problem and encourage a better way of life for these teenage prostitutes, some girls looking for drugs, others unemployed. She put the Army's views and case strongly to the government and in the end influenced modifications of the legal proposals.

In an instance in which the language on a radio program was obscene, the Army along with other church leaders protested to the broadcasting authorities. The result was tempered language on the program.

During Eva's term in Australia, unemployment jumped, especially among young people. Ranks of the unemployed had swollen the lines of people coming to the Army for help. She said, "While the politicians are counting the economic consequences, I want to look at the social consequences of unemployment." She had her social services staff study the effects of unemployment on individuals and families. They found not only that people were short of money, but also that their home situations were chaotic. The research revealed that the most urgent need was for a training scheme to assist unemployed youth.

Eva took action immediately to provide funding for a pilot project named "Employment 2000," a highly imaginative scheme first suggested by Captain Brian Mundy and designed by Salvationist Bob Risden to help young people who had been out of work for more than six months. Unemployed youth enrolled for three months, with mornings devoted to learning skills that would make them employable and afternoons given to improving attitudes about life and work.

The project achieved a high success rate. The wide acclaim for the program and its impact was such that the government asked the Army to organize similar training schemes for adults and for Vietnamese refugees.

Opposing the Tax Bill
In 1985 the Australian Government convened what it called the Tax Summit, an assembly of the country's highest level experts, with a

Commissioner Eva Burrows admires work of trainees in Employment 2000 in Melbourne.

proposal that would have levied a heavy burden on the poor. Having spoken out on the Australian government's proposals for taxation reform, Commissioner Burrows was invited to the nation's capital, Canberra, to address a national forum in Parliament House.

She monitored the discussion over several days of deliberation. When it came her turn to speak, she gave one of her most influential speeches, a classic of advocacy on behalf of the poor.

As she began to speak, a hush fell over the assembly. Here was a voice of compassion, of authority, one who was not speaking as an armchair observer, but one who knew the poor by name and need. Her speech that day had great pathos and power. The following are excerpts.

Here in this forum of influence and power—money power, political power, people power—I must raise my voice. A voice not strident, but pleading; pleading for the poor, the disadvantaged, the despairing, the unemployed.

If anyone knows the pain of suffering poverty, it is The Salvation Army. If anyone knows the deep unhappiness of the young unemployed who are becoming an angry and violent generation, it is The Salvation Army.

Let me ask you some questions.

How many of you in this chamber are paid under $200 a week? How many of you think you spend under $80 per week on food, drink, and cigarettes?

The greatest problem we have in representing the needs of the poor in Australia today is trying to help the rest of us realize how rich we are. Eighty dollars per week is not considered to be an excessive food bill by many Australian families and $50 per week is about an average for low rental. These two figures add up to $130 per week. This is $2 less than the supporting parent benefit for a single adult and two children.

How then can this parent pay for fuel and clothing, shoes and school supplies? The most austere level of the poverty line is still $50 above the meager supporting parent benefit. The queues at our welfare centers are still long, demonstrating a poverty unparalleled in the Australian scene. These are fellow Australians who have never had to beg before, never had to ask for a handout. It is our belief that a broad-based consumption tax will increase the length of these queues.

No one in Australia should have to beg. No one should have to live below the poverty line. . . .

Poverty is not just having a low weekly income or a social security benefit. It also means having a lack of cash after paying the rent, having a lack of capital for satisfactory housing, adequate diet, and sound health, a lack of good credit standing. Then, when a family crisis arises or there is a sudden health problem, the poor have no resistance, no escape from the vicious circle that imprisons them. . . .

Before Burrows finished, she offered alternatives for providing sufficient revenue for the government. "Have a crackdown," she challenged, "on evasion and avoidance," which she said, with effective methods to audit assets, would reap more than $1 billion. "Thank you, Prime Minister," she concluded, "for this opportunity to speak in this forum and for your willingness to listen to a passionate voice on behalf of the poor."

Her eloquence had captivated that audience of politicians, trade union delegates, and leading businessmen. Her point had been cogently made, that indirect taxation disadvantaged the poor. As she finished, her audience erupted with "thunderous applause," and the government abandoned its unbefitting proposals. One news commentator said that she would have been swept into political power had she been willing to stand for election.

At the conclusion of the hearings, the Tax Summit modified its proposals in regard to charitable organizations, responding to the opposition the Army had voiced.

Church Growth

Life in Australia had become secular throughout and bordered on the pagan. People were caught up with sports, going to the beach, or whatever provided a good time. An awakening within the church and the Army in Australia was desperately needed.

A dynamic concept called Church Growth had begun to take root in the Army in the U.S.A. The movement was the brainchild of Donald McGavran, a product of his observations as a third-generation missionary in India. He had coined the title to escape some of the negative baggage of conventional terms. In the 1970s Church Growth became the subject of books, films, and seminars, largely popularized by Peter Wagner and Carl George in America, and was making its way into the mainline denominations. When Eva Burrows came to Australia, she was quick to discern that Church Growth was a hot topic.

The Army had become much more effective at getting decisions and converts than at making disciples. Church Growth was about discipling, enlisting every member to reach out and win others to Christ through proven growth strategies.

One Australian officer had attended the Fuller Institute in America. His impressions aroused some discussion among officers that this might be something that the Army in Australia should look at. When Commissioner Burrows heard that the movement had become prominent in The Salvation Army in Canada, she sent two officers there to one of the seminars. They returned enthusiastic and thought its principles could be the means of reviving the evangelistic thrust of Salvationists. They made their recommendation and Burrows agreed to set up the Church Growth seminars.

While on vacation, Eva was reading Church Growth literature "until it came out of my ears, because I agreed to a seminar, and I wanted to see for myself that it wasn't an American gimmick." She studied the movement cautiously to insure that the Army would not be carried away by the enthusiasm of pragmatics at the expense of real dependence upon God. She was not one to be motivated merely by a lust for success or to use methods that invite superficial spiritual results.

She felt an affinity with Peter Wagner's philosophy that "strategy is never intended to be a substitute for the Holy Spirit, but to be Spirit-directed." The more she read the books on the subject, the more it sounded to her like the Salvation Army of earlier days. Research had revealed that 85 percent of new Christians came to faith through personal contact with relatives and friends. Eva heartily agreed with the emphasis on the use of lay people and their spiritual gifts, the significance of prayer as part of that growth, and the pastor as the organizer. "Church Growth," she concluded, "is about evangelism and discipling by the church members, and that has always been a strong point with me and the Army."

She fervently believed in, and had always preached, the theology of growth. Her own unflagging passion for evangelism led her to accept Church Growth as a new approach for the Army's spiritual life and outreach. And when Eva Burrows gets turned on by something, things start to happen. "Church Growth excites a church," she said. "It is The Salvation Army's original motivation updated and fitted into new terminology."

Eva said, "We had to be honest to say that we had become a bit comfortable in our worship. We went to our services, had our wonderful music which everyone enjoyed. We could almost go to The Salvation Army as if it were a social club. We had our friends there, enjoyed fellowship with them, and went home. But Church Growth asked if each of us had introduced someone to the Lord."

To give momentum to the program, she appointed Church Growth officers in Australia. Seminars were set up for the officers and lay Salvationists with Peter Wagner and Carl George invited to conduct seminars.

Salvationists were motivated and went out to share their faith and bring others into the church. Meeting schedules were being changed for effective outreach. Attendances climbed at corps that had been static for years. Home Bible study and prayer groups were organized with one corps in Camberwell having thirty cell groups in homes. Salvationists experienced an infusion of new life and became involved in outreach evangelism. Some Army halls became so packed that members wondered if their citadel was going to be large enough. Commissioner Burrows had brought the dynamic concept to the Army in Australia and exciting new growth was taking place.

Moving Ahead
The territorial headquarters building into which Burrows came had been occupied by the Army for almost a century. It had a great tradition and sentimental attachment, but was hardly the functional facility for the Army of the '80s and the vigorous leadership of the new Territorial Commander. With characteristic ability to enthuse others and undertake a seemingly impossible project, Commissioner Burrows sought Melbourne's top property adviser and town planner, A.T. Cocks. With a select committee of the Advisory Board, she guided the Army in the selection and purchase of a new building. She then presided over the plans for furnishing and equipping the first new headquarters of the territory in almost 100 years. Those who did not want to see the Army give up the historic old building were also satisfied as it was refurbished and used for the Army's social services and expanded Divisional Headquarters.

Annual Congresses had been a feature of the Territory for many years. By the time Burrows arrived, the Melbourne Congress, the largest and most important, had lost some of its appeal. Interest waned and attendance declined. She called a meeting of heads of departments to discuss plans for a "new look" Congress. There was little enthusiasm. The usual response was, "That wouldn't work here." Finally she disposed of any further equivocation by appointing the Field Secretary Lt. Colonel John Clinch to meet with the four state divisional commanders to formulate plans for her consideration.

Plans were presented to her for a totally new style Congress — different venues, programs, timetables. The entire program would be based on corps or local sponsorship rather than by territorial headquarters directive, bypassing planning "from the top down." There was much skepticism. Throughout, Commissioner Burrows gave the committee her full support, doing everything she was asked, including traveling to centers to meet with local corps organizers.

Opening night, usually a poorly attended event, attracted four times the number of people than the previous year. Sunday meetings tripled in attendance. The music festival doubled, and the number of seekers — those who come to the altar in dedication — quadrupled. This "new look" Congress in 1984 was a resounding success and revitalized the annual event for years to come. Sharing this report years later, Commissioner John Clinch says, "It was a perfect example of her ability to inspire others, to do something different, then give them total support, even at the risk of her own reputation."

Expansion projects were the order of the day. Always having a keen sense of stewardship, her dictum to the staff in fundraising was, "We must be totally honest with the public. Whatever we use as publicity must always be the truth."

Salvation Army retirement villages in Australia are major programs, hosting as many as 800 senior citizens in attractive small cottages, a nursing home, and hospices for the later years. In Perth, Commissioner Burrows arranged for a large residential program for the aged, with the government building small cottages and the Army conducting the program. Before leaving Australia she launched a $10 million residential program for the aged in Melbourne. A program of help for aborigines with alcohol problems also became a major thrust under her leadership.

When General Jarl Wahlstrom visited Australia and saw all that was happening under Burrows' leadership, he said to her, "In driving a car, the foot is used for both the accelerator and the brake. But you never use the brake."

The Order of Australia

The Order of Australia is one of the highest recognitions given citizens in that country and permits the awardees to add the letters A.O. after their names. It recognizes those who have made significant contributions to the community. Eva Burrows received the formal invitation from the office of the Governor in Melbourne to receive on May 30th, 1986 the appointment of the highest among the distinctions of the Order, the *Officer of the Order of Australia.*

Each honoree is allowed to invite four guests to the Investiture. Eva brought Bram and Margaret Southwell, her personal aide, Brigadier Jean Geddes, and her niece Claire Southwell. The guests took their places among hundreds assembled in the ballroom of the official residence of the Governor. Recipients were called individually to stand before Governor David McCaughey. The citation for Eva stated that the award was "For service to the community in Australia and to humanity at large as a member of The Salvation Army."

Melbourne newspapers ran stories on the Army leader, and she was featured on radio and television. An editorial in *The Age* read: "Having spent thirty years overseas, she admits to special pleasure from an award that acknowledges her commitment to the local scene—something she has expressed by speaking out at the tax summit on behalf of the poor and by tackling other issues such as unemployment and prostitution."

Just four weeks earlier Eva Burrows had become the General-elect of The Salvation Army. From the Australian award ceremony she returned to the Officers Councils she was conducting in Melbourne. She would shortly leave to take up the office of the General. A proud council of officers greeted her return with a sustained standing ovation. In that electric moment, she quipped, "Well, there's only one thing left for me to do, and that's to get married!" The comment brought the house down.

Before leaving for England, she summarized, "My time in Australia has given me immense satisfaction and it has brought a great enrichment to my own life. There has been a maturing in my leadership style and a deeper consciousness of the Holy Spirit's presence and authority in the direction of my life and leadership."

"Nor Lose the Common Touch"

At her first corps visit as Territorial Commander, Eva had vowed she would open a new hostel in Fitzroy if it were the last thing she did in the Territory. Eva Burrows takes her vows seriously. In one of her last acts as Territorial Commander, she opened the new homeless youth hostel at Fitzroy. These were street-hardened teenagers, caught up in prostitution and criminal behavior, but reachable by genuine care and interest. She had a rapport with these streetwise kids and they would never forget The Salvation Army woman who cared for them and did so much to help them find themselves.

One of those teenagers was Jodie Smith who looked older than her seventeen years. She had been taken from her mother at nine months and brought up in orphanages. By the time she was thirteen she was a child of the streets addicted to heroin and speed. For Jodie, homelessness meant not just rootlessness but also no one to care about her. Commissioner Burrows, in opening the new center, made an eloquent statement that the Army cares deeply for Jodie and other homeless young women. The center is a house with a comfortable and attractive home atmosphere. When someone complained that it was too good for a hostel, Commissioner Burrows replied, "If we give the young people a decent, clean, and tidy enviroment, they are more likely to want to keep the place tidy." At the dedication Jodie

Jodie Smith says to Commissioner Burrows: "It is somewhere I can call home for the first time."

said, "It is somewhere I can call home for the first time in my life."

Brigadier Jean Geddes remembers a telling incident on that occasion. She had just seen the Commissioner invested with the *Order of Australia* and observed the dignity and grace she displayed on that occasion. Then, shortly following, she observed her in a dramatically different setting. Instead of high officials and national leaders, she was among the street kids. Geddes recalls, "I saw her in conversation with a girl who obviously had a 'chip on her shoulder.' As Eva talked with her, I could sense the girl relaxing and responding. With her arm round her shoulder I saw Eva bend and gently kiss the girl on the cheek. I shall never forget the look, first of amazement and then of utter joy, on the girl's face. My thought immediately was, she can 'walk with kings—nor lose the common touch.' "

Soon kings and queens, princes and princesses, presidents and prime ministers, the homeless and the hurting, the lost and the lonely, and a world fellowship would come to know the special touch of Eva Burrows. Destiny was just a step away.

Left: Official photo.

Right:
In tropical uniform.

Portrait by well-known artist Anita Watson-Amos. The theme is hope for the children of the world and the painting hangs in the entrance to The Salvation Army's Social Services Headquarters on Judd Street in London.

*Upper left: At National Advisory Organization
Conference in Washington, D.C., 1992.
Upper right: At 1988 International Leader's Conference.
Center Bottom: With representative world leaders at 1988
International Leader's Conference.*

Above: The author interviews General Eva Burrows for the biography in her office.

Left: The General from across the desk.

Right: General Eva Burrows leads the 1990 International Congress.

Below: General Burrows with her three predecessors: retired Generals Erik Wickberg, Jarl Wahlstrom, and Arnold Brown.

A Citizen of the World

Top and center: Colorfully welcomed and garlanded in India.
Left: Adroit with chopsticks in Japan.
Right: Wearing a sombrero in Latin America.

General Eva Burrows at the 1990 International Congress admits into the Order of the Founder *Salvation Army heroes Major Yin Hung-shun (above) and Brigadier Josef Korbel (below).*

At the front lines of the world's tragedies

Left: General Eva Burrows "goes on a shopping spree" at the Mkwayi Refugee Camp in Malawi.

Below: General Eva Burrows with a Salvation Army sponsored school class in the Mkwayi Refugee Camp.

General Burrows during her return visits to Africa meets former students, now in high positions of national leadership.

With Envoy Z. Gwindi and S.S. Mutowembwa.

With David Ndoda.   *With Lezinah Sibanda.*

Above: General Eva Burrows prays with President Ronald Reagan in the White House in 1986. Sharing in the visit were Colonel Ernest Miller and Commissioners Norman S. Marshall and Andrew S. Miller.

Left: General Eva Burrows meets with Mother Teresa in Calcutta, 1990.

Captain Eva Burrows with her Girl Guides in Africa.

Captain Eva Burrows, corps officer, visits in a village in Zimbabwe.

Ingrid Lindberg and Eva Burrows at Usher Institute, ca. 1953.

Mistress of the media

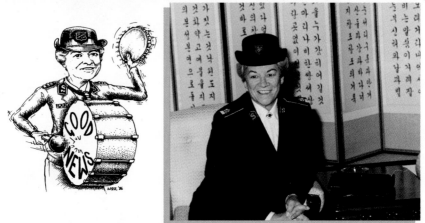

A Young People's General

A commemorative stamp.

The "Captain and her Lieutenant" General Burrows with Colonel Lilian Glase (R), to whom General Burrows was appointed as a newly commissioned lieutenant.

General Burrows, following a ceremony where she was honored as an Officer of the Order of Australia, *with sister Margaret, Margaret's husband Dr. Bramwell Southwell, and daughter Claire Southwell.*

PART THREE

★ ★ ★ ★ ★ ★ ★ ★ ★ ★ ★ ★ ★

THE GENERAL

15

★ ★ ★ ★ ★ ★ ★ ★ ★ ★ ★ ★ ★ ★ ★ ★ ★ ★ ★ ★

ELECTING A GENERAL

"I would want my leadership style to be like that of Jesus."

Forty-six leaders from the Army's eighty-nine countries and territories convened on April 25, 1986 to elect an international leader to succeed retiring General Jarl Wahlstrom of Finland. Five of the forty-six were women. They met at Sunbury Court, the Army's conference center in a secluded country mansion by the Thames just outside of London, for eight days. Eva Burrows was now a "veteran" of High Councils, having attended in 1977 and in 1981.

The Army's High Council meets only to elect a General. Its purpose and procedure has been compared to the Roman Catholic College of Cardinals. The pattern has served the Army well since its inception in the year of Eva Burrows' birth. The leaders at this summit meeting were greeted at a reception by the Prime Minister of the host country, Margaret Thatcher.

The backgrounds of the High Council members read like a *National Geographic,* for they came from such far-flung and diverse places as Australia and Africa, Japan and Jamaica, the Americas and Scandinavia. They epitomized the internationalism of The Salvation Army—a spiritual bond that spans and transcends all continents, races, and cultures, and preaches the Gospel in 116 languages of the world. Even in an era when many Third World countries have become independent and moved away from old colonial systems, the international bond of the Army has remained unbroken. The office of the General is a cohesive influence on the Army's worldwide fellowship.

Theirs was a sacred and challenging task—to elect for up to a five-

Commissioners Eva Burrows and Harry Read talk with Prime Minister Margaret Thatcher at the reception for the High Council.

year term a person to lead the world's foremost combined evangelical and social service organization. The requisites were formidable. The person elected would be the spiritual leader of the movement, exemplifying the highest standards of holy living. The position would require vision and vigor to meet the challenges of a tumultuous world, and astute administrative skills to manage the sensitive areas of personnel, finance, organizational and structural details. Conviction and courage were needed to address the critical issues of the day, and to inspire the troops.

The High Council members knew their task to be beyond human wisdom. Thus they came together in prayer, seeking divine guidance for their mandate. Tens of thousands of Salvationists around the world were also praying for God's direction. They came together from diverse cultures and national backgrounds in a bond of the spirit and a unity that would make the United Nations blush with envy.

Procedure and Speculation
The initial days were spent establishing procedure, electing officers, becoming better acquainted, and devoting ample time for corporate

prayer and meditation on God's Word. Although precedent carries weight, the High Council is not bound by it. A free-ranging discussion on matters of concern affecting the Army world was skillfully guided by the president elected by the Council, Commissioner Norman S. Marshall (U.S.A.).

The worldwide membership of The Salvation Army eagerly awaited the Council's decision. Within Army circles there was the usual speculation as several names were mentioned as logical candidates for the office. But, as former General Frederick Coutts had observed, "The only thing predictable about the outcome of a High Council is its unpredictability."

Eva Burrows' name was on the lips of many as the High Council convened to elect a General. Retired General Coutts was not one to discuss personalities or to speculate on their future. But there was a lapse in this reluctance one day as the 1986 High Council drew near, when he could not repress his intuitive prescience of the history about to unfold. Of the one he had first seen as a missionary in Africa, he said in a rare moment of conjecture in private conversation, referring to his anticipation of the outcome, "It must be this time." Mrs. Coutts, widow of the General, reflects, "There were many who thought she was young for the appointment then. But how right he was!"

Commissioner William Rivers, who had worked with Eva in Scotland, comments that "Eva Burrows could have been perceived as a General in the making. Her intellectual prowess, personal charm and charisma, good appearance and variety of leadership appointments, besides her Third World experience, made her a most electable person for the generalship."

There is no politicizing about the election. Nominations are made with strict anonymity, so no one knows who has offered them. But the Army was abuzz with informal speculations that invariably had Eva Burrows' name among the expected nominees. Election would be for a five-year term and some thought Eva was a bit young. Others thought she ought to go in now while young and still energetic. "Why wait till she's sixty-one? Why not now?"

Nominees have the option to accept or refuse nominations. The late General Clarence Wiseman turned down the nomination at the High Council prior to the one at which he was elected. At this 1986 High Council, a gifted leader who would have been a strong contender declined when nominated, indicating he did not feel he could adequately handle the demands of the office.

During a break following her nomination, Eva retired to her room to pray. She monitored her motives. "Do I want to accept this because it would be the crowning pinnacle of my life? Do I want this to show that a woman can do it?" Having crystallized and chastened her own motives, she was led to an awareness that it was right for her to accept the nomination.

"When I accepted nomination, I did not say to myself, 'That means you're going to be in, you're going to be the General.' No, I think I was very prepared, saying, 'Lord, I'm ready to be accepted, but if I'm not, it's all right.' I was so happy in Australia and really enjoying that demanding leadership role. Church Growth was taking off, the social work projects were moving ahead, and I had a great working relationship with the men around me. I would have been perfectly happy to go back to Australia. So I was quite at peace, whatever the decision."

Each nominee was asked to provide answers to a series of questions set by council members. A question was directed to Eva on the status of her health. She replied straightforwardly about her heart attack, but stated that she had made total recovery and had received a clean medical bill of health a short time before.

Nominees were also asked to prepare their views on the role of the General, to be given the following day. Working late into the night on the topic of leadership, Eva became uneasy. She prayed about her speech. Even though the hour was late, she felt led to scrap what she had been preparing and start over, this time on the leadership of Jesus. Once she came to this concept her thoughts flowed. The next day she spoke on how she would want to pattern her leadership style after that of Jesus.

The Balloting

Following the days of prayer and interludes of worship, the first ballot was cast. A two-thirds majority is required for election on the first or second ballot with the bottom candidate eliminated after each vote. After the third ballot, a majority vote of the High Council members is needed for election.

A tradition-breaking High Council of thirteen nominations included the first Colonel nominee, the first woman nominee outside the Booth family, and the first nominee from the Third World. Six nominees declined, leaving seven candidates to be voted on: Commissioners Eva Burrows (Australia), Francy Cachelin (Switzerland), William Cairns (Australia), Andrew S. Miller (U.S.A.), Harry Read (U.K.), Mannam Samuel (India) and Colonel Wesley Harris (U.K.). Following withdrawals and a second ballot, there remained three nominees — Burrows, Miller, and Read. After the third ballot Miller's name was deleted.

Read was highly respected. He had a warm personality, was a proven spiritual leader and capable administrator, with solid international leadership experience. He was also well known for his poetry and verses of song. He was a strong candidate for the office of the General.

Eva also came to this final ballot with an impressive portfolio of assets. In prior positions she had displayed an energetic style of leadership and an infectious enthusiasm. She manifested an immense optimism regarding the Army's role in God's plan for the world. An accomplished communicator and astute administrator, she had extensive international experience, having served on four continents. Her sensitivities had been tempered in the fires of Africa's aspirations and Sri Lanka's strife. Her leadership skills had broadened in top command positions at the International College, in Social Services, in Scotland and Australia. None could but be impressed by her striking appearance, and the excellent impression she made when representing the High Council in welcoming Prime Minister Margaret Thatcher to their gathering. Thus her innate abilities and acquired skills established her as a strong nominee for the Generalship.

Eva Burrows also came to that final ballot with some debits. First, she was a woman. Forty-one members of that High Council were men, and although devout, some may not have been quite ready to see a woman at the helm of their worldwide movement. The Army, while offering marvelous opportunities to women, was nonetheless dominated by male leadership at the top level. Second, Eva Burrows was only fifty-six years of age. A General is elected for up to five years and required to retire at age sixty-eight. No prior Generals had been elected younger than in their sixties. Thus there were those who well could have thought, "She can still have a go at it next time." Third, she had suffered a heart attack six years earlier. Although she received a medical report of total recovery and sound health, there were bound to be lingering questions that could influence some votes.

Near the end of the High Council proceedings, as delegates were seated around the table in prayer, Eva suddenly heard a voice that whispered, "Eva." She turned and saw that it was not the Commissioner next to her. She perceived it as an affirmation that she would be elected General, and in that moment had a deep sense of God's peace. "Hearing my name," she says, "was not a delusion so much as an assurance that everything would be all right in God's will and direction of my life. It is the only time in my life that I had an experience like it."

The moment had now come for the final and historic ballot to be cast.

16

★ ★ ★ ★ ★ ★ ★ ★ ★ ★ ★ ★ ★ ★ ★ ★ ★ ★ ★ ★

"WE HAVE A GENERAL"

"I hope to be a General of great compassion."

The fourth ballot revealed that Eva Burrows was elected the thirteenth General of The Salvation Army by the narrowest margin in the movement's history. Commissioner Norman S. Marshall, President of the High Council, formally announced, "We have a General."

At fifty-six she became the youngest person elected to that office in the Army's 121-year history and the first woman elected since Evangeline Booth in 1934. In that moment she became a citizen of the world, and the spiritual and administrative leader of the international Salvation Army. The result was dispatched to the Army's territorial headquarters around the world, "Eva Burrows elected General of The Salvation Army. God bless the General." On July 9, she would succeed General Jarl Wahlstrom who would retire on his sixty-eighth birthday.

Burrows set some precedents as the Army's international leader. Besides being the youngest elected General, she became the first one to have a degree in education and the first to have served for many years in the Third World.

In Africa the news of her election brought great jubilation. Jonah Matswetu echoed the joyful sentiments of many of her former students at Howard, "When the young Eva Burrows left the land of her birth and came and settled among our people, little did we know that the Lord Almighty had in His good grace chosen this woman, armed with a Bible and a tambourine, to arise from among His black Zimbabwean people and finally send her as an ambassador to the world. Her election speaks volumes for the progressiveness of the Army. One can safely conclude that leadership in our Army is not the exclusive preserve of a certain nationality, race, color, or sex, but that it can be for all men and women, from all four corners of the world, who have been chosen by God."

About the vote that elected her General, Burrows says, "I believed it was God's will and that He would see me through. I had a great sense of reliance on God. I would never have chosen to be the General. It was really as if God had chosen me. And when He chooses you to do something, He qualifies you, gives you what is needed for that task. So my confidence was in God rather than myself.

"One of the beautiful things at the High Council is that once the General is elected, total loyalty is expressed. When the final vote was counted, I was called to come to the head of the table and, following a prayer, each one of the members came to greet me, sharing a personal word of encouragement and support. And those who had themselves been nominated said in a very deliberate way, 'I give you my total loyalty.' It was a very moving experience. There had been no lobbying, no competition; it was all conducted in the spirit of love and unity."

The First Communications

As Eva Burrows stepped forth to be presented as the new General, an embarrassing moment took place. The media was not on hand as in previous elections. But once the word got out that the new General was a woman, a media blitz ensued. Newspapers around the world and leading magazines carried the news. She was deluged with requests for interviews from journalists. *Time* magazine devoted a full page of text and photos on Eva Burrows as the new head of the international Army.

The first person the new General rang by phone to break the news was her sister Margaret in Australia. Margaret's husband, Dr. Bramwell Southwell, a corps sergeant major, answered the phone and became the first, outside the Council members, to offer words of congratulations before Margaret came to the phone.

Then Eva phoned her sister Joyce and other family members. Their excitement was irrepressible. Joyce recalls, "When the phone rang to give me the news that Eva was General, I was both glad and sad. Our family was exultant but I also wept, because the one who

The General-elect is welcomed by Junior Soldier Elizabeth Putbrace (above) who greeted her on behalf of all the Army's young people and by the General in office, Jarl Wahlstrom (right).

had prayed, worked, and sacrificed could not share in our greatest joy. The radiant life of our mother that showed us all the Christlike example could not see this beautiful fruit of her labors, sacrifice, and example. Our parents would have felt their life's work and self-denial had achieved the ultimate, that their labors had been crowned with triumphant joy."

Upon hearing his successor had been chosen, General Jarl Wahlstrom came immediately from International Headquarters in London to wish her well and to pray with her. Burrows reported, "He quoted Solomon and prayed that I would have wisdom, patience, and joy in my leadership."

One of the persons Eva Burrows admired most at the High Council was Commissioner N.J. Samuel of India. The Commissioner, who had been a teacher and was a brilliant manager and leader, evoked an instant respect from all who met him. The last day at Sunbury Court—venue for the High Council—he and General-elect Burrows sat on a bench in the garden. It was springtime and a lovely almond tree was just coming into bloom. The Commissioner looked up at the tree and said to his friend, "Your becoming the General is like a springtime in The Salvation Army."

Commissioner Caughey Gauntlett, Chief of the Staff, had prepared a letter addressed to the final two nominees, just before the last ballot of the High Council. One would be given to the person elected, following the tradition of the second in command, expressing his willingness to accept another appointment should the new General wish. When the final ballot results were announced to Council members, Burrows received the letter. Not many minutes later, in the whirl of events which are unleashed when the General-elect is announced, she whispered to Gauntlett, with characteristic humor, "You're staying, boy!" Thus there took place the informal announcement of retention to her first Chief of the Staff.

For the next several days Eva remained in London, conferring with her predecessor and the Chief of the Staff on pending leadership appointments and other international matters.

The New General's Philosophy

General-elect Burrows made it clear at her first press conference that people are her top priority. "I hope to be a General of great compassion and love for the people."

"How do you feel on the verge of this big step into leadership?"

she was asked. "It is very awe-inspiring. But my confidence is in God because we believe that the High Council is Holy Spirit-directed. We spend much time in prayer and seek the mind of God for our movement. Although I was selected through what you might call a very human process of an election, I nevertheless have my confidence in Him."

"Do you feel that you have been destined for your position as General?" she was asked early in her term as General. "I must say, 'Yes, I do.' Since I've been in this office, I've really felt that God's hand has been on my life. That period when I was disobedient to Him, He has turned to good.

"Now I don't think in The Salvation Army that the leaders from the past sat down and said, 'There is Eva Burrows. We'll see that she goes to Africa and we'll see she goes to Great Britain.' I don't think that there was that deliberate plan, but I think it was in God's plan. In The Salvation Army we accept the fact that the Army cannot send us anywhere where God could not work out His purposes in our life. So in that sense, if that is destiny, then yes, I have a sense, not of fatalistic destiny, but of God's hand."

In interviews with the press, General-elect Burrows said, "I never preach Christianity, I always preach Christ." She emphasized that Jesus Christ should have first place in The Salvation Army and in the heart of the General. Her priority for the Army as it prepared to move into the twenty-first century was "to continue doing what The Salvation Army has been doing, with greater effectiveness and relevance to the modern situation."

She reaffirmed her belief in and commitment to the internationalism of the movement. She emphasized her concern that all Salvationists share the burden of bringing people to a personal knowledge of Jesus Christ, and she announced that she would implement the proven strategies and principles of the Church Growth movement to further the Army's evangelistic outreach among its soldiery. Her priorities embraced the involvement of youth—"for the views of young people to filter through to the top. Young people have some of the best ideas in the Christian church today." She expressed her commitment "to keep the total concept of the Army as a strong spiritual force and a compassionate social service agency, with both aspects inextricably joined together."

In an interview for *New Life,* Australia's weekly evangelical newspaper, she was asked whether she had aspired to leadership roles in the Army. She responded, "I can honestly say that when I received promotions I have always been surprised, because I give myself entirely to the job I'm doing at the time. I find intense satisfaction in doing what I'm doing. I have never looked to see what would be my next assignment. You may say that is more feminine than masculine, and I think that is true. Men seem to think more about their future, planning where they are going. I certainly have never done that. The deepest satisfaction is to do well what you're doing and to please God. I've always liked to feel that my life pleased God. If ever I have an epitaph on my tombstone, that is what I'd like it to be, 'She pleased God.'"

A news reporter asked, "It seems you have reached the highest pinnacle in The Salvation Army. What do you aspire to next and what does your election mean to you?" She replied, "I haven't aspired to this position. In The Salvation Army we don't look upon life as a career but a commitment. I have been brought to this position by God, so therefore I am completely content to do what may please God in my life. The General is the world leader of The Salvation Army. It is a high office, a noble office. To aspire to such an office would be unbecoming to any Salvationist, but if it falls upon you, as it has for me, it is an awe-inspiring experience. One has to have spiritual authority to lead this church of God in the world, and then also the sanctified commonsense to administer a movement with the many ramifications of social services which we have.

"I want to make sure we get out among the people with the message of Jesus Christ. We are an evangelical movement with a social conscience. Former Prime Minister of Canada, Arthur Meighan, defined us as 'a vital spiritual force with an acute social conscience.' These two aspects—faith and practice—are indivisible."

Burrows the activist likes what has often been called a "Christianity with its sleeves rolled up" image for The Salvation Army. The Army's practical ministry is viewed as a vital arm of the Christian church, serving in the trenches of human need. But she also longs to see the movement receive more recognition as a church.

Following her election as General, one Australian colleague confided that he was delighted she was elected but was sure he would live to regret it. He was referring to his feeling that her standards and expectations were so rigorous and demanding.

In Australia Burrows had become known for her outspokenness on social and moral issues. After her election when she was asked if she would still speak out as an international leader, she replied, "I definitely feel that the Army should not be involved in partisan politics, but I believe strongly that we should be prepared to speak out as Christ did. It is the role of church leaders to show the compassion of Jesus and to quicken a government's conscience about the needs of the people. We will encourage world leaders to see the needs of the people who are at the bottom of the heap."

A Grand Sendoff

On her return to Australia as General-elect, she received a rousing welcome at Melbourne Airport. Young people with flags waving and timbrels flashing lined the sides of the footpath as she moved to where a large company of waiting officers and cadets were singing a joyful Army song accompanied by the cadet band. Commissioner Burrows expressed her appreciation for the welcome and her confidence in God for the task ahead. The event was covered by teams of Melbourne television stations and journalists.

A dinner honoring the General-elect was held in Melbourne, hosted by leading citizens and church leaders. The Governor-General of Australia Sir Ninian, with Lady Stephen, flew from Canberra to be present, and spoke of the pride of Australians in the election of Commissioner Burrows.

The General-elect gave her Army a major scare just before she left Australia to take up her duties as General. Commissioner Gauntlett, Chief of the Staff in London, received an urgent phone call from the Chief Secretary in Melbourne. He was informed that Burrows had collapsed and been rushed to the hospital during the mammoth parade march of the Territorial Congress. There was grave concern. What would happen if she were unable to take up her global leadership? Army leaders could only rest upon the assurance that God had everything under control. When the diagnosis proved it to be exhaustion rather than a cardiac problem, all were enormously relieved.

Never before had an Australian born General-elect been farewelled from their homeland, and Australian Salvationists made the most of it. A 2,000-seat auditorium in Melbourne was rented for the June 23, 1986 event, and those involved say that for every ticket available they could have sold three. People came from far and wide to give their Aussie General a royal sendoff, to express their love and enthusiasm for her as a leader and their pride in her election as General. The atmosphere was electric in what was described as "a fabulous night, full of life, color, and excitement." Tributes were expressed to Burrows for her energy, enthusiasm, vision, Christ-centered messages, friendliness, and interest in youth. To Australia's favorite tune, "Waltzing Matilda," the gathering sang "God bless our General." Almost an hour after the meeting she was still standing in the foyer greeting individuals from the vast crowd of people eager to have this final contact with their leader.

"My strength is in God," the new General affirmed. "I have always found in my leadership role that the grace of God empowers me to do what I, of my own natural abilities, may not be able to do."

17

★ ★

GENERAL OF GOD'S ARMY

"I want us to set our sails to the wind of the Spirit."

No one can examine the role of General without being impressed by its diversity and demands. The General is the ceremonial head of the movement, the authoritative exponent of its policy and mission, and in international matters the source of legislative action and final executive decision. To combine these roles with the mantle of spiritual leadership of a worldwide flock is to make a stupendous claim upon the energies of a single person.

The First Days

The arrival of the new General at International Headquarters in London was met with enthusiasm and formalities. A brief meeting took place in the foyer with the singing of the Army Founder's song, "O Boundless Salvation," and greetings and a prayer from the new General. Later, in Bramwell Booth Memorial Hall, General Burrows was warmly greeted by officers and employees of IHQ and NHQ.

Commissioner William Roberts had worked closely with Eva Burrows as her Chief Secretary (second in command), for two and one-half years when she was the territorial leader in Australia. Serving at International Headquarters upon her arrival, he was selected to speak at her welcome. His words presented a graphic insight to her new associates at the international office.

"She is obsessed with Jesus," he said. "She is a people person. She is always caring, never too busy. When we were in public meetings and people asked her whereabouts I would say, 'Check the doors.' She was either greeting people or saying good-bye. She was always the last to leave. The young, old, and those in between are important to her.

"She knows what is happening. I predict she will know what all of us do before she is here very long. She has a great sense of humor. She makes things happen. Status quo is not in her vocabulary. We are in for some great days in this Salvation Army with her to the fore."

The Saturday evening public welcome meeting at Westminster Central Hall, led by the Chief of the Staff Commissioner Caughey Gauntlett, was charged with excitement and expectancy. As the General mounted the platform, stood beneath the flag and gave the Army salute, an avalanche of applause showered her with love and loyalty. Representative Salvationists expressed words of welcome as the Army began a new chapter in its history. Several Australian Salvationists were on hand, including her sister Margaret. When Eva rose to address the audience, she avowed her rededication "to the positive evangelistic stance of the Army and that great purpose of our movement—to proclaim Jesus Christ and to win people to Him."

The new General faced busy initial days of welcomes, media interviews, and pressing duties of her now global leadership. In her first week in office, she was subjected to intense questioning by radio and television reporters. The Anglican Church in Britain at its annual synod had just decided to take no action on the admission of women to the priesthood. The General was questioned on the Army's role for women, its military terminology and uniform wearing, its work in South Africa, its association with the World Council of Churches, and about social problems of poverty, drug abuse, and unemployment.

Among the many messages received was one from Prime Minister Robert Mugabe of Zimbabwe. He wrote, "I would like to congratulate you on your recent election as thirteenth General of The Salvation Army. Being a woman of outstanding leadership qualities, your strong convictions and vast experience as an administrator will guide you through the task that lies ahead. I take this opportunity to thank you for the work you did in Zimbabwe during your seventeen-year tour of duty with us. Your teaching career here had a positive influence on many young men and women who have since taken up prominent roles in our newly independent country."

Agenda for the Future
Eva Burrows lost no time in communicating with her troops around the world. While on her first vacation as General, she spent two

weeks crystallizing priorities for her leadership and the worldwide
Army God had given as her parish. She issued her *Agenda for the
Future,* published in Salvationist media, outlining her challenge to
Salvationists.

> Our manifesto is found in the Gospel of Christ, in His powerful
> teachings and clear challenges. It is most succinctly expressed in
> His great commission to go into all the world and preach the
> Gospel and make disciples. I commit myself to that commission
> with all the vigor and zeal that I can command.
>
> We need an agenda for the future to make us aware of what
> we stand for, to direct our thoughts as to where we are head-
> ing, to set our priorities and the issues we really feel strongly
> about, and to be a means by which we can evaluate our efforts.
> I have sought the illuminating guidance of the Holy Spirit, and
> now set down in faith and love what I believe should be the
> basic agenda for The Salvation Army as we move through these
> final years of the twentieth century into the twenty-first. May
> this agenda help to define our purpose, shape our mission,
> guide our planning and activities, and direct our prayers as we
> venture forth with vision and commitment.

Her agenda highlighted six priorities for The Salvation Army.

1. *To emphasize the supremacy of evangelism* in fulfillment of the
   Lord's great commission, "Go forth therefore and make all
   nations My disciples." To evangelize, to share the good news
   with an understanding of the social and cultural context of
   those being reached. . . . To have a vision for growth and
   actively work to bring that vision to reality.
2. *To call the Army to spiritual renewal.* To reemphasize the
   possibility of holy living and spiritual maturity through the
   resources of prayer, worship, Bible study, sacrificial giving,
   and Holy Spirit power.
3. *To reaffirm our basic stance on the authority and validity of the
   Scriptures,* both as a basis for our faith and as a guide for
   Christian conduct. . . . To deepen our understanding of the
   truth of our doctrines in experience as well as in intellect.
4. *To emphasize the Christian ethic* as the significant influence in
   establishing a moral society. To assert the value of marriage

and family as God's plan for society. . . . To oppose the enthronement of the physical body. . . . To withstand the acceptance of lifestyles postulated as "alternative sexual preferences." . . . To acknowledge Christ's lordship in every area of life. . . . To challenge social evils from a Christian conscience.

5. *To support efforts for peace in the world,* and champion the principles of justice and equity. . . . To oppose all forms of man's inhumanity to man. . . . To withstand every form of prejudice. . . .

6. *To reaffirm the importance of our young people.* . . . To be aware of our need to show them how important they are to us and God.

A Pivotal Position

A General's performance as international leader requires a strong supporting cast. There is a reliance on capable and dedicated Army leaders around the world as well as the IHQ team.

The selection of her direct assistant, her aide-de-camp (ADC), was an essential early decision. The ADC arranges the General's schedule, travels with her around the world, manages the secretarial staff, and coordinates the communications and business of the General's office. The position requires relational skills on sensitive matters with Army leaders around the world. The General's ADC both prevents and solves problems. The requirements of stamina, efficiency, and dedication are daunting. The position is demanding administratively, physically, and emotionally.

The new General had earned the reputation of not being the easiest person with whom to work. She was as demanding and unsparing of others as she was with herself. More than one person who had worked closely with her in the office had suffered elevated blood pressure.

Since 1980, Lt. Colonel Jean Issitt had shown outstanding efficiency in the responsible position of Assistant Chief Secretary to the Chief of the Staff. Working just down the corridor from the office of the General, she was well versed in the business and procedures of IHQ. When General Burrows had been appointed leader of the Women's Social Services in the United Kingdom, she first observed Colonel Issitt as one of her staff leaders who had been in administration since 1960. Colonel Issitt led one of the sessions of Councils conducted by Burrows for officers in the department. Burrows also had observed Issitt's efficient management of the secretariat at both the 1981 and 1986 High Councils.

The General-elect invited Colonel Issitt to be her ADC. Discerning the demands that would devolve from both the office and the person, in response to the invitation Issitt said, "I reckon if you can cope with me, I can cope with you."

Colonel Issitt became the first woman ADC to a General in the over 100-year history of the Army and the first ADC in recent Army history to hold rank above that of a Major. She has handled with utmost effectiveness the multitudinous duties of the General's office, including the most extensive travel schedule in the history of the movement. By her gracious spirit, efficient and hard work, and quiet authority, Jean Issitt has endeared herself to Salvationists throughout the Army world.

For seven years she has served in the background, subordinating herself, performing any task needed, including that of the General's travel agent, valet, buffer, shield, minesweeper, adviser, listener, and companion. At one point during their travels, the General appropriately presented her in a meeting as "the one who patiently and painstakingly looks after me." In this pivotal role, Colonel Issitt has made an inestimable contribution to the Generalship of Eva Burrows and to the international Salvation Army.

Consultative Leadership
General Eva Burrows describes her leadership style as "consensus in the Spirit." She prefers to work with groups, to consider carefully the ideas and suggestions they put forward before making her final decisions. She can command her staff and forces all over the world but describes the Army system as "a benevolent autocracy." "My leadership style," she says, "is after the pattern of Jesus Christ, where a leader is not an autocrat, but a servant of all."

Eva's devotion to the grail of consultative leadership was kindled during her earlier leadership positions as she worked closely with staff members. She encouraged frank discussion rather than to have staff posture or say what was expected of them. She did not look for "yes" persons and was happy to have someone contradict her with an idea that had merit. This egalitarian approach added both spice and creativity to the input of her staff.

Her mode of consultative leadership, she believes, helps the worldwide forces move together. Once a decision is made, individual differences are subordinated to the purpose of the movement. Commissioner William Rivers observes, "A very alert mind enables her to quickly assess a situation and come to a decision without dithering. In this she is probably the General who has been most like the Founder, who wrote the following in my mother's autograph album, 'Make sure of the rightness of the path you are treading and then let the cry be *Forward.*' "

A close associate observed that once General Burrows set her mind on a plan of action, few could deter her from following through. Even if support was not forthcoming, she would often stay with her own decision. On three occasions she decided contrary to an Advisory Council recommendation and followed her own judgment. This was, of course, her prerogative and one exercised by previous Generals as well.

She is well aware of the danger of a leader in her position becoming autocratic and domineering. "If a Salvation Army General prostitutes that leadership position," she says, "then there is a structure in the Army which can have that person removed, if they no longer serve the purposes of the Army. The same High Council that elects the leader can also meet to adjudicate the fitness of the leader. The people who handle the things of God must be accountable."

In an interview she described her concept of the power of the General's office. "In theory, I am very powerful. I have, according to our constitution, the sole oversight, direction, and control of this movement. In that, I'm like the Pope. But in practice, authority is given to the national leaders. My word is final, but I would be a very foolish leader if I didn't have the mind of the people. I am no autocrat. I like to feel the vibrations and respond to them. In the end, a decision would be mine, and I would not avoid making it or be afraid of making it. But it would be a decision which emerged from discussion. And we have a big plus factor in the Army. We seek the guidance of God and always pray before every board meeting."

Commissioner Gauntlett, her first Chief of the Staff, acknowledges, "I had to be on my toes at all times. Nothing escaped her observations and awareness on all kinds of matters. But the depth of her intensity to serve God with her whole being, and the breadth of her mental and spiritual horizons, together with her feminine intuition in matters relating to human nature, were an inspiration for me and for many others. I shall always feel privileged, with a deep sense of enrichment, at having been able to share in this remarkable woman's ministry as the Army's General."

Challenge to Salvationists

As she took up the responsibilities of world leadership she wrote a message published in Salvationist media around the world, outlining her challenge. She based it on the Apostle Peter's text, "Think what sort of people we should be." The following is abridged from her clarion call and challenge.

Salvationists should be people who hold strong convictions, unswervingly convinced that Christ's way is the way for mankind. We have a faith which says that through Christ a man can be transformed, radically changed, born again. We believe also that by the power of the Holy Spirit we can live pure, uncompromising lives in today's world. That belief is based on the Bible and on our personal relationship with Jesus Christ. May your faith hold firm, despite the onslaught of the materialistic and humanistic attitudes in many areas of the world. May it hold up against the opposition of anti-Christian fanaticism and atheistic ideologies in other areas of the world. May it stand up and be counted in an environment of moral pollution where distorted values have an especially persuasive influence on the minds of the young.

Salvationists should be people of compassion. Our Army began among a people in need—the poor and the lost, the deprived and the depraved of the east end of London. Such are "our people" still today. A Salvationist is a person not afraid to be involved, reaching out in caring concern for those whose lives are messed up and mismanaged through sin, of those who are hassled and tense because of family breakup or unemployment or poverty. These people are looking for answers. We have the answer in Jesus Christ to share with them.

Salvationists should be people who communicate the good news of the Gospel. Evangelism is our supreme purpose. Remember that the most powerful, relevant communication takes place when one person shares Christ with another! Make Jesus Christ a natural part of your conversation, and help your neighbor, your workmate, your colleague to rediscover Christ and become His disciple!

The secret for our success is the Spirit-filled life. Conviction comes when the Holy Spirit opens our mind to the truth and gives us the assurance by which we stand firm. Compassion comes when the love of Christ is shed abroad in our hearts by the Holy Spirit and He stirs within us a burning love for souls. And the Holy Spirit is the greatest communicator. He never speaks of Himself, but always of Christ. He prompts us to speak of Jesus. He gives us courage and power to witness.

May we all be Spirit-filled, fire-powered Salvationists! During these early days of my leadership, I shall be seeking the Holy Spirit's guidance as to the direction our Army should be taking, the priorities we should be setting. I want that we should set our sails to the wind of the Spirit.

Thus the new General set the Army sails to catch the powerful wind of the Spirit for the uncharted waters of days and challenges to come.

18

★ ★ ★ ★ ★ ★ ★ ★ ★ ★ ★ ★ ★ ★ ★ ★ ★ ★ ★ ★

A DAY IN THE LIFE OF THE GENERAL

"Most of all, I am accountable to God."

The day-by-day life of General Burrows is a balance between office and pulpit, home and abroad. She spends about half of her time in London and the other half traveling to visit her troops in near and distant places of the world.

Daily Schedule

When in London, her average day begins at 6 A.M. She first carries out her physical and spiritual exercises — the latter being a period of prayer, Bible reading, and reflection, which she considers vital if the day is to start well.

Her breakfast at home invariably consists of half a grapefruit, toast, and lime marmalade. She shares each morning at breakfast in a family altar with a reading and a prayer with the officer who lives with her as a housekeeper-companion. Lt. Colonel Leah Davids, who in retirement lived with Burrows in London from August 1988 to August 1991, recalls that the time for morning prayer was always a priority and set the tone for the day.

A staff member calls for Burrows at 8 A.M. for the ten-minute drive to the seven-story International Headquarters on Queen Victoria Street, nestled between St. Paul's Cathedral and the River Thames. The edifice affectionately known as "101" serves as a combination "Vatican" and "Pentagon" for the Army, housing headquarters for the United Kingdom as well as the international Army. The spartan grey building hosts the General's office on the second floor, in the center of a suite of offices occupied by her closest executive and support staff. In the corner of the office is the General's Salvation Army flag, a gift from the U.S.A.

On the wall are photographs of herself with Mother Teresa and various heads of state, including Ronald Reagan, François Mitterrand, Robert Mugabe, George Bush, and Bob Hawke. Her bookshelves and cabinets are studded with Salvation Army volumes, references, and working volumes. On the left of her large desk sits an illuminated globe, next to a new computer that silently waits for its owner to stop long enough to "have a go at it."

At 9:30 each morning she consults with her second-in-command, the Chief of the Staff. His agenda for their discussions could take most of the morning. They discuss such matters as a new strategy for India, promotions and placements of senior officers, progress or problems of the Army's medical or educational work, the agenda for an international conference, problems arising from domestic turmoil, political developments or natural disaster somewhere in the world where the Army is at work. She says, "We have 2 million Salvationists throughout the world in ninety-seven countries, and keeping abreast of current situations and coming to the right decisions is a major task."

At midday she has lunch in the small dining room next to her office, often a "working lunch" with guests. Once a week she lunches with staff in the canteen. "I like to be a visible General," she says. Afternoon visitors may include staff for official conferences, Salvationists from anywhere in the Army world, former acquaintances, or the constant stream of the media.

On Thursday morning there is a half-hour worship program in the lower level of IHQ, the Bramwell Booth Memorial Hall. The General attends as a member of the congregation.

At 4:30 or 5 she leaves the office, but her workday does not end. Much of her evening is devoted to writing speeches, dictating letters, and preparing for future engagements. A cup of tea breaks up the evening at 9 P.M. and then it's back to the study to prepare her messages, until bedtime around midnight. She tries to manage six hours of sleep. Most weekends are spent preaching and leading Salvation Army meetings in England or overseas.

"To Fill the Unforgiving Minute"
A compulsion drives Burrows "to fill the unforgiving minute with sixty seconds worth of distance run." But the busyness of the office

does not preclude her taking time for people.

One of her overseas staff members at IHQ had the onset of a debilitating disease. Informed of this, the General sat down with her, talked, listened, asked if there were any way the Army could help, and then prayed with her. "I was very touched by this," says the officer. "Her schedule is crowded, but again and again she makes time for individuals." Later, as the disease progressed, the General arranged for her to have an appointment back in her homeland.

Accountability

Former General Arnold Brown, eloquent elder statesman of the Army, had written, "I cannot stress enough the importance of this principle of accountability. It should run like a living vein through the whole anatomy of the Army. No leader who demands accountability from those he leads can regard himself as exempt." General Burrows, who has no equals in rank, was asked to whom she is accountable. She replied, "I am accountable to The Salvation Army and its principles. I see myself being accountable to the people, the Salvationists whom I lead. But most of all I am accountable to God. The principle of accountability is a sine qua non within The Salvation Army."

Although a people person, General Burrows takes seriously her responsibility as an administrator. "Mission and administration are not mutually exclusive," she wrote in the July 1986 issue of *101,* the house magazine for IHQ. "Though we are a spiritual movement, the principles of good management apply to our administrative procedures as much as to any business organization." In management talks she often quotes from the Peters and Waterman best-seller, *In Search of Excellence,* citing some of its principles as relevant to the Army. "If, in our search for excellence in administration, we uphold these principles, but add prayer for God's guidance and the creative power of the Spirit, then we've got it made!"

Always having a strong sense of accountability in fiscal matters, she early undertook to understand the complicated international finances of the Army. Meetings were scheduled with the Army's Chancellor of the Exchequer and other finance staff to help her grasp the IHQ fiscal structure and the budgets that had great impact on the world services of the Army.

Funding is an ongoing concern for the General as she looks out upon the needs of the world where the Army works. She says, "I want to challenge Salvationists to live simply so that other people can simply live, and to challenge our Third World Salvationists to support the ministry of the Army. While they may receive funds from abroad for projects and for capital funding and new developments, yet the maintenance of The Salvation Army itself should be a spiritual imperative for them."

To help her understand the mechanics of IHQ and prioritize her work, every department head received from her an invitation for a conference to describe their area of work and ministry. She sent them such questions as, "What gives you the greatest challenge in your leadership? What gives you the greatest pleasure? Are there problems in your work that you feel you can't resolve?" They came to the General's office one by one and brought their comments on paper to discuss with the General.

On the Soup Run

Referring to the American *War Cry,* General Burrows says, "American Salvationists call me 'The People's General,' and I rather like this tag, because I do try to get into the front lines as much as possible to see how our work is going." General Arnold Brown had said that "the front lines of The Salvation Army run through the tragedies of our world." General Burrows is a front-lines General.

In January of 1988 London was gripped in the deep freeze of an arctic weather spell. Local Salvationists conducted a nightly soup run, dispensing besides soup, sleeping bags, heat packs, and blankets to the homeless sleeping out in the cold. The General wanted to see this for herself and was escorted by Majors Robert Street and Jorge Booth.

The report of her midnight visit described her moving among the human wreckage, dispensing hot soup and a word of cheer. Strangers in this venue are unwelcome and photographers have had their cameras bashed. But here The Salvation Army uniform is a passport. Eva Burrows peers inside the small opening of a box and calls, "Hello, Tom." Everybody was "Tom." That way she gets to know their name when they respond, "My name's not Tom, it's Bill." "Bill, give me your hand," she says. A grimy hand emerges; hot soup is handed over. Then she asks, "Bill, may I pray with you." Hesitation, then a reluctant, "Okay." She leans forward, kneels on the ground, using her gloves as a mat on the snow, her head almost disappears in the box. From inside a voice exclaims, "Good God, lady, I didn't

General Burrows visits inside a "residence" of Cardboard City.

know you wanted to get in bed with me!" She replies, "O Bill, I should have known this is your bedroom!"

The last stop is underneath the Royal Festival Hall, the area known as "cardboard city." As she visits those living in the boxes she is shocked to suddenly hear a voice call out, "Hello, Eva." She can't imagine who it would be. "Do you remember me?" he asks. Eva recognizes him as a former night watchman at the William Booth Memorial College where she had lectured. This knight of the road is now past seventy, widowed, has fallen on hard times, and sleeps "in" under the arches of the Royal Festival Hall. She puts her arm around him, talks with him, prays with him, kisses him, and walks slowly away.

Major Street, observing the tears Eva has not been able to hold back, keeps a respectful distance until she has collected herself. She is deeply moved in finding the night watchman, for now the homeless are no longer just anonymous people but have faces and names. She returns home from her rounds at 4 A.M. Her driver consulting her diary for the next day sees the General's next appointment is at 10 A.M.

The midnight patrol to pockets of human need was not a new

experience for Burrows. Lt. Colonel Lucille Turfrey recalls an experience when she was her ADC and lived with her in Scotland. Occasionally when the hour reached about 10:30 P.M., Eva would say, "Come on, let's go down to Lauriston," a deprived area of Glasgow where the Army had a lodging for the down-and-out.

"One such night," recalls Turfrey, "I stood watching the Territorial Commander and saw her combing the hair and then caressing the brow of a poor, emaciated frame of a woman who visibly relaxed into the arms of the one bringing such gentle, tender care into the early hours of the morning. This, I thought in wonder, is her true greatness! As good, as competent as she is behind the office desk so strategically handling the affairs of the Army, here is where her greatest qualities are to be found—among the people, and people most in need. Here is where Christlikeness really shows! Away from the cameras, the T.V. and newsmen, in a quiet corner of human need."

A Revolving Door

Eva Burrows is not a cloistered executive. Her days in the office are filled with interaction with people. She thrives on having people around her and her office becomes as a revolving door with persons coming and going throughout the day.

When Commissioner John Nelson, the International Secretary (IS) for South Asia comes for his appointment, discussion centers on problems in Burma and the suffering of children there. The IS reports on how Singaporean Salvationists have raised funds to help Burmese Salvationists. The General shares she has received $20,000 from a generous donor and wants it used to help in Myanmar. Discussion then focuses on the forthcoming appointment change in Mizoram, India with the IS making his proposal. They discuss the qualifications of prospective leaders, including health status. General Burrows is very knowledgeable of the persons discussed, remembering one Indian officer from when he was a delegate to the International College some twenty years earlier, "as a shining example of integrity." She and the IS arrive at a consensus and she reminds him that the proposal needs to go to the Advisory Council along with a health certificate. Their conference concludes with discussion of the need for leadership development, the Conference for Asian Leaders (COAL), and a letter from a man who wants the Army to start up in Thailand.

Her next appointment is with Commissioner Frank Fullarton, the IS for Europe. They discuss the biennial zonal conference coming up and the Army's recent reopenings in Eastern Europe. The General indicates she is pleased about the development of social services there which are addressing alcoholism, unemployment, child abuse, and AIDS. Reference is made to NORAD, the Norwegian grant program that sponsors many overseas projects, and the fact that Norway gives more overseas aid per capita than any other country. The agenda also includes the forthcoming Social Work Conference in March sponsored by the Army in Moscow, and the "Hallelujah Trams" that advertise the Army in St. Petersburg. They refer to a consultant hired to keep the Army informed on legislation and developments in the European Community and its impact upon the Army's work. The General sighs when reference is made to a promising officer for that area who has just suffered a heart attack.

The International Secretary for South Pacific and East Asia, Commissioner John Clinch, takes up a sensitive subject with the General—a discipline problem with a leader. Later, Commissioner Stanley Walter, the IS for Africa, reviews developments in the Congo and the problem of devaluation in another African country, and responds to a query about the condition of an African leader friend.

Her next visitor is Commissioner William Rivers, in the pivotal position of International Secretary for Administration. This day he represents the Chief of the Staff who is conducting meetings in Sri Lanka and India. The General has read beforehand the daily agenda, and she listens as the Commissioner courteously expresses his difference of opinion on a proposal that the General had found favorable. After listening to his reasoning, the Commissioner carries her judgment and she changes her support in favor of his recommendation. At one point when an unreasonable suggestion is said to be made by an officer, Burrows reacts, "How could he expect to do that? Rubbish!" Substantive subjects are discussed including dates for the next High Council that will elect her successor, the possible need for a new edition of the doctrine book, and proposals of appointments and promotions to go to the Advisory Council.

Office Style

As a leader she invites and enjoys a give-and-take with her staff. She probes and challenges them in their work and welcomes a good debate or constructive argument. She likes to work with people of similar strength who express their disagreements and she appreciates what comes from the cut and thrust of argument.

Commissioner Peter Hawkins, who served as her Chancellor of the Exchequer when she became General, says, "She enjoys frank discussion on any subject. The General doesn't like weakness in her subordinates. She wants them to come to her with well-considered opinions and balanced points of view and be prepared to debate the issues very openly." The Commissioner, answering a question as to how she relates to fiscal management, says, "She has a very shrewd idea of where we should go and a pragmatic sense of management."

To be fully informed on the executive business of IHQ, she reads copies of correspondence that go out from the office of the Chief of the Staff. Upon returning from an overseas trip she has her secretary bring the files of correspondence, both incoming and outgoing, for her to take home and read. Before coming to the office the next morning she will have read all correspondence and business and made notes of any questions or comments on them.

Her approach is always direct. One of her colleagues writes, "One of the things I appreciated very much in dealing with the General was that I always knew where I stood. She spoke what was in her mind. In administration, she is very much the headmistress and little eludes her eagle eye."

No one who works closely with Burrows pretends it is an unbroken idyll. Captain Sylvia Burt, her confidential secretary shares that Burrows expects things to get done at the office. "Her presence is pressure. She is demanding, commanding. She knows what she wants and she puts it to you. Responding to her leadership is a challenge."

Captain Burt shares the further insight, "She's not mechanical. She does not hand me the dictation and just say, 'Here's your work for today,' but discusses letters with me. She doesn't just give me a folder with the material but lets me into that folder with the sharing of information and background." Major Mrs. Margaret Goffin, who had served as her private secretary in Australia, echoes this mode of office style. "Often she would ask us to draft a letter or summarize contents of a long letter so she could handle it more quickly and efficiently. We were encouraged to think and share with her in the work process, which we appreciated."

Captain Burt further speaks from close everyday observation, "She is an action lady with a great capacity for work, an ability to accomplish a task, and an extraordinary drive and executive courage. She has a thin line of patience, and can be reactive and volatile. I don't know how it is God has gifted her with so much talent and capacity. She is leadership personified. It is a growing experience because you can't work with her without something rubbing off on you."

One person who worked in the office with her in earlier years shares, "There was one particular day when I felt that nothing I did would please her. The Lord really dealt with me on that and made very plain to me that all I had to do was please Him in this appointment. That was a turning point for me, because I then did just try to give my best and to please God, and that seemed to suit the Commissioner as well." The person adds, "She could be hard at times and demand a lot, but she also was an encourager and was grateful for what you did for her."

Burrows' secretaries were never at a loss for work, except perhaps, once. Burrows always kept ahead by doing dictation at home late at night and bringing it to the office in the morning. Major Mrs. Goffin remembers the day when Burrows came in and just stood in front of her typewriter and dolefully announced, "I do not have any tapes today." For Burrows, that was a type of frustration — she could not stand to see work come to a standstill.

Instead of doing the dictation, she had spent the night in prayer. She faced that day a major decision relative to the discipline of an officer. Goffin recalls, "It always stood out in my mind that she was prepared to let all that office work go, which she was usually so concerned about. She let it all go, spending the time in prayer that she normally would give to work, so that she would know the Lord's guidance in this matter. I really admired her for that, and my estimation of her as a spiritual leader went up on that occasion."

One day in the life of the General is never the same as any other. About half of her days she will be traveling, often to distant countries and diverse cultures. But each is filled with daunting challenges and, in the perception of a buoyant General, "with wonderful opportunities for service to God and the Army."

19

★ ★ ★ ★ ★ ★ ★ ★ ★ ★ ★ ★ ★ ★ ★ ★ ★ ★ ★

THE GENERAL–PHILOSOPHICALLY SPEAKING

"Evangelism is our supreme purpose."

In her tenure as General, Eva Burrows has made many pronouncements and has been quoted numerous times from her addresses, interviews, and written communications. Her statements reveal her philosophy about herself, the Army, and a wide range of topics on Christian living.

She recognizes the positive profile the Army has with the public but warns, "We must not rest on the public image of ourselves. We must be more self-critical. In the public's eye we're often seen as a social welfare agency, not as a church. We need to be sure we really fulfill the evangelistic purpose of our movement."

General Burrows reacts against any impression of the Army as old-fashioned, a slightly quaint organization with a strict moral code. She does not apologize for the Army's trappings and rejects any suggestion that it is outmoded or Victorian in its approach. "I would hate to think we were old-fashioned and fuddy-duddy," she says. "I like to think we are adaptable. We don't want to be trendy for the sake of just being trendy. We must be relevant. We need to communicate in the language that people understand."

Some have suggested that the Army's paramilitary uniforms are a Victorian appendage. In response, Burrows has said, "The principle of having a uniform is standing up for what you believe. It means we're available if someone wants help. Our uniforms are adaptable, tailored to suit the climate and customs of those countries where Salvationists are based." She cites a West German Bishop of Berlin who congratulated the movement for the uniform. When asked why, he explained that there were too many anonymous Christians in the world.

In response to the question, "Has The Salvation Army had its day or is it getting a second wind?" she said, "I think every organization does have a tendency to wind down like a mechanical toy. But we are not just an organization; we are an organism of the Holy Spirit. If we're open to renewal by the Holy Spirit then I think you could call what happens to us our second wind. We are looking more critically at the way we've done things and we're not holding onto things just because they belong to our past."

To the question, "How much scope is there for the individual within the Army system?" she answered, "I think far more than would appear. We are not a sausage machine turning out Salvationists all the same. Even though we have the uniform appearance of a quasimilitary movement, we encourage individual style. We are looking for and encourage people with creative ability. Yes, there is the needed obedience to our orders and regulations—our guidelines for conduct which are constantly reviewed. But within the Army there is still plenty of scope for creativity."

Theology and Ecumenism

On the subject of theology and ecumenism she has said, "We are not very interested in theological debate. As Bramwell Booth once said, we carry our theology in a knapsack because we are always on the move. Our theologians within the movement are prepared to argue our points if necessary. We would not want to spend our time in committees because we are a bit impatient with just talk. But where there is a mission or an evangelical purpose, such as the Billy Graham crusades, we have been very active and supportive.

"When it comes to denominational differences we have always been tolerant of other approaches, and have never expressed ourselves in a judgmental way on other denominations. We have our own standards, and our nonsacramental stance, but we don't expect others to hold to that. Perhaps we have been led to do that so God will use it to help others who need that example.

"We need also to show love and tolerance to those of non-Christian faiths. I don't think we should be dogmatically aggressive, but on the other hand neither should we be compromising about the Christian faith. Personally I cannot accept multifaith worship. 'There is one name given among men by which we must be saved.' But that does not give me reason to stand and judge a Muslim or a Hindu—

I've lived with them too long. I leave that to God's wisdom and love. My challenge from God is to proclaim Christ. I believe that Christ is the Light of the World, and any other truth followed is only a step toward that ultimate truth."

A Practical Holiness

General Burrows' exegesis on the Army's doctrine of holiness is not couched in boilerplate pietism or mystical abstractions, but is geared to practical everyday life. "I believe that holiness — holy living — is a practical experience. If God calls us to holiness, it must be possible. Holiness is sometimes made to sound like a special code of spiritual etiquette that you must follow. That's rather negative. I believe that holiness is a very positive, wholesome experience which is not so much what you do, but what you are.

"To me, holiness is approximating the ideal of a Christlike life. Holiness is not a gloomy pietism or an unattractive self-righteousness, but a goodness, a shining quality.

"Sanctification also includes my mind, for God works through my thinking. I open myself to the Holy Spirit working in my mind, and as I have advanced in leadership I realize more and more that God doesn't just whisper the answers to us, but expects us to work with Him in our decision-making."

Her preachment on holiness refers to the Holy Spirit as the agent and enabler of our sanctification. "What we are depends on the Holy Spirit in our life. It's absolutely amazing what the Holy Spirit will do through a life given to Him. The Holy Spirit helps us to be Christlike in our everyday life and work. I believe that in today's environment, which is often very sordid and unholy, we can shine like Christ. Jesus Christ did not avoid contact with the things of the world. Only if we live in the world, unsullied by its sordidness around us, can we really witness to true Christian living. The Holy Spirit gives us power to overcome and live a Christlike life. The cost for receiving the Holy Spirit is yourself — given in self-surrender.

"We have our Sunday morning holiness meeting to encourage Christlikeness in our people. Holiness is not some kind of spiritual aristocracy for the few; it is God's will for everyone."

The Army's Compulsion

Burrows often refers to the Founder to illustrate the mission of the Army. "When William Booth worked among the deprived and the depraved of the east end of London, he had a clear perception that you cannot preach to a man about wearing heavenly robes if he does not have a shirt on his back. Neither can you speak of feasting in paradise if a person has not had a meal for a week. So you have this hallmark of The Salvation Army, which is to meet the physical, mental, and social needs of a man while you are meeting his spiritual needs. We feel that is a distinctive purpose, and that again was under the leading of the Holy Spirit."

Her sermons inexorably move toward a point of decision and dedication. "Right from the beginning," she says, "we've had this compulsion of the Gospel, to preach for a verdict. In other words, when you give a message you expect people to make a decision about it."

One of her major concerns as General has been to assure a proper balance between the Army's evangelism and its social work. "I'm trying to put before them the fact that our charitable work must be linked with our Christian commitment. I would like to get it all back into balance. It isn't that I don't regard the social work. I often tell leaders when I'm speaking that if we are just a religious movement without any social dimension, we would become a back street mission. Yet if we are a social agency without our spiritual work, then we become a professional agency that is one among many. The fact that we are both together makes The Salvation Army what it is. Therefore, if I seem to overemphasize the spiritual, it is in order to correct the imbalance.

"The average Salvationist in the Western world has climbed up several notches in the social scale since the early days of the Army. Today we find doctors, lawyers, accountants, businessmen, who are the children and grandchildren of early Salvationists. We are grateful for their involvement, but we need to guard against losing touch with working-class people."

She tells the story of Major Joy Webb, outstanding musician and recording artist in the Army, who was practicing to sing in Westminster Abbey. As she was standing there with several clerics, one of the guides from the Abbey came straight down the aisle to her and said, "There's a man out there who needs help. Can you come?" She makes the point that the clergymen were also standing around in their robes, but the guide came to the one Salvationist in the group. Major Webb helped the man, taking him to an Army hostel near the Abbey. Burrows concludes, "We are still going for the lonely, the lost, the worst. They are still our parish."

One of her major emphases for the Army has been spiritual renewal which she interprets as "a greater awareness of the place of the Holy Spirit in life enrichment as a Christian." She sees it as discovering and developing the gifts of the Holy Spirit and then using them for the building of the body of Christ.

Homelessness and Alcoholism

In an interview with a journalist from East Germany, the topic turned to what the Army was doing for the homeless in its hostels. Understanding Britain to be a welfare state that provides for all the problems and needs of its people he asked, "Why in Britain are there still homeless people?" She pondered, "Well, you say to yourself, 'Why? If government provides the welfare of the state and we have all this provision, everything on tap for people in difficulty, why are there still people wandering around homeless? Why are there people sleeping in the streets?' It is because there are so many people whose psyche is out of tune. Because they have deep psychological problems, hangups from their unhappy home life, breakups of families. Although you may provide all the homes, there are still going to be people whose lives are messed up and shattered. I believe that if you could get to the base of people's problems and help them spiritually, they would come through."

She often quotes a statement she once heard on the different approaches to treating an alcoholic. "In a rehabilitation program, if you take an alcoholic to a doctor, he will become a healthy alcoholic. If you take him to a psychiatrist, he will become a balanced alcoholic. If you take him to Alcoholics Anonymous, he will become a sober alcoholic. But if you take him to Jesus Christ, he will become a transformed person with a whole new direction in life. He's a new creature in Christ Jesus.

"Jesus said the experience of being transformed by the spiritual relationship with God is as radical as being born again. I believe there are deep problems beneath the surface when people come to us for help. It's not just a case of saying, 'Be saved.' But we do believe that if they can get their spiritual life right, they can cope with some of the big distresses of life."

Army Symbols

The Army's mercy seat, or altar, is seen by the General as not only a place to come and kneel in seeking salvation, but also as a place for covenanting, for reconsecrating, or even for celebrating.

She often has led Cadets in their covenant service, a time just before their commissioning when they sign their covenant promising to serve God faithfully all their days and to make the salvation of souls the supreme purpose of their lives. She would sit at a nearby table and sign their cards as witness to their covenants. Then, before she proceeded to the platform, she herself would kneel at the mercy seat and renew her covenant with God. Many were surprised to see the General herself kneel there in prayer. On one occasion she received a letter from a Cadet saying, "I was very moved that you knelt at the mercy seat, because it reminded me that even the General needs to renew her covenant with God."

Colonel Lyndon Taylor, who served with her in Africa, remarked that when she was a young officer he had seen Eva Burrows at the mercy seat more than anyone else.

"Our mercy seat is the place where we kneel in communion with God, where we often make our sacred decisions and dedications. I remember Commissioner Catherine Bramwell-Booth [granddaughter of the Founder] when as the principal I invited her to lecture at the International College. She spoke to us about an hour and a half and challenged us about what we should be in today's world. She said we mustn't idolize things, even great things of The Salvation Army. As she talked she walked down in front of the mercy seat and she then sat down on the mercy seat as she continued speaking. Everyone was thinking that perhaps she was tired because she was getting very old. But I think she was saying to us that you could sit on that bench because there is no virtue in the wood or in the place. It's what happens in people's hearts when they come there."

Eva Burrows has a strong belief in the destiny of The Salvation Army, under the initiative and empowering of the Holy Spirit. Although she has a great love for the Army, she realistically sees its weaknesses as well as its strengths. "I wouldn't say I'm so overawed by the Army that I don't see its faults. The analogy I use is that 'we have this treasure in earthen vessels.' There are imperfections because it is run by imperfect human beings. Yes, we are fallible, we are vulnerable, but our great purpose is to reveal Christ.

"I believe this movement was called into being by the Holy Spirit for a purpose, with an identity separate from others. Our Founder, William Booth, did not sit down with a group of people and say, 'We will have a Salvation Army.' But in a wonderful way, the Holy

Spirit brought to light the concept of an army of soldiers of Jesus Christ waging a war against sin. To us there is no doubt that the origin of The Salvation Army was definitely under the Holy Spirit's leading."

In her visits around the world she often shares her perception of the kind of Salvation Army she wants to see. Her points include: (1) a Spirit-Filled Army with members sanctified by the Holy Spirit; (2) a Soul-Saving Army with every member seeking to win the lost to Christ; (3) a Serving Army that is concerned for the lost, homeless, poor, serving as Christ served, with all Soldiers joined in the task; and (4) a Solidarity Army with all nations joined in one bond of fellowship and purpose. She challenges, "Be true to what the Army stands for. By the power of the Holy Spirit, go forward."

Preaching is a very sacred and serious business for General Burrows. She diligently prepares herself for every engagement. In addition to her large number of sermons that she varies in her preaching, she has a basic outline for different functions that she modifies and adapts to the local situation, such as building dedications, centennials, annual meetings, enrollments, presentation of awards. She believes sermons should be biblically based and relevant to people where they are. Media such as drama, choreography, and music are methods she strongly endorses. Realizing that television has made audiences visually oriented, she speaks with an effective reliance on illustrations from real life. She sets a consistent standard for brevity, never preaching for more than twenty minutes.

Youth Emphasis

As General she has placed a great emphasis on young people. When asked why she identifies so closely with youth she gave several reasons. "One was my own rebellion in my teen years. If it hadn't been for the understanding of my mother during that period, I would have had great difficulty. So I appreciate that some young people do rebel just for the sake of rebelling. Then for seventeen years I worked with young people in Africa. I have great faith in young people and I feel that I must stand up for them when their elders criticize them. I don't excuse them in such things as drug-taking, but I do want older people to realize that young people have good ideas. Their adventurous attitude, their willingness to take risks and go out and do things—we lose a lot of that as we get older. As the young venture forth, we older ones become more comfortable as we look for security.

General Burrows always has time for youth.

"The Salvation Army really began as a youth movement, with many of our early leaders as commissioners and commanders before they were thirty. So much of the vigor of our early days was because our leaders were young. All the time I have my antenna up to see that the young people are given opportunity. And possibly, I'm still young at heart. I can enjoy new things. It's no problem for me to enjoy the new music they have. Some people grind their teeth over it, but I kind of enjoy it."

She gives a caveat, though, in her outlook on youth. "The thing that makes me a little anxious about young people these days is their view of freedom. True freedom is not just claiming, as Frank Sinatra sings, 'I did it my way.' Freedom is to find the guidelines within which to direct your life. And I think sometimes our kids don't understand that. I get anxious when their concept of freedom leads them to drugs and an undisciplined life. There is nothing lovelier than a young Christian who is full of the joy of his faith."

As General she has often surprised people by coming to the Sunday School. She says, "It is a pleasure to go in and see the young people studying the Bible."

Prayer Power

Throughout her life General Burrows has had a deep commitment to prayer. She said early in life, "I want to be a graduate in the school of prayer." With the increasing burdens of leadership she had to come to a greater reliance upon the guidance and strength found in prayer. She frequently refers to prayer in her discourses and pronouncements, often more as a testimony than a treatise.

Prayer has been a major emphasis of General Burrows in her messages around the world. "There is no substitute for prayer, for it links us with the wisdom and the power of God." At a leader's meeting in the U.S.A., she shared that she had given sixty-two talks in four and one-half weeks, only ten of them repeaters. She said, "It is the sustaining grace of prayer that keeps me going." She challenged a congregation in Africa, "Brothers and sisters, we must live in the climate of prayer. Vision comes in our solitude with God. If we're a praying Army, we will be God's Army, and a growing Army."

She has had a profound sense of prayer support from her Army around the world. She often says, "I doubt that I ever get a letter, even from Army leaders around the world, where they don't finish by saying, 'Do be assured, General, we pray for you.' I have a great sense of being sustained by the prayers of the people. When the sun rises in the eastern islands in Australia, then moves to Asia and Africa, as the sun rises around the world, prayer is said for me in every time of the day. In many homes the General is prayed for every day. That would not just be our clergy—officers, but also our soldiers—lay members. I know in my own family that the General was someone who had our respect and love. But when it happens to you, yourself, it is really overwhelming. It does not matter really who the General is, it is the office of the General. It is the one who stands for what The Salvation Army stands for.

"Because the spiritual demands are very great, I am always thrown back on the resources of God. When you are at the end of your own strength, you lean so much more on God. The Holy Spirit seems to get hold of you in those times in such a way that afterward you say, Wasn't that amazing? I would not be able to live up to the spiritual demands if it weren't for the Holy Spirit working through me. My human resources are limited, but God's resources are unlimited."

Her own deep commitment to prayer found expression in declaring a worldwide Prayer Vigil Day to be held on April 1, 1990. "A praying Army is a powerful Army," she emphasized. She designated the first Sunday in April of each year as a day of prayer for Salvationists around the world. "This will create a stream of prayer," she announced, "flowing continuously from the rising of the sun in Fiji to its setting in Hawaii. God is waiting and longing to hear from His people."

20

★ ★ ★ ★ ★ ★ ★ ★ ★ ★ ★ ★ ★ ★ ★ ★ ★ ★ ★

MOVING GOD'S ARMY AHEAD
"Go for growth!"

There are said to be three kinds of people: those who make things happen, those who let things happen, and those who say, "What happened? Eva Burrows became known as a "Get-it-done General." She is a leader who makes a difference and has set a new course for the international movement she has led for seven fruitful years.

International programs have been a hallmark of the Generalship of Eva Burrows. Her strong emphasis on the internationalism of The Salvation Army engendered an International Congress, two International Conferences of Leaders, and the setting up of international seminars and councils. These all served to strengthen the Army's worldwide fellowship and give impetus to the fulfillment of its mission.

At the time of her election, the Army's forces and ministries in then ninety countries came under her command. It was imperative to secure a quick grasp of the people, settings, needs, and potential of this vast international network of people and programs. She wasted no time in gaining a knowledge of her worldwide Army.

An invaluable foundation was laid by visits in her first year to four of the five Army zonal conferences, meeting with leaders and discussing needs and recommendations. These contacts and discussions would serve her well throughout her Generalship for decisions to be made on policy, program, and personnel.

1988 International Conference of Leaders
General Burrows convened an International Conference of Leaders at Lake Arrowhead, California, in September of 1988. A proposed

agenda was sent to her leaders around the world, requesting comment for deletions or additions. The final agenda was set, taking into consideration the ideas and suggestions that had been forthcoming. Through the Army media the agenda was disseminated around the world, inviting direct input. Also each territory was expected to discuss the agenda with working committees. When the leaders came to the Conference, they brought not only their own ideas, but the thinking of the rank and file of the Army.

The Conference agenda included such vital topics as "Our Human Resources," "Spiritual Renewal," "Evangelism," "Church/Corps Growth," "Social and Moral Issues." Many practical recommendations were forthcoming that would ultimately bring creative change in some of the basic procedures and policies of the Army. The nine days were spent mostly in twenty-six working sessions, each day commencing with devotions and ending with prayers.

"We have the destiny of The Salvation Army in our hands," Burrows told the leaders. "We must ask God to give us a vision and the courage to take risks. People of vision need to be people of action." She commented on the Founder's warning that the Army should beware of three dangers: stagnation, secularization, and self-satisfaction. She said that these were still pertinent dangers and that the Army could not relax its vigilance in any of these areas.

To assure that the results of the Conference would not be just filed away in reams of minutes, Burrows appointed a commission to review the decisions and recommendations of the Conference for the purpose of implementation. Following the Conference the commission met for four days at IHQ and prepared a set of proposals for action.

The Conference included a united rally at the famed Crystal Cathedral in California, overflowing its capacity of 4,000 in an international salute. When leaders from around the world graced the immense platform for this International Salute, the variety of uniforms and saris, rich ethnic backgrounds and colors, eloquently testified to the multinational miracle of the Army. A mammoth flag—thirty by fifty feet—was raised from the stage to the vaulted ceiling of the cathedral, loftily adorning the festive occasion as a symbol of the Army's crowning glory—its internationalism in Christ.

The large gathering witnessed a presentation of the *Order of the Founder* by the General to Mrs. Commissioner Grace Sughanantham of India for "her peerless example to Indian officer wives, beautifully demonstrating the spirit of caring for the destitute through half a century of active service."

General Burrows preached compellingly on the Conference theme, "Toward 2000 — Vision and Task." At the end of the stirring rally, everyone in the audience stood in response to the General's invitation for rededication to Christ. It was a night to be recorded and remembered in the annals of Salvation Army history.

A New *Articles of War*

The *Articles of War* is one of the most sacrosanct documents of The Salvation Army. For over 100 years it has been the covenant signed by every Soldier at the time of enrollment. General Burrows, congenitally incapable of being satisfied with the status quo in a fast-changing world, thought it was time to update the century-old wording in the covenant. For some in The Salvation Army this was akin to taking on Holy Writ.

General Burrows considered the wording of the promises to be somewhat Victorian and not adequate for today's challenges. She had suggested that a revision was overdue for the Army document, but nothing came of it. So she had a text drawn up from discussions with some officers, with helpful input especially from Colonel John Larsson. The text was then submitted to the General's Advisory Council for discussion. Amendments were made and sent to all the Army territories. Many of the territories set up commissions to study the text and make their proposals, suggesting additions, amendments, etc. These all came back for further review by the Advisory Council.

Each command leader of the Army world was then sent the recommendations for reaction as to how the new wording would affect their territory. The matter was slated to be a major agenda item at the forthcoming International Conference of Leaders.

The revised *Articles of War* would retain its two parts — the doctrines or beliefs of a Salvationist, and the promises that define the behavior of a Salvationist. Thus belief and behavior are wedded in the document as in life. The doctrines would remain the same, but the outdated and legalistic language of the covenant would be updated. The old document had contained no reference to some of the wider range of issues faced today, such as sanctity of marriage, pornography, the occult, and concern for the needy.

The final text was adopted at the 1988 International Conference of Leaders held in California and chaired by General Burrows. A Soldiers' Renewal Sunday was projected to launch the Army's revised *Articles of War*.

Women and Families

One of the concerns Burrows sought to address is the role of officer wives. Male officers, especially those who leave corps work, often receive appointments designed for the man without a comparable position of significant leadership for the wife.

The International Headquarters under Burrows would serve as a model for utilizing the dedication and skills of its married woman officers. She established the policy that the wife of each IHQ officer should have a meaningful appointment and opportunity of service. For example, Colonel and Mrs. David Edwards came from significant dual leadership positions in the United States, for Colonel Edwards to serve as Under Secretary for the Americas. General Burrows arranged for an appointment for Mrs. Edwards, who had been trained as a nurse, in the medical section of IHQ.

She likewise established for the first time appointments for wives of the five International Secretaries serving at IHQ. Each was appointed as Assistant Secretary for Women's Organizations for the part of the world for which her husband was responsible. The wife of the Chief of the Staff was given the appointment of World Secretary of Women's Organizations. The first appointee, Mrs. Commissioner Cox, is acknowledged by Burrows to have been an enormous asset in this capacity. Another first for women's leadership under Burrows was the appointment of an officer wife to the Advisory Council to the General, perhaps the most influential international council of the Army.

Although unmarried herself, Burrows recognizes the demands of marriage and family life. "All officer wives are ordained as officers and enter into a joint ministry with their husbands. They have to work out their role as mother, wife, and minister of the Gospel. I remember a young married woman officer asking, 'Which is more important, my role as an officer or my role as a mother?' Both are important. The priorities may change at different times in life. When the children are younger, you may have to give more time to them and limit the ministry role. Later, when the children are more independent, the opposite occurs. We in the Army would very much emphasize the significance of the mother's influence on the family, and stress the priority of that role."

A common criticism during General Burrows' term has been that she did not advance women in top positions of leadership as much as many had hoped. The number of women eligible for the High Council declined from five at the time of her election to three near the time of her retirement. Burrows responds to this criticism by pointing out that in recent years unmarried women on the High Council had come to their positions primarily by advancing through missionary service. Also she had mandated Army territories to promote women to the top echelon of leadership and that each territory should have at least one unmarried woman officer elevated to the rank of Lt. Colonel. Territories often responded with reasons why they were not able to comply, or in some cases responded with token appointments or promotions. Although the General set the pattern at IHQ and issued a policy statement, her cause met with little overall success, due to limitations or lack of initiatives within some territories. She takes pride in the fact that she has appointed more women as Chief Secretaries—second in command of territories—than any previous General.

Restructuring the Advisory Council

One of the major support groups to the General is the Advisory Council, composed of ten senior officers from around the world. It provides the General with advice and guidance in the formulation of policy on a wide range of matters affecting the Army. The Council is advisory and does not detract from the executive and legislative authority of the General.

The Council meets up to four times a year and covers a broad scope of subjects. Items for the agenda may be proposed by any Salvationist to his or her territorial command leader. Among the forty-two subjects considered in 1991 were the appointments of top leadership, proposed admissions to the *Order of the Founder,* restoration of rank to former officers in Czechoslovakia, Hungary, and China, marriage of retired officers, proposed changes in *Orders and Regulations,* possible preparation of a new Doctrine Book, High Council membership, and an international commission to study all aspects relating to the ministry of women officers. The Council may also study such matters as trends in the movement, moral issues, ecumenical relationships, officer personnel, and convening of international congresses and conferences. Though purely advisory, the Council is very influential.

In her third month as General, Burrows appointed a blue ribbon commission under the chairmanship of Commissioner Norman S. Marshall, the eighth such group in the forty-year history of the Council, to study ways to increase its effectiveness, or suggest changes in its constitution. She challenged the group, "I would not like to see the Advisory Council merely as a rubber stamp on the General's decisions. I want to make the fullest use of the Council." The Commission responded to the challenge with creative input that enhanced its supportive role to the General.

Burrows is intolerant with the status quo when she believes there can be improvement. Five years later, as a result of the historic changes in the administrative structure of IHQ, she launched the ninth Advisory Council Review Commission in June of 1991 under the chairmanship of Commissioner James Osborne, who is highly respected for his management expertise. Burrows advised the Council that she did not expect a "business as usual" routine, but would welcome "radical suggestions" that would be for the good of the Army. She stated, "It could well be that this is now the occasion for a radical rethinking of the role and scope of the Advisory Council. I want you to feel free to bring as fresh an approach as possible at this crucial time in our history."

There resulted a major restructuring with new initiatives and a broader international input and agenda for advising the General. One innovation was a new requirement for a minimum of two women as members of the Council.

Chiefs of Staff Selection

Perhaps no other decision of leaders is as important as the selection of staff. The choice of Chief of the Staff, second in command of the international Salvation Army, is the most important staff selection by the General. This officer works closely with the General in the administration of international affairs, acts on the General's behalf, and carries a major responsibility of spiritual and administrative leadership within the organization.

General Burrows retained one and selected two Chiefs of Staff during her tenure. She acknowledges that the position is just a step away from the Generalship, and that factor is one to be considered in the selection. "You have to be careful that you are not seen in some way to be trying to influence the selection of your successor." She also considered it an advantage for a Chief of the Staff to have had some prior experience at IHQ.

Caughey Gauntlett was due to retire in August 1986, but she asked him to stay on for an additional year. Upon his retirement, Burrows chose Commissioner Ron Cox as her second Chief. She respected his international experience in Europe and Africa and former service as an Under Secretary at IHQ. His integrity and administrative skills were complemented with an equable temperament and a refreshing sense of humor.

In 1991 Commissioner Cox came to retirement and General Burrows had to select her third Chief of the Staff. The selection for this position was a decision to which she gave much prayer. She had pledged at the High Council that she would consult with at least four other leaders on the appointment, although the ultimate decision would be hers. On this occasion she consulted with six leaders and her choice was unanimously approved.

She selected Commissioner Bramwell Tillsley, Territorial Commander for Australia Southern, known as one of the most effective preachers and Bible teachers of the Army world. The Chief of the Staff position requires managing the International Headquarters and its business when the General is away, which is more than half of the time.

A crisis struck IHQ and the Army world in March of 1992 when Commissioner Tillsley suffered a heart attack. Burrows was stunned. Tillsley had been the picture of energy and vitality. But to the relief of the General and Salvationists around the world, it was termed a "mild heart attack." Within a matter of weeks the popular Chief returned to the office, but two weeks later had to undergo a triple bypass. Crisis once again struck the office of the General with the international business of the Army coming under great pressure in the absence of the Chief of the Staff. Burrows' leadership was put to a severe test.

This breakdown and the heavy burden of administration without a Chief of the Staff seemed overwhelming. Eva Burrows, in this moment, was constrained to lean on her greatest resource—prayer. In taking the burden to the Lord she found the guidance and assurance that would get her through. "The Lord said to me, 'Do not worry. This is My Army. I will give you strength and take care of it. I will guide you through this crisis.' "

Commissioner William Rivers and the executive staff helped carry the extra workload throughout the four months of Tillsley's absence.

Burrows was led to take the unprecedented step of calling from retirement her former Chief of the Staff, Commissioner Ron Cox, who stepped in for three weeks as "Acting COS" until Bramwell Tillsley was able to return. The crisis passed and her third Chief of the Staff returned healed and applied his sensitive and sagacious skills during the final period of the history-making Burrows era.

Church Growth on an International Scale

The Church Growth movement which she had discovered to be so effective in Australia received international impetus within the Army. "There is a new air of expectancy," she announced, "a sense that we are going to accomplish a great evangelistic purpose through this awakening. Also that the primacy of evangelism will be achieved through the members of The Salvation Army and not by organization from the top." She brought into the worldwide Army the missiological principles grounded in Scripture and practical strategy, as developed and articulated at the Fuller School of World Missions, believing it would powerfully impact the Army in renewing its mission of evangelism and discipling.

She stated, "I think The Salvation Army has made many advances in the social services field. We have also made great advances in fiscal support and the sacrificial giving of our people. These areas of progress have thrilled us. However, we have been groping for a new expression of evangelism within The Salvation Army, and we believe it will come through the use of church growth principles. They are what we used to call in the early days of The Salvation Army 'the compulsion of the Gospel.' We remember the parable of Jesus when He said, 'Go out and compel them to come in.' That really was a great motivation in the early Salvation Army and I believe it is coming back again."

She viewed church growth not only in terms of numbers but as a seedbed of renewal for the spiritual life of Salvationists, with individual lay members becoming involved in evangelistic outreach and discipling. She underscored her commitment for church growth within the Army by calling an International Strategy for Growth Conference in the summer of 1989 to be held in London, with Colonel Ian Cutmore serving as Principal of this historic conference. The fifteen-day conference was filled with presentations and discussions by officers and soldiers from around the world in the format of a working group for strategy rather than a series of lectures. "The

Army has always been in the business of evangelism," she emphasized. "It is our very raison d'etre." She challenged the ninety-six delegates from forty-nine of the Army's territories, "Go for growth."

Cross-Pollination of Ideas

While she was principal at ICO, she came to an interesting discovery. A delegate from Australia would share some excellent brochures and material and another delegate would say, "Oh, I wish I had known that, because it would have saved me a lot of work and expense." She perceived the potential of a forum to share ideas and material that could be helpful in mutual areas of ministry.

One of her initiatives to address this need was the setting up of international councils to bring together representatives from different parts of the Army world for a cross-pollination of ideas in such areas as literary matters, music, and public relations. From the broad spectrum of the international movement there came together experts in their respective fields, as well as representatives who would benefit from their expertise. Some ninety-seven countries and territories would no longer "do their thing" in isolation from the Army's family of nations. One outgrowth was a projected International Literary and Publishing Conference that would share the Army's worldwide resources for training and enhancement of the Army's literary and publishing ministries.

Internationalizing the Army

Historically, the International Secretaries, responsible for the five major areas of the Army world, came primarily from Western cultures. In her campaign to internationalize the IHQ administration, General Burrows made appointments to these important posts that gave a balanced representation from the diverse cross-sections of the world they administered.

She appointed the first Hispanic leader, Commissioner Carl Eliasen of South America, as International Secretary for the Americas and Caribbean, and forged a truly international roster of Secretaries. She brought from Ghana the first African, Major John Amoah, to the position of Under Secretary for Africa, and from Japan the first Japanese, Major Makoto Yoshida as Under Secretary for South Pacific and East Asia. Captain Jayaratnasingham became the first Sri Lankan to serve in the office for South Asia. Under the internationalization program of Burrows, IHQ became cosmopolitan with accents and racial distinctions that gave a new color to this epicenter of the Army world. A seasoned observer states, "More than ever before, IHQ has indigenous representation from around the world."

Under General Burrows' direction, interchange of personnel between countries accelerated. For example, several Korean officers were appointed to the United States to help develop the Korean ministry that was taking hold there. A Singaporean officer went to Australia to develop the work there among refugees, and a Hong Kong Salvationist went to Sydney to help with the growing Chinese ministry.

She recognized that in addition to the inspirational qualities of leadership, Third World leaders need to be well trained in management and administration. To achieve this, she arranged for officers from developing countries to spend a period in Great Britain, the United States, or Australia to gain an intercultural and management training experience.

One of her goals was to have one national and one missionary officer in the top two leadership positions in a developing country. This would assure national representation as well as provide complementing leadership skills. The international Salvation Army during the Burrows era took a quantum leap toward becoming more truly international.

IHQ Mission Statement

The later restructuring of IHQ led General Burrows to carefully examine the essential purpose and role of The Salvation Army's International Headquarters. Now no longer encumbered with the administration of the Army in Great Britain, it could focus its attention and energies to worldwide needs.

In January 1992, the International Management Council chaired by the General adopted a Mission Statement, defining clearly the purpose and functions of the International Headquarters, as follows:

The International Headquarters of The Salvation Army acts on behalf of the General:

To affirm that The Salvation Army, an evangelical part of the universal Christian church, is motivated by love for God and its mission to preach the Gospel of Jesus Christ and meet human need in His name without discrimination.

To provide leadership for the international Salvation Army and set its overall strategy.

To develop policies that can be applied internationally while taking into account local culture and thinking.

To preserve the doctrines, maintain the standards, protect the interests and manage the resources of The Salvation Army.

Strategy for India

India, the Army's oldest mission field, was among the countries General Burrows visited in her first year. She observed that in India The Salvation Army had not kept pace with the changing times in its social or its evangelistic work.

The Army's social work in India had largely focused on hospitals and had made a significant contribution to the health and healing ministry of the nation. But times had changed. Community social care, private and government hospitals were emerging with Indian doctors replacing the former missionary medical staff. Army hospitals began to suffer from low occupancy rates. Problems were exacerbated by reduction in foreign assistance and severe visa restrictions. The number of missionary officers dropped from 200 in 1970 to 20 in 1988.

General Burrows responded by setting up in 1988 the ten-member All-India Strategy Commission under the chairmanship of Lt. Colonel (Dr.) Paul du Plessis. The word *strategy* denoted its purpose to be more than just a study and analysis. She challenged, "I want to see decisions emerge from the conference, and not just recommendations; concrete lines for action and not just suggestions. We want to achieve something and not just talk." The Commission's objectives were to adopt a mission statement, mobilize personnel through leadership training, adopt a policy of graduated financial autonomy, strengthen international coordination and the Army's place in the church, evaluate social programs and problems, give special attention to the rural and urban poor, enhance worship, and improve the program for soldiership.

The Commission visited the five Army Territories in India, researching the input of Army staff in those areas, talking with people at all levels of involvement, and returning to IHQ with a detailed report and recommendations. General Burrows responded to the Commission's findings with a Manifesto to all Indian Salvationists, articulating eight points for action in line with the stated objectives and research, and culminating with an Indian Mission Statement that incorporates their emphasis on holy living.

The work of this Commission comprises one of the major accomplishments of the Generalship of Eva Burrows. It is expected to enhance the Army's ministry throughout India for decades to come.

1990 International Congress

"In all my years in The Salvation Army, I've never seen anything like this." These words of Commissioner Ron Cox, Chief of the Staff, echoed the sentiment of the estimated 20,000 Salvationists who came from fifty territories of the Army world to the 1990 International Congress. It was convened from June 29 to July 8 in London, birthplace of The Salvation Army. The Congress was the most spectacular event of Burrows' Generalship and was an international extravaganza of historic proportions.

The multinational composition of the Army and yet its unity in Christ was a hallmark of the Congress. Translators communicated to delegates in Dutch, Finnish, French, German, Japanese, Norwegian, Spanish, and Swedish. Delegates came from as far away as Australia and Argentina, China and the Congo, India and Italy, Jamaica and Japan, Zaire and Zimbabwe. Their spirit of unity transcended their multinational and multilingual backgrounds as delegates shared in a grand celebration of their faith in Christ.

" 'With Christ into the Future' is a theme to match the times in which we live," declared General Burrows at the opening ceremony. "We must be a forward-looking Army," she added in her welcome to "this largest International Congress in our history with a record 3,570 registered delegates," augmented by ticket buyers to each program.

"We come seeking God's will for the future," affirmed Burrows. "God is challenging our Army today. The Holy Spirit is working in our midst. Let us open our minds, our hearts, our ears, to catch what God is going to say to us." Her message on the opening night challenged the audience to claim the threefold security of The Promises of God, The Presence of Christ, and The Power of the Holy Spirit.

Burrows outlined the purposes of the Congress: to renew commitment to the mission of the Army, to strengthen the bond of international unity, to challenge each delegate to a new level of dedication to Christ, and to look to the future with vision and realism. She summarized, "This is going to be a time of celebration and of dedication to launch our international Army into its final decade of this millennium with a vibrant faith for yet greater conquests for God."

This sixth International Congress was without peer in its variety of offerings. The "schoolteacher General" designed it as a "Congress with a curriculum." Educational and motivational components were prominent throughout, including thirty-two three-day seminars on vital and practical subjects led by top experts of the Army world.

In response to Burrows' appeal, over 14,000 persons from sixty-four countries returned cards with a promise to pray for the Congress. A cruciform altar, in the center of the two main venues at the Royal Albert Hall and Wembley Arena, became for thousands a sacred place of dedication. Delegates from varied national backgrounds and races knelt side by side in divine communion. "We are separated by great distances," said the General, "yet here the cross joins us." On the final Sunday night at Wembley, delegates from all parts of the vast arena queued up some twenty deep around the cross, waiting to kneel and sign the covenant card. Well into the prayer meeting, Burrows turned the leadership over to retired General Arnold Brown (R) as she left the platform and herself stood in line to kneel and sign her covenant card.

Tonal opulence enriched the programs, with offerings from the premier bands and choral groups from around the Army world. Delegates were inspired by the quintessence of Army music including the 1,400 voice Congress chorus, historic highlights, multimedia presentations, a new musical, a festival of Gospel arts, a total of four admissions to the *Order of the Founder,* and creative worship. Fellowship Day on the first Saturday featured a kaleidoscope of captivating events in the alfresco settings of London's beautiful parks. An awesome parade on the second Saturday, 6,000 strong including seventy bands – the biggest Army march since the Founder's funeral procession – marched on London's historic Mall toward Buckingham Palace. A swirling sea of flags and placards flowed down the Mall, as throngs photographed the stirring sight.

In surprise ceremonies, and what became for many the most memorable moments of the Congress, Burrows bestowed the *Order of the Founder* on two Army heroes. Major Yin Hung-shun of China had maintained his faith and Salvationism, surviving fifteen years in a labor camp, and is the subject of a biography by General Arnold Brown. Summarizing his story of heroism she declared, "And brothers and sisters, he is here today, Major Yin of China." The full attendance in Wembley Arena detonated in a prolonged ovation as the Major, eighty-five years of age, came and stood beside General Burrows. She concluded, "Your faithfulness to God and the Army, your endurance under persecution, and the inspiration that you have been to Salvationists would have commended you to our Founder William Booth. Therefore today it gives me great pleasure to admit you to the *Order of the Founder.*"

What then followed became one of the peak moments of inspiration at the Congress. Major Yin stepped forward, thanked the General "for this great honor" and the delegates for their welcome. He then sang in a confident, resonant voice, the chorus, "All my days and all my hours . . . shall be Thine, dear Lord." Those who knew his story remembered it was the singing of these words, as at the end of each day he lingered behind in the fields of the labor camp, that helped keep alive his faith and Salvationism. Burrows then invited the great international congregation to join Major Yin in singing those words of consecration. A wife of a divisional commander later commented, "It was during the singing of that chorus that my love for the Army was renewed."

Later in the Congress General Burrows admitted to the *Order of the Founder* another Army hero, Brigadier Josef Korbel. Now eighty-three, he had paid the high cost of discipleship with ten years of imprisonment under communist oppression in his homeland of Czechoslovakia. The Brigadier had just come from his native country where he had helped with the Army's reestablishment there. Following a standing ovation there ensued a classic moment in the history of Burrows' Generalship and of The Salvation Army. Yin and Korbel had known of each other's stories but had never met. Major Yin was called forward and there on the platform they met for the first time and spontaneously embraced, fellow-sufferers for the Gospel. It was a moment enshrined in the devotional experience and memory of each present.

A General's Dream
Addressing 5,000 officers in Councils in the Royal Albert Hall, General Burrows shared her dream for the worldwide Army.

I have a dream of an Army renewed in spirit and zeal, multiplying and growing, with a harvest of souls in Christ from all nations. I have a dream of Salvationists gathered around the Word of God in groups, small and large, coming alive from

God's Word in a new way, and inspired by His Word to new ventures of faith. I have a dream of Salvationist young people being challenged and encouraged to devise new ways to win their peers from worldly apathy and indifference into the love and service of Christ. I have a vision of the Salvation Army in Great Britain on the march. . . . I have a dream of China, released from the atheistic tyranny of communism, and opened as never before to Christian influence. . . . I have a dream that as our Army moves again to Eastern Europe, our Salvationists of Western Europe will experience resurgence of faith and spiritual power. I have a dream of a Spirit-filled Army ready to sacrifice and to serve in obedience to Christ's Commission, an Army open to changes which the creative Holy Spirit is wanting, so that our strategy for the future is Spirit-directed and Spirit-controlled. May God help me to bring that dream to reality.

Centuries ago, the preacher of Proverbs declared, "Where there is no vision, the people perish." On that July morning in London's Royal Albert Hall, General Eva Burrows gave to her worldwide Army a vision, resplendent and venturesome.

21

★ ★

ADDRESSING THE ISSUES

"I want to get something done."

Burrows is unfazed by controversial subjects and makes her voice heard through the media on such volatile issues as abortion, homosexuality, and human rights. "I believe we should feel strongly about social injustice," Burrows asserted. "As an Army leader I must be prepared to speak out, as Christ did. If 'political' means speaking out on issues such as prostitution or abortion, poverty or homelessness, if political means speaking out to quicken the conscience of the government on the needs of the people, then I'm political. I'm not just protesting for protesting's sake. I want to get something done!"

In November 1987 General Burrows set up a Social and Moral Issues Council to study issues in the United Kingdom and the world at large. The Council's fifteen members are officers and soldiers from a broad spectrum including law, genetic engineering, teaching, medicine, psychiatry, and social service. They meet five times a year and give valued recommendations to the General, enabling her to make informed and searching comments on the issues.

Statements prepared by them are addressed to the British Prime Minister and other world leaders on topics such as abortion, alcoholism, euthanasia, capital punishment, unemployment, homosexuality, embryo research and biotechnology, the place of the family, and nuclear disarmament.

Human Rights

• **Apartheid.** As a young missionary, Eva Burrows reacted strongly to the racial segregation she witnessed in South Africa. She deliberately stood in the queue at the post office counter set aside for blacks. When she was told she should be in the area reserved for whites, she would not change lines, but left.

"Apartheid is anathema," declared General Burrows shortly after taking office. It became one of the strongest statements issued in the history of The Salvation Army against a social evil backed by political power. Even some Salvation Army leaders and members in South Africa and elsewhere took exception to the General making this statement on a political issue in violation of the Army's apolitical policy. However, Burrows astutely discerned that most issues cannot be divorced from politics today. Abortion, homosexuality, racism, and nuclear disarmament have all become politicized. She responded, "I say that apartheid is not just a political philosophy. It's a philosophy of life that is contrary to the teachings of Christ."

She nonetheless emphasized the Army's nonconfrontational policy. "I could never see Salvationists or myself being like Archbishop Tutu. I believe God uses people like Tutu to be outspoken, but I do not see The Salvation Army in that role. Our role is working with the people, whether they be white or black, whatever the philosophy of the country."

• **Women's Rights.** On the issue of women's rights, General Burrows believes women's leadership can improve a world that has become overly competitive and aggressive. She sees that feminism can disrupt family life as well as threaten women with the loss of their true and precious feminine qualities. "We are the people," she says, "who are picking up the casualties of broken homes. I often congratulate mothers who don't go to work too early because of the desire for material things and the competition to keep up with the Joneses." She also opposes any thought of a statutory woman on boards and councils. "I think," she says, "women have to take their place by reason of their gifts and abilities."

Burrows disclaims being a feminist in the extreme sense. She says, "Even though Catherine Booth was a strong advocate of women having the right to preach, she was not a radical feminist. She urged the church to allow women to use their God-given gifts. She was also very much the mother of her household, the educator and trainer of her children, with strong views on home and family life. She was a wonderful mother who at the same time could go off for preaching expeditions every now and again."

The media asked, "As a woman do you think you can bring some different qualities to the job?" She replied, "Mrs. Catherine Booth, wife of the Founder, said that women are not in competition with men, they complement men. I agree with the Jungian psychology that man and woman are of two different psyches, and each has its own gifts to bring. I see a difference in the style of leadership. Men are more ambitious and plan ahead. Women are more involved and concerned with people. It isn't just culture-conditioning, it is their nature. I wouldn't think of myself as leading in a masculine way, which is normally aggressive and competitive. Women have more sensitivity to people and a greater tolerance than men. We have a responsibility to use our feminine gifts, and not our wiles."

Burrows often refers to Catherine Booth, who is considered the cofounder of the Army and who had challenged, "If there is in Jesus Christ neither male nor female, who shall dare thrust woman out of the church's operation or presume to put any candle which God has lighted under a bushel? Why should the swaddling bands of blind custom be again wrapped around the female disciples of the Lord?" General William Booth was certainly convinced by his wife's logic and himself said, "Some of my best men are women."

• **Abortion.** Writing to the Prime Minister of England, General Burrows suggested changes in the Human Fertilization and Embryology Bill that came before Parliament in early 1990. She stated, "The Salvation Army believes in the sanctity of human life and therefore views with concern any procedures knowingly undertaken that damage or destroy the human embryo. Although some medical benefits might follow such procedures, they should not be pursued at any cost. It is the Army's view that the controls presently offered in the Human Fertilization and Embryology Bill are far from adequate and should be amended."

During her term as General she strongly upheld the Army's sanctity of life position and carefully monitored proposed territorial Position Statements to assure adherence to the Army's pro life stance. Territories had returned to them any proposals that had equivocal wording on the issue. She with the Army affirmed "the sanctity of all human life from the moment of fertilization. It considers each person to be of infinite value, and each life a gift from God to be cherished, nurtured, and preserved."

She states, "There is a clear scriptural teaching that the sanctity of life commences before birth and God's compassion is for all creation, particularly for the defenseless. We emphasize the need for provision of skilled counsel, and compassionate practical care for women with an unplanned or unwanted pregnancy and the need to give counsel and ongoing support for women who choose abortion, without condoning the decision."

Burrows does acknowledge that there are extreme circumstances in which an abortion might be justified, such as danger to the life of the mother. But her position leaves no loopholes for quality of life ethics over sanctity of life.

The Family

"Those who think the family has had its day should think again," asserted General Burrows. "I have seen for myself The Salvation Army family success story in the Army's worldwide family." She affirms, "The trust and love found in a Christian home provide a secure base from which all family members may play their various parts."

Strengthening family life was a major plank in General Burrows' platform. She stated that she considered divorce and family breakup as one of the greatest problems facing society. "Down the road we are going to reap a terrible harvest." In the new *Articles of War and Soldier's Covenant* which is signed by every soldier of The Salvation Army, she incorporated a commitment to family life and marriage.

Marriage enrichment seminars, for officers as well as lay members, received her strong advocacy. "It's better to help a couple look at their marriage and strengthen it, than to try to patch it up after everything is broken down. The people we encourage to go to marriage enrichment seminars are not those whose marriages are in trouble, but those who want to enrich and improve their marriages. This is necessary in the Western world, not in the Third World, because this problem hasn't yet struck Africa and Asia." In Australia, she had officers trained to conduct these seminars for officers and soldiers. Her brother-in-law, Dr. Bramwell Southwell, was among those who conducted marriage enrichment courses and counseling for burnout in marriage.

One of the most sensitive and troubling issues General Burrows would have to deal with during her term as General was the Army's position and regulation concerning divorce and remarriage. The sensitivity of the issue was complicated by the multinational and cultural diversity within the Army. In India, Salvationists remained strongly opposed to divorce, whereas divorce on certain grounds gained increasing acceptance in the Western world. To come to a consensus on regulation for the issue was indeed a difficult task, and recommendations of the Advisory Council did not have concurrence from all world leaders of the Army.

In September of 1987 General Burrows urged the British government to give its backing to a proposal being made by the United Nations for an International Year of the Family. In a letter to Prime Minister Margaret Thatcher, the General shared her concern and also chided the government for its neglect of the family issue.

Through our membership in the International Council of Social Welfare, we have been made aware of the current proposal for a United Nations International Year of the Family (IYOF). We understand that Her Majesty's Government has been invited to express a view on this proposal, and I write to urge that the proposal be received with warm enthusiasm.

We find ourselves increasingly concerned at the ever-accelerating rate of marital and family breakdown in this country and elsewhere. An IYOF would present timely opportunities for reemphasizing the indispensable importance of families and family life to the successful development of every individual and of society as a whole.

An IYOF would also prompt a serious review of how far the concept of the family has been relegated in recent decades from a central and key position in social policy-making. We noted with considerable dismay that none of the major political parties in their recent General Election manifestos had anything positive, systematic, or constructive to say about family policy.

It is the Army's intention to offer strong support to the proposal for an IYOF and I very much hope that you will be able to respond similarly on behalf of the people of the United Kingdom.

Unemployment

Unemployment had long been an issue addressed by General Burrows. In Australia she had made a major impact by her Employment 2000 scheme. As General she wanted someone to research the needs and determine what could be done in this area of need. A lay Salvationist, Barry Mitchell, who had professional experience in social work with involvement in government, was engaged for one year as a consultant for services to the unemployed and to explore resources. Arrangements were made for him go to Australia to study the Employment 2000 program. He was also asked to research the possible use of the Army's property in Hadleigh in the U.K., remnants of a 3,200-acre farm purchased by William Booth in 1891 as part of his great social scheme for practical training in agriculture and industry.

The result was an employment training scheme at the Army's Hadleigh Farm and an Army social services center. At the latter, 150 long-term unemployed people were trained. General Burrows inspected the complex and found men who were jobless being trained up to City and Guilds standards in the construction industry. She observed skills being taught in painting, decorating, and bricklaying. In the woodworking shop she saw trainees making window frames and doors. In an office women were taught clerical skills. The project was a model scheme, jointly funded by the private sector and the Army.

Interchurch Relations

In response to an interviewer's question on ecumenism and the Army, General Burrows said, "The Salvation Army has always been open to interdenominational and interchurch relations. I would say that on the local level we have always been happily involved. Perhaps a controversy came about because of our stance in the World Council of Churches, but that in no way reflects the local situation. The one thing about The Salvation Army is that we like to achieve things, we like to get things done, we're activists. Therefore, we don't always sit easily in committees where they talk endlessly and accomplish nothing. However, if we feel we can take part in an ecumenical group for initiatives on evangelism or growth, we'll be there.

"The Salvation Army moved from full membership in the World Council of Churches to what we call 'fraternal status' for several reasons. One was that we felt the WCC was too much involved in the politicization of its activity. Also, the stress on a eucharistic fellowship made us wonder if perhaps The Salvation Army were being pushed out of the Christian family. We also thought that the World Council of Churches was not giving enough significance to the evangelistic purpose of the church. Whilst I agree that we should speak against injustice in the political arena, we also need to be known as an evangelistic church, seeking to build up the kingdom of Jesus Christ."

When asked what her word would be to the churches at large today, she responded, "I feel that what we must do is lift up Jesus Christ, because the problems of the world are so great. Where do you start to meet the world's needs? The crisis of famine, the tragedy of homelessness, the acceleration of technological and scientific changes—all bring major moral issues to the fore. Where do you start? I think if every Christian lifts up Christ and offers Christ to his neighbor, they will accomplish something. We need to get back to the Great Commission, to go into all the world and preach the Gospel."

When the Jim Bakker and Jimmy Swaggart scandals rocked the Christian church in America, she did not add to the Cassandra cries or published polemics of the day, but did give her own watchword to the Army from this tragedy. "Many have asked me about this topic since I've been in America. It should remind us to keep the element of sacrifice and self-denial in our ministry as Salvation Army leaders. For example, I have done many television interviews and have received generous monetary responses for them. But I never accept these for myself. They all go to The Salvation Army. A self-denying lifestyle, not a luxurious one, is the calling of The Salvation Army officer. We need also to maintain a strict accountability and integrity before God and each other."

A Voice in the Halls of Power
In May 1988, after all other approaches had been unproductive, General Burrows appealed to Prime Minister Margaret Thatcher for her intervention with an amendment to a bill coming before the House of Lords. This Local Government Finance Bill would have a damaging impact upon the Army's rehabilitative work in its fifty hostels throughout England and Wales offering care for almost 4,000 persons. The Bill would force the Army, as an agent of government, to collect public tax from its residents and clients, many of whom are social casualties with psychological problems.

Burrows' letter emphasized that the attitude of trust, so essential to the Army's effectiveness, "depends to a very significant extent upon the fact that we are not perceived as acting on behalf of the authorities for any purpose whatsoever. The collection of a public tax from residents and clients in our social centers would have a subtle but profoundly damaging effect upon the relationship with the people we are trying to assit. Her letter of advocacy for the Army's clients concluded, "We do believe that we have a very strong case to be made on compassionate and commonsense grounds."

After intense lobbying of Parliament and the personal appeal to the Prime Minister from General Burrows, an amendment to the bill exempted clients in the types of residences run by The Salvation Army.

"Increasing numbers of people in debt are turning to the Army in desperation," General Burrows told Prime Minister Margaret Thatcher, in a letter calling for more control of credit card companies and rates of interest. "Can it be right," she asked, "that credit is so easily obtainable, when for so many the end result is family stress and even breakdown?" The main culprit, Burrows advanced, is "that dubious wonder of our age — the credit card. We are at a loss to understand why the banks and business houses issuing cards have not been brought into line. The government must assume responsibility. Action is urgently needed."

She urged early action such as statutory regulation of interest rates used by credit card companies, a requirement for the companies to make known in plain English their interest rates, and a statutory system to be followed in screening applicants for credit-worthiness.

The *Last Temptation* Film
When in 1988 many Christian leaders remained silent about the release of the film, *The Last Temptation of Christ,* General Burrows fired one of her most explosive salvos. She called for a boycott of the film, strongly condemning it.

> It is morally offensive in the extreme. Devout Christians will be shocked and saddened by the film's blasphemous claims and sick distortion of the truth. There is no basis whatever in Scripture for Martin Scorsese's grossly distorted representation of Christ's sexuality and human relationships, which is completely at variance with the Gospel record of Christ's life and teaching. We cannot remain silent in the face of such blatant misrepresentation and exploitation.

Alcoholism
When the British government became concerned about the eruption of violence traced to alcohol consumption, General Burrows presented a four-point plan for combating the effects of alcohol abuse. She wrote to Prime Minister Margaret Thatcher:

You have our support and prayers in tackling this frighteningly difficult problem. At a time when the government is giving consideration to taking strong measures to combat the damaging and sometimes tragic effects of growing violence and hooliganism, usually prompted by alcohol abuse, The Salvation Army expresses the hope that measures taken will tackle the wider alcohol issue and not concentrate only on the immediate problems relating to football games and public order. Indeed, it would be unfortunate if national humiliation and embarrassment were seen to be the motivating forces for dealing with the alcohol problem, rather than deep concern for the immense human suffering and ongoing damage to individuals and families, and thereby the nation, caused by everyday alcohol abuse. Such abuse is a major cause of domestic violence. It destroys family life, often causing serious injury and sometimes death. Alcohol abuse is at the heart of various forms of violent crime.

The British government was urged to give serious consideration to strong specific proposals. First, a total review of advertising of alcoholic beverages. Burrows stated that a ban on television advertising of alcohol was long overdue, particularly when it is noted that advertisements give a false and glamorous picture of the effects of alcohol. She said it should be borne in mind that alcohol is a dangerous drug, and nothing less than a total ban on the advertising, except at the point of sale, is acceptable. Second, Burrows advocated that health warnings should be made obligatory on all containers of alcoholic drinks. Third, she proposed the excise duty on alcohol beverages be increased immediately. And fourth, she urged random testing of drivers to be introduced with a lowering of the legal limit of blood alcohol level from 100 mgm to 50 mgm.

Burrows concluded her letter with a note of authority, "We believe that long experience of rehabilitation programs for alcohol dependents, and of conducting educational courses for the prevention of alcohol-related problems, makes us highly qualified to offer these recommendations."

AIDS

The pandemic of AIDS emerged as a major world issue during Burrows' tenure as General. Its challenge did not escape her attention and commitment. She sent out word that "every territory in the

General Burrows visits people with AIDS in their London home.

Army world is asked to make its response to this crisis."

In England she became a patron of the organization ACET (AIDS Care, Education, and Training). To demonstrate the Army's caring response to people with HIV and AIDS, and to their relatives and friends, she spent an afternoon with AIDS patients and with those who care for them. Later she visited an AIDS ward of a London hospital and spoke with the nursing staff, patients, and volunteers.

She also agreed to the convening of a medical conference in Zaire, with representation of Army medical units from throughout the world. The number one item on their agenda was AIDS. She asked for guidelines to be drawn up for counseling AIDS victims. She called on the Army not to be judgmental, but to love and help the victims. In Zambia where three in ten persons are affected, a section of the Army's mission hospital at Chikankata that for so many years had served lepers was adapted for AIDS patients.

Under Burrows, the Army organized an international conference on AIDS, held in Switzerland in June 1991, with joint sponsorship by the United Nations and development agencies from a number of countries. Its theme, "From Fear To Hope—An Integrated Response to AIDS," set the tone and direction of the conference. The social, medical, community, and counseling aspects of AIDS programs were represented. Before the conference, Captain (Dr.) Ian Campbell, the IHQ Medical Adviser, stated, "It will not be simply a time of good discussion but will be a fusion of minds from diverse backgrounds to clarify specific guidelines that can be put into practice, allowing for the cultural, economic, religious, political, and geographical differences of each country." The conference provided practical insights and guidelines for those seeking to address this worldwide health menace.

In speaking to the AIDS crisis, Burrows stated forthrightly, "Let us keep something else in mind. Let us stand up and be counted for Christian moral standards. Let us uphold the standard of chastity before marriage, faithfulness in marriage. Don't say, 'Choose chastity so we won't get AIDS,' but, 'Choose chastity because it is God's will for us.' "

Nuclear Disarmament and War

Nuclear disarmament was high on General Burrows' agenda of issues that require a voice from the Christian community. She urged world leaders to take steps to avoid the catastrophe of instant apocalypse.

In the summer of 1988 she delegated Commissioner Andrew S. Miller, U.S.A. National Commander, to represent her in addressing world members at the Third Special Session in New York of the United Nations General Assembly Devoted to Disarmament. She had the Commissioner read the statement that had been formulated by her predecessor, General Jarl Wahlstrom. It appealed to the Assembly to call on all governments to reduce weapons and lessen the peril of nuclear conflict. It advocated the reallocation of the world's finite resources from excessive military expenditures to alleviation of world hunger, poverty, and removing the deep scars of human suffering.

Miller concluded the message to the Assembly saying, "The Salvation Army reaffirms its belief in the love of God for all peoples, and the standards of righteousness and justice set forth in the Bible and revealed to mankind in Jesus Christ as the basis for harmonious interpersonal and international relationships. . . . Today, General Burrows pledges the moral resources of more than 2 million Salvationists to world disarmament, peace on earth, goodwill to men."

When finally a treaty was signed by the United States and the

Soviet Union, the General wrote to both President Reagan and General Secretary Mikhail Gorbachev expressing gratitude for eliminating all intermediate-range nuclear weapons. Her letter concluded, "You have won the esteem of people of goodwill everywhere. Be assured of our prayers in your continued efforts with other world leaders for international peace and the safety of our beautiful planet."

With the outbreak of the Gulf War in 1991, Burrows called on her worldwide Army to pray.

> Pray for peace, that the fighting will be brief, and with a minimum of casualties. Pray for those caught up in the fighting, that they will realize God's presence and the realities of His love.
>
> Pray for all the world leaders involved in decision-making, including Saddam Hussein. Whilst we do not condone his intransigence and unwillingness to accept the United Nations resolution, we must pray for him, that he will see that peace is the desire of the world, and that his withdrawal from Kuwait is essential to that peace.
>
> Pray for our officers assigned to work in the Gulf, and for all chaplains and other personnel involved in such tasks. And pray for all the peoples of the world, that in their longings for peace they may resist all feelings of animosity and reach out in love to one another.

The Environment

She encouraged her troops to give an important place to the issue of the environment. In a letter of July 1991 to her world leaders, she urged them to "keep alive this subject in your own teaching ministry. It has vital implications for all Christians."

She is sympathetic toward environmentalists, but emphasizes that they need to think more about who made this beautiful world, and bring the Creator into their platform. "The care of God's creation is a significant concern for us all. The stewardship for this wonderful world God has given us is a very important plank of the Christian faith. We must challenge Salvationists around the world on the significant issue of ecology."

Poverty and Homelessness

"It is right that we meet here in a Christian church because Jesus Christ was a champion of the disadvantaged and oppressed," asserted

General Burrows in her travels visits the homeless and people in difficult circumstances in the inner cities.

General Burrows in addressing a meeting of Christian service workers in London. "He challenged us not to close our eyes to the inequalities of a needy world. He quickened our conscience about the plight of the mentally ill, the homeless, and the hungry. Of all people, Christians should be the ones stabbed awake to the needs of their neighbors, and then to go and do something for them."

At a press conference in January of 1992, Burrows announced on behalf of the U.K. Territory a multimillion-dollar, five-year program called *Strategy for Change* to help the homeless population of London. The program was designed to provide a continuum of services with transitional housing and other assistance leading to different levels of independence according to the need of the individual. She expressed the concern not just to provide emergency housing for the homeless, but to have a problem-solving approach that would deal with causes as well as effects.

A low cost advertising campaign including thirty-second spots was launched to help raise the ambitious funding goal, far more than ever before undertaken by the Army in England. But Burrows has never thought in small terms when it comes to addressing the critical needs of those who in desperate straits comprise the Army's parish.

"Homelessness is not just an isolated social evil. It is the catalyst and the breeding ground for other problems such as marriage difficulties and family breakup, unemployment, stress, health problems, and alcoholism. Emergency shelters for the homeless can provide a roof over the head, but they cannot provide an appropriate home. And homes are what the homeless need."

IHQ media director, Captain Charles King says, "Burrows has been more political than any General in recent times. She has spoken out publicly in very critical ways of the government in areas of unemployment and poverty. She hasn't pulled her punches." Indeed, in the area of social and moral issues, the General seems to have fulfilled her vow "to get something done."

22

★ ★ ★ ★ ★ ★ ★ ★ ★ ★ ★ ★ ★ ★ ★ ★ ★ ★ ★ ★

THE RESTRUCTURING REVOLUTION

"This should be not merely an administrative exercise,
but a spiritual one as well."

The international press of the Army headlined it "Revolution," the
term coined by its chief architect, Colonel John Larsson. "With characteristic boldness," wrote Larsson, "the General has launched the
Army's most fundamental administrative change in the movement's
125-year history." The restructuring of the Army's International
Headquarters and its British Territory was indeed revolutionary and
radical. The ultimate aim was to increase the Army's effectiveness in
its mission. The key issue was the dismantling of the outmoded
relationship between the Army's international office and its work in
the United Kingdom.

The Problem
For decades there had been questions and concerns about the close
alignment of the British Salvation Army with the International
Headquarters. The historical and legal reasons did not quell the dis-
quiet about the control that International Headquarters had over the
Army in the United Kingdom, and the claims the national office
made on the time and energies of the General and international
leadership of the Army. Questions were raised both in Britain and
from abroad. Previous Generals had looked at the possibility of a
separation of the United Kingdom from IHQ's direct control. Commissions and working parties also studied the problem, but no work-
able plan ever emerged.

However, General Burrows had promised at the High Council to
once again consider the issue. She knew the problem firsthand from

when she served as head of the Social Services and later as Territorial Commander in Scotland.

Many daunting obstacles stood in the way of bifurcating the administrations. One of the fears was that the office of the General would lose its power and prestige by not having a working base. The analogy was made with the Pope, who is very much in charge of the Church in Italy while holding the Catholic Church's post of international leadership. In England the Archbishop of Canterbury is head both of the Anglican Communion and of the Diocese of Canterbury. It was feared that the General might, by losing this home base of operation, become merely a figurehead.

Another obstacle was that the international and British administrations were intertwined at the highest levels. Key leaders and their staff had both international and national administrative responsibility. The General and Chief of the Staff wore two hats, international and British. When they wore their British hats, they became the National Commander and Chief Secretary for Britain. Leadership positions normally related to Territorial Commanders reported directly to the Chief of the Staff, positions such as Social Services leader, Training Principal, Editor-in-chief, Secretary for Public Relations. Larsson pointed out that nearly two-thirds of the personnel of IHQ also worked directly with the British operation.

The problem was further compounded by the extent to which British and international finances were intermingled, with the sharing of a common purse. The international office of The Salvation Army was heavily dependent on this support.

Historically, Bramwell Booth, son and right arm of the Founder, and also the second General, is said to have run the Army in Britain with one hand and the Army in the rest of the world with the other. For the next forty years, 1929 to 1969, all Generals with the exception of Carpenter were British, with three of them having been former British Commissioners. A remarkable degree of control was exercised by the Generals over the British scene, including approval of every property transaction.

Increased international travels and demands, more funding from outside Britain, and no British General since 1969 had steadily worked toward disengaging the generalship from the British scene and making it a predominantly international institution. This development, positive in many ways, nevertheless left a leadership vacuum. As Larsson described it, "There is no one in effective charge of the Army in Britain. Britain is like a body without a head." The Army's managerial efficiency in Britain was compromised in such areas as planning overall strategy, allocating resources, setting priorities, coordination, communication, personnel welfare, and fundraising.

The Potential

Following the Second World War, the Army in Britain suffered decline. But by the time General Burrows took office, winds of renewal and growth were blowing across the landscape of the Army in Britain so that it seemed there was a readiness for a whole new and radical structure that could become as a sail hoisted to catch the wind of the Spirit.

In 1988 Colonel John Larsson, then principal of the International Training College, was summoned to the General's office. Burrows shared with him that she had been considering ways to tackle this question of separating the U.K. Army from the international administration. Since previous commissions appointed to study it all came up with no results or negative conclusions, General Burrows told the Colonel she was now ready to try the old Salvation Army style of asking one person to look into it. She was subscribing to the axiom, "A committee of one gets things done!"

In that meeting Colonel Larsson received his appointment as Assistant to the Chief of the Staff for United Kingdom Administrative Planning—a long title which essentially meant he was charged with the daunting restructuring project. The General's intuitive discernment led her to the man supremely qualified for the task. Larsson's name was a household word around the Army world. He had a background of Third World experience, was the noted author of Army books, and composer for the internationally popular Gowans and Larsson Army musicals. He brought to this project an articulate voice, an analytical mind, a nonconfrontational approach to sensitive issues, and an intimate knowledge of the problem, having served in the U.K. as well as under IHQ.

"The Die Was Cast"

The statement by General Eva Burrows on May 16, 1988 disposed of any equivocation about the problem being addressed. The announcement of the appointment of Colonel Larsson was significant, in that it was the first public acknowledgment that a problem existed.

She described the administrative situation in Britain and the relationship with International Headquarters as a "puzzle to many." Larsson
observes, "When she went public that she had appointed someone to
look into it, in a sense the die was cast."

A time frame of two years was allotted for the task. General Burrows said she wanted the project to be completed in time to handle
its implementation rather than to "leave it to someone else to handle"
after her retirement. Larsson fully measured up to the confidence of his
General in producing a brilliant plan that would achieve the most
radical administrative change in recent decades of Army history.

Historically the timing was right. In prior years various segments of
the Army in Britain and at IHQ were headed by commissioners, with
no fewer than sixteen commissioners in 1948. A new territory taking
over these IHQ departments then would have had quite a surplus of
commissioners. In more recent years non-British Generals regarded the
office of the General as running the international Army, not Britain.
"Nevertheless, it needed executive courage to make the change," says
Commissioner Larsson, "and the General wasn't short of that."

In his ninety-seven-page comprehensive briefing, Colonel Larsson
summarized the challenges and benefits of restructuring. "It would
provide an historic opportunity for everything that is best in modern
management technique to be brought into service. . . . It would be
the time for barriers to be dismantled and unnecessary red tape to be
burnt. It would be an opportunity to release creativity and possibility
thinking and the potential within the ranks of both officers and lay
Salvationists. . . . There are many indications that there is an upsurge
of spirit within the Army in the United Kingdom. It now needs the
administrative machinery that can take hold of that upsurge."

When it was clear that the restructuring would be legally, constitu-
tionally, and financially possible, and detailed draft proposals had
been drawn up, the management consultants Coopers & Lybrand
were engaged to conduct an independent study of the proposed
international and British administrations. Burrows did not ask them,
"Come and show us what we should be doing." Larsson had already
spent eighteen months interviewing people, discussing his findings,
setting down an outline of options. The Army's perspective had been
carefully forged; the management consultants were called in to assess
the viability of the Army's ideas and to conduct interviews and research. General Burrows along with Colonel Larsson and other
Army staff met many times with the consultants who said that they

never had any company work so closely with them. On one occasion during their four-month study, a difficult question confronted them and the Army. General Burrows said, "I will need to pray about that and seek the Holy Spirit's direction." One of the consultants countered, "My goodness, we're up against some pretty strong competition, aren't we!"

The Impossible Is Done

Following the many consultations and reviews and the final endorsement by the Advisory Council to the General, on November 1, 1990 the establishment of the United Kingdom Territory and a reorganization of International Headquarters to be effective February 1, 1991 became fact. Under the leadership of General Eva Burrows, the Army in Britain became a unified entity, disentangled from the international administration.

In the process, International Headquarters was streamlined in its leadership of the worldwide Army. An International Management Council was set up as a forum for guiding strategies, policies, and plans, and for discussing key issues. "My original prime motive," says Burrows, "was to allow The Salvation Army in Britain to become more effective in its mission but, in fact, this has also helped our IHQ administration to become more effective and efficient for our Army around the world."

General Burrows courageously transferred financial assets to the Territory, perhaps the hardest and stickiest issue of the project. IHQ needs a bedrock of assets, not only a capital base but also a revenue income. All income for the United Kingdom Territory would now come to it directly, whereas previously everything flowed to IHQ first and then was proportionately allotted to the various segments of the Territory.

At the historic Public Inauguration of the United Kingdom Territory, held in Westminster Central Hall on November 6, 1990, General Burrows quoted from the Old Testament, "Consecrate yourselves, for tomorrow the Lord will do amazing things among you." She described the restructuring as "not merely an administrative exercise but a spiritual one," challenging the new Territory to "be more effective in evangelical mission so that our compassionate concern for the least, lowest, and lost will be quickened and that the Army will be mobilized to new endeavors." She concluded with the statement, "I charge you to keep as your priority the winning of souls."

Larsson observes, "For at least thirty years people had been saying something ought to be done. At five or six successive High Councils, candidates for the General had been asked, 'Will you look into this possibility of separating the administration?' And all the candidates had said, 'Yes.' But all those persons were men! It took a woman to say 'Yes' and actually make it happen."

A former British Commissioner, who had lived with the frustrations of leading the British Territory with its entanglements with IHQ, tells of a previous General who had spoken very sympathetically of the problem prior to taking office. After being elected and studying the situation, he called in this British Commissioner and confessed to its intractable nature. The retired Commissioner summarizes, "Now the massive adjustment has taken place and it is General Eva Burrows who has brought it about. When I expressed my admiration of her leadership in this regard to an officer involved in the intricate process, he remarked, 'She specializes in pulling hot irons out of the fire.' "

Lt. Colonel Malcolm Bale, one of the senior staff involved in the restructuring program comments, "Her most courageous act of all is this whole new setup in the U.K. I know she gave a commitment to the High Council to look at the question, but it's been talked about for decades. And here she comes in and does it and does it thoroughly, and is prepared to stay on and meet the consequences of it. You could see Generals making a move like that six months before they retire. And I have been amazed at the thoroughness with which the transfer has been done, things that we thought IHQ would hold on to at all costs she has relinquished."

Commissioner James Osborne, U.S.A. National Commander, stated, "I cannot commend our General enough for the courage of this approach and for the manner in which it was carried out. We believe the restructuring will enhance The Salvation Army around the world." Leaders of the Army echoed Commissioner Rivers' assessment, "I suppose her greatest accomplishment will have been the separation of the U.K. Territory from IHQ. This has exacted a personal cost from the General, and she still agonizes in her attempts to get it right."

Streamlining the Reorganization

Upon discovering ways that the new structure could be improved, Burrows wasted no time in streamlining the IHQ reorganization. A vacuum for IHQ in areas of practical management was filled by the establishment of the International Management Council (IMC). The formation of the IMC was a fundamental part of the reorganization of IHQ and became the vehicle by which further streamlining could be undertaken. In her remarks at the first meeting of the IMC, General Burrows emphasized, "We want this new administration to succeed. We must be flexible—ready to adjust, evaluate, and modify."

General Burrows and her staff showed the executive courage to acknowledge the weaknesses and imperfections that emerged, to address them with correction and refinement as needed in an ongoing commitment to the success for this quantum leap forward in the history of the Army.

The landmark and radical restructuring decision would never totally be "put to bed" during her Generalship, but would impose a continued demand on her leadership and energy to assure the most efficient implementation. General Burrows maintained an active role of nurturing this child of her own doing to maturity.

23

★ ★

MASTERING THE MEDIA

*"I take every opportunity for TV because
it is the most powerful medium today."*

In her seven years in office, General Eva Burrows has communicated with more persons than all previous Generals combined. A virtuoso in communication, she has used modern technology and the media to optimum advantage.

She has displayed a well-honed skill at fielding and finessing the routine inquiries as well as the tough or "clever" questions put to her. If an interviewer gave her nothing to hit but softballs, she would obliquely target a subject of import, and perhaps pose a question such as, "Would you like to know what we are doing about the AIDS problem?"

She has had hundreds of press and media conferences and interviews during her term, reaching millions of people around the world. She knew that often "the media was not interested so much in the fact that I was the leader of a church, but that a woman was a head of a church." Thus she anticipated their questioning along that line and prepared herself to answer. Her responses have never been boilerplate statements, but have flowed with spontaneity and bordered on eloquence.

In December 1991 an estimated 30 million people around the world heard General Burrows give the Army's viewpoint on a wide range of issues when she was the special guest on a live phone-in program on London's BBC World Service. The hour-long program on the world's most listened to radio station was judged an outstanding success by the BBC. Far more calls than could be dealt with flooded in from every continent.

224

Topics ranged from the Army's policy on cooperation or confrontation with repressive governments, social issues such as poverty and unemployment, moral issues such as homosexuality, and theological questions. She had no advance knowledge of the questions. The estimated audience represented the largest "congregation" addressed by any Salvationist.

Mesmerizing the Media

Captain Charles King, the IHQ Media Relations Director who accompanied her on interviews and appearances in London, sums up her skills. "She is extraordinary with the media. I've never known her to be outsmarted by even the brightest of journalists. She anticipates the questions they are going to ask, can see the direction they're taking, and when they are working toward a very ticklish question, she often gets there first. She's extremely well read and informed with a wide knowledge of the secular world as well as the religious world. She has a good knowledge of literature, classical music, drama, and musicals that enables her not only to be up-to-date and perceptive, but also to communicate."

King describes her personal qualities for the media. "She has a charisma that comes across the airwaves just as it does in her personal appearances. Her charisma is not just a matter of gesture, but had to do with her very nature. She is someone people are drawn to. She has tremendous stamina. A tired mind is easily identified in an interview. I have not seen this in the General. She retains a tremendous clarity of thought and freshness and enthusiasm, even though she may be answering the same questions that have been asked many times before. She's a master—or a mistress—of the 'sound bite,' that ten-second quote or perhaps thirty-second statement which sums up everything that needs saying.

"She always does her homework, wants to know a lot about the person who's interviewing her and the outlet of their media. She expects me, before a journalist interviews her, to give them a basic knowledge of the Army and of herself so they don't ask questions which reveal too great an ignorance.

"She's very courteous and warmhearted in interviews. Everyone ends up liking her. She's very professional. Her timing is impeccable, her delivery is excellent, and her broadcasting voice is good. The BBC has two forms of microphones. One they call 'an actor's microphone' and the other is for everyone else. They always use the actor's microphone for the General. I've been told that she would make an excellent interviewer or announcer. I would rate her as the very best communicator with the media that we've had."

In the early stage of her Generalship, she was besieged with requests for interviews. Although she wanted to seize every opportunity to communicate to the general public, she found it difficult to fit them all into her schedule. "I take every opportunity for TV," she says, "because it is the most powerful and effective medium today." Radio was next, with a more selective availability for press interviews.

Of her handling of media in Australia as Territorial Commander, Lt. Colonel Ernest Lamotte who served on her staff says, "Skilled media personnel were mesmerized by this lady's charm and ability in answering the trickiest of questions. She is a quick wit who enjoys having someone to laugh and parry with. General Eva Burrows is one of God's remarkable women."

Lt. Colonel Malcolm Bale reflects from his position as having been her editor-in-chief at International Headquarters and in Australia. "From an editorial point of view she has been much more permissive, both in Australia and here, than is usually the case. English language papers have sometimes suffered from a kind of close censorship or cautiousness from leaders. I found it most remarkable in Australia and here that I could speak on quasi-political issues in the paper, provided they were things that the Army could get wholeheartedly behind. And we had some hard-hitting articles in *The War Cry*. We were sometimes actually slighting the government and she was allowing us to do it. That was very refreshing."

The story is told of a Scottish man who was watching Sunday afternoon football when the television announcer said, "Now there will be an interview with Commissioner Burrows." He said to himself, "How boring." But he was too lazy to get out of his chair and turn off the television. As he watched and listened, he was led to ask himself what he had done with his life, and he became convicted. He found The Salvation Army, started to attend, and one day came to the mercy seat and gave his life to God. General Burrows enrolled him as a soldier in full uniform. The story was later aired on a television weekly program with the title, "A Man Who Became a Christian."

This man worked at the Grangemouth Oil Refinery and his wife was a schoolteacher. After his conversion, he said that the Lord had changed him and healed him of his prejudices. "I despised the down-and-outs, people who were drunks. One great thing now is that I really care for them and want to help them." This man went every week to the Army Hostel for the Homeless in Edinburgh, talking to men and influencing them for Christ.

A Shaper of Events
Early in her Generalship, the Institute for Oral History at Baylor University in Texas invited Burrows to do a series of two-hour interviews on her life and work. Institute interviews preserve the memories of individuals who have shaped events of the past. The six interviews with the General commenced in June 1988 and continued during subsequent visits to the United States.

The edited transcripts are to be deposited for research in the National Archives in New York, the International Archives in London, and at Baylor University.

A Publication Coup
A communications fallout occurred for the office of the General following the restructuring of IHQ and the U.K. Territory. The weekly sixteen-page *Salvationist* had heretofore served as the international and the U.K. periodical of The Salvation Army. The editorial department came under IHQ administration with its staff and publication available to the General. This left the editorial department at times with a somewhat schizophrenic relationship between its dual masters of NHQ and IHQ.

Upon the inauguration of the U.K. Territory, *Salvationist* became the U.K. Territory's newspaper, and the General and The Salvation Army suddenly no longer had an international publication voice. For all practical purposes *Salvationist* mutated from an international to a national periodical, with reports of Burrows' comings and goings noticably declining in its pages. And the General was more than a little discomfited by this seeming "editorial secession."

But General Burrows was not to be daunted by the challenge. Sensing the vacuum she then resorted to her "consultative leadership" strategy and put the matter to the International Communications Council (ICC).

The ICC recommended and received the General's approval for a monthly column to be written by the General and sent to territorial and editorial offices of the Army throughout the world, to be published in all official Army periodicals. The column was titled, "From the General's Desk" and photos of General Burrows at her desk were dispatched to be used with the columns.

The results were astonishing. Now instead of one periodical being the publication voice of the General, every major periodical throughout the Army world received a monthly column with news of her travels and her message to Salvationists. Instead of communicating officially through one publication with a circulation of less than 25,000, she was now communicating with her troops in Army periodicals around the world with an almost 1 million circulation.

A further development was the transmission by fax of the ongoing *International News Release* (INR) by Lt. Colonel Cecil Williams, reporting on news and events around the Army world. Taking advantage of the technology of instant communication, it became a vital source for reportage in Army periodicals and served as a further bonding for the internationalism of the Army.

Thus the Army's "Mistress of the Media" overcame what seemed an irrecoverable loss to achieve one of the movement's major communication coups.

24

★ ★ ★ ★ ★ ★ ★ ★ ★ ★ ★ ★ ★ ★ ★ ★ ★ ★ ★ ★

EXTENDED TERM

*"In a world where secession and fragmentation are rife,
the solidarity of the Army remains firm."*

General Eva Burrows was due to retire at midnight on July 8, 1991, at the end of her five-year elected term. A letter of April 10, 1990 from Commissioner Ron A. Cox, Chief of the Staff, informed world leaders of a formal proposal to extend for two years the term of General Burrows. The proposal had been initiated by Commissioner James Osborne, U.S.A. National Commander, with the required five Commissioners as signatories — Cox, Hawkins, Osborne, E. Read, H. Read. Reasons for the proposal were:

1. The General would be well below the normal retirement age when her present term expires.
2. A medical examination reveals the General to be in excellent health.
3. The General's leadership under God has had a profound worldwide impact.
4. Continuity of leadership is needed to work through the changes of the proposed restructuring of the U.K. Territory and IHQ.

Postal ballots under confidential cover were sent to the forty-three world leaders eligible to vote, to be marked either favored or opposed. A two-thirds response favoring the proposal was required for the extension. On May 16 the Army's solicitor, Mr. Giles Ridley, opened the unidentified sealed envelopes to tally the ballots. On May 18 a letter from the Chief of the Staff notified Army leaders around the world that the poll had been conducted according to the Army's prescribed process, with a copy of the results enclosed.

The vote favored that the General be asked to continue. This message was conveyed to her, and her acceptance was received. Commissioner Osborne, in his bulletin announcing the result, stated, "This ensures that the bold, dynamic and Holy Spirit-directed leadership of General Eva Burrows will continue." Her seven-year tenure would be the longest in three decades for a General of The Salvation Army.

The final tally was an overwhelming vote of confidence and mandate for General Eva Burrows. Only two of the forty-three ballots opposed. Four were ineligible due to "spoilt papers"—not properly filled out. General Burrows who had originally been elected by the narrowest of margins—on her potential—had her term of office extended on the basis of her performance.

When asked her reasons for agreeing to the extension, she said, "First of all I felt divinely led to agree. I consulted the Lord and asked Him to guide me. Several practical reasons were also involved. I had set in motion these radical administrative changes and it seemed only fair that I remain in office to see the new United Kingdom Territory and IHQ through the initial growing pains of implementation. Also I had a thorough health checkup and the specialist pronounced me to be in amazingly good health. And I felt two years would be adequate to accomplish my goals for the future. Finally, I felt honored by the overwhelming mandate that was given to me by The Salvation Army leaders and felt almost duty-bound to respond positively to their request to stay in office."

She set down seven priorities for this final period: (1) a forum for an International Conference of Leaders; (2) emphasis on the imperatives of evangelism, renewal, growth; (3) to bring the new IHQ structure into effective operation; (4) to ensure the work in Central and Eastern Europe is well established; (5) to strengthen the Army's internationalism; (6) to continue emphasis of work among youth; and (7) to continue the development of indigenous leadership.

One of General Burrows' visions for IHQ was that it would be a resource with modern ideas and materials for the worldwide Army. To achieve that, in her extended term she established the International Resources Department that offers a resource of materials and data on programs, management, communications, church growth, training, and development, and all aspects of Army life and ministry.

1991 International Leaders' Conference

Burrows convened an International Leaders Conference in London of July/August 1991 with the theme, "Mission and Growth Today." It expressed her perception of the underlying dynamics which drive the Army in every age. A great deal of her energy in the past had been focused on the radical restructuring at the U.K. and IHQ, and the reopening of the work in Central and Eastern Europe. She structured the 1991 Conference to review principles and establish priorities as the basis of future growth for the worldwide Salvation Army.

The agenda was set by a task force and based on suggestions received from all territories of the world: the need for Salvationists to develop an effective prayer life, to nurture family worship, to make the best use of Army periodicals, to instruct new converts and to provide ongoing teaching at every level. The agenda also included subjects of worship, evangelism, candidate recruitment, literature, training programs, stewardship, human resources, communications, AIDS, youth programs, and social action. The Conference was addressed by one of the General's favorite authors, Dr. John R.W. Stott, who presented an exposition on the Christology of evangelism.

The "Teacher General" adopted a new format for the Conference, proposed by the task force headed by Commissioner John Clinch—the syndicate system—in order to tap the collective experience of all the delegates. Rather than a lecture method, delegates remained in the same six syndicates throughout for discussion. Recommendations from the syndicate groups and general discussion took place in the plenary sessions.

A major outcome of the Conference was a reaffirmation of the solidarity of the Army and a Manifesto by the 105 delegates calling Salvationists to be true to the historic mission of the Army for holy living and a caring ministry. This statement read, "The International Conference of Leaders has confirmed that in a world where secession and fragmentation are rife, the solidarity of The Salvation Army remains firm." Indeed, in the time when the international map was being radically revised with secessions, God's Army and its miracle of internationalism was being expanded and strengthened.

The two-year extended term for General Eva Burrows turned out to be more than a consolidation of the gains already achieved. During this period she led her worldwide Army to new and exciting frontiers of service for God.

25

★ ★

ON THE PERSONAL SIDE

"My ambition is just to please God."

Eva Burrows stands out in any crowd. Smartly attired in her tailored uniform, she presents a striking appearance. She has a healthy complexion without the use of cosmetics. Her hairstyle has changed little over the years, the style that at IHQ has come to be referred to as "the E.B. roll." She is never seen to look at any time other than perfectly coiffured.

Eva Burrows is a person people cannot be neutral about. "When she walks into a room," observes Commissioner Ron Cox, "you know she is there. She doesn't have to draw attention to herself. You can't ignore her."

She says, "I suppose good appearance always seemed important to me, because I believe Christians should be attractive and well groomed. A friend who had been a missionary for many years was on a train going to South Africa. Walking past her in the aisle was a poorly groomed woman. The woman sitting next to my friend said, 'You can tell she is a missionary by the way she dresses.' The idea that Christians must look old-fashioned, fuddy-duddy, is one I've always tried to dispel. I've never been outlandish in following fashions, but I always like to look up-to-date, in my uniform as well."

Wherever she goes, people tend to be smitten with Burrows. Her brown eyes, warm smile, and charming manner have melted hearts on six continents. A magazine reporter described her as "having the warmest smile imaginable." But as her associates know, her determination and aggressiveness in crucial moments give a glimpse of the steel beneath the calm exterior.

232

Her official photographer, Robin Bryant, has seen her with a photographer's discerning eye on many occasions. His portraiture of her graces the frontispiece of this book as well as Wedgewood plates and postcards used around the world. He observes, "General Burrows has a commanding and immaculate image; she is an attractive woman with a personable approach which immediately puts one at ease. I have seen people waiting to see her, full of nervous excitement; yet the moment they walk into her office they are immediately put at ease with warmth and sincerity. Her greeting goes beyond the formal handshake, with a hand placed on an arm and the individual made the center of interest and attention."

Bryant further recalls, "Always perceptive of what might be required to make a good picture better, with a keen eye for composition and symmetry, she has been most helpful in orchestrating people and movement into the best position, making my work relatively easy. I also appreciate her courtesy in introducing me to her guests, often making the photographs seem secondary to the moment, when of course I had no other reason to be there."

The Salvation Army bonnet is still in vogue in Britain, but most other countries have contemporized the uniform, adapting it to their cultures. When General Burrows visited those countries, she often donned their uniform. In India and Sri Lanka she wore a sari, and in the U.S.A. she was shown on the cover of the *War Cry* wearing the American uniform hat. She received a letter from a veteran Salvationist chiding her for not wearing the bonnet.

"To Whom Much Is Given"

"She has received many natural gifts," says her friend, Ingrid Lindberg, "but she also has received many gifts of the Spirit. Everything she has is dedicated to the Lord. She's absolutely single-minded in her service to God and the Army."

Regarding her gifts, Burrows says, "The gifts from God are not something to be proud of, because they're given. If you are a gifted person, you can be tempted. This is an area of vulnerability. Helen Prosser, my American colleague with whom I shared a house when I first went to Zimbabwe, was good to live with because she would bring me down a peg or two in those early days when I needed to learn the lesson of humility. I will have to stand before the throne and answer for my gifts." She often quotes the text, "For to whom much is given, of him much will be required."

Prayer Life

How does the activist Eva Burrows, carrying the heavy administrative and spiritual burden of a multinational movement, maintain the priority for prayer? She admits it is not easy. But she acknowledges her heavy dependence on prayer and the Holy Spirit, and her commitment to a regular tryst with God in prayer.

The question, "How do you make time for prayer?" elicited an illustration from her early life. She recalled that when she was quite young, she had been asked to do something and replied, "I will see if I can make time for it." She was gently chided, "You can't make time. You can only reorganize time according to your priorities." That became one of the seminal insights that has guided her through life, especially in the area of her communion with God. "Prayer is a priority," she says, "and I organize my life to assure my time with God, for I am very dependent upon the Holy Spirit.

"As I listen to what God says, God's purposes seem to seep into my mind, through my devotional life and through my constant contact with Him. I do not hear God's voice in an external sound. It's much more an internal awareness of what God wants that seems to crystallize in my mind.

"God has shown me that I must emphasize our need for renewal in The Salvation Army. God seems to have said, 'You've tackled several administrative challenges, you've done quite a lot of clearing away of the organizational problem; now it's time to center down and focus on the great issue of renewal within The Salvation Army and on the mission for which I called it into being.' "

Preaching and Theology

Burrows does not rate herself highly as a preacher, saying on occasion, "I wish I could preach." She does not consider preaching to be one of her gifts. She teaches more than preaches, in a straightforward and conversational style. She is a master in the use of illustration, drawing from her contemporary experience and keen observation.

Exuberant gestures are her trademark, with ambidextrous slashes punctuating her sermons throughout. Although her manuscripts are carefully prepared, she speaks with freedom and without noticeable reliance on her notes. An unusual clarity of speech, resonance, and inflection of voice enhance her delivery.

As a storyteller she can be scintillating, even side-splitting. She usually uses humor at the outset of a talk, as a bonding device. Her audiences laugh generously, and the teacher/preacher arrows the truth to their hearts.

Eva is relentless in her search for information to equip herself for visits and talks, giving the most diligent preparation for an event. Yet she keeps herself flexible right up to the moment of presentation, to allow for change and adaptation.

She exhibits an extraordinary ability to think and adapt on her feet, often introducing something of local or topical interest and responding to the needs of her hearers. Responses to introductions that will precede her presentations are also prepared. When speaking in a situation that requires translation, she will plan something she can say in the language of the people. Often she will have these remarks translated and written out as well as recorded, for her to practice over and over until she gets it just right.

Burrows' theology is a simple subscription to the Army's basic eleven tenets of faith; Christology is the heart of her theology. She proclaims her convictions with sincerity and urgency and invariably emphasizes salvation in Christ and holiness as a practical experience through the power of the Holy Spirit.

There is no room for a "prosperity theology" in Burrows' preachment. She calls her hearers to a full surrender to Christ and the cross. But she is quick to point out, "Any sacrifice or suffering that you go through in Christian leadership and service is not a penalty but a privilege. I hold very dear that beautiful promise, 'My grace is sufficient for thee.' I have preached several times on the enriching grace, the enabling grace, and the enduring grace."

Encounters Incognito

While principal of the ICO, Eva took an evening off to attend the theater with her sister Joyce who was visiting her. En route, a Salvation Army open-air meeting was in process and she stopped nearby to listen.

One of the cadets approached and, not recognizing her in civilian dress, asked, "Are you saved?" She responded, "What do you mean by 'saved'?" There ensued a serious dissertation by the cadet and a promise by Burrows that she would give careful thought to the young man's witness.

Imagine the cadet's surprise when later his peers asked him if he knew that he was trying to convert Colonel Burrows! The cadet had been a farmer and upon inquiring about him later, Burrows learned that he had been appointed in charge of the Army's farming program at Usher School in Zimbabwe.

On another occasion, in London's Soho quarter, mecca for connoisseurs of its cosmopolitan culture as well as for deviants, Eva with Margaret and Bramwell, were en route to a theater to see *The Mousetrap*. They were not in uniform and on the way they came across an open-air meeting conducted by cadets from the International Training College. A large crowd had gathered around the circle and Eva and her party were able to watch without being recognized. "What is this? Who are these people?" she asked of a well-dressed onlooker. "Don't you know?" was the surprised fellow's reply. "The Salvation Army. Where have you been? Haven't you heard of them?"

The question invited a "Yes" or "No" reply, but what followed was a little more than the Southwells expected. "I've been living in Africa for many years," she said by way of explanation for her apparent ignorance of such a well known organization. But the man was her equal. "I'm sure there would be a Salvation Army in Africa." And so the conversation went on. Never would the man have imagined that he was talking with a future General of this Salvation Army!

Other People Matter

Lt. Colonel Almey Morris (R) tells of a time when she was still serving at Usher Institute in Africa and Eva Burrows was the principal at the International College in London. "On the sudden death of my father in London, just prior to a long-awaited visit of my parents to Africa, it was Eva who encouraged my mother to fly out to visit me. She helped with her passport and with other practical details. I even discovered later that Eva slept on the cushions on the floor to give my mother a bed for the night. When I eventually came home, Eva met me in the early morning at the airport."

Almey Morris shares a further memory. "When stationed at the International College and still new to England, she went out herself to enroll the gardener's little boy in his first school. He is now at university and a keen Salvationist. These personal contacts mean so much. There is always the feeling that other people matter to Eva."

It is told that the Poet Laureate Tennyson recognized the genius of the young Rudyard Kipling and paid him a compliment. To this word of appreciation, Kipling replied, "When the private in the ranks is praised by the general, he cannot presume to thank him, but he fights the better the next day." There are many in The Salvation

Army troops around the world who are fighting a better fight because of the encouraging word they received from their General.

A Sacramental Experience

Eva had visited the Holy Land in 1982 and felt strongly led to revisit its gaunt hills and ancient ruins that represented the primordial landscape of her faith. With her friends Ingrid Lindberg and Lucille Turfrey, she took a tour in Israel in the summer of 1987. They stayed in Jerusalem for a week, walked to the Mount of Olives, and on the ramparts of Jerusalem. By car they traveled to Beersheba, through Bethlehem, and across the desert to the Dead Sea. They visited an archeological museum and took a tour to the Lebanon border to see the source of the Jordan. A highlight was a week in a hotel on the shore of the Sea of Galilee. Burrows swam each day, often at sunrise with the sun streaking across the water.

At the site where Jesus had fed the 5,000, Eva and her two companions shared in a time of devotions which she described as a sacramental experience. "As we looked out at the Sea of Galilee, we read the text where Jesus took the bread, broke it, blessed it and fed the multitude. It expresses what we want our lives to be — placed in Christ's hands for Him to bless and use to feed others. So together we sang what has become known as the Army's 'sacramental song,' written by the late General Orsborn. That song expresses our view of the eucharist; its words epitomize the Salvationist belief that our whole life is sacramental for Christ."

> My life must be Christ's broken bread,
>   My love His outpoured wine,
> A cup o'erfilled, a table spread
>   Beneath His name and sign,
> That other souls refreshed and fed,
>   May share His life through mine.

They walked to a nearby chapel built on a large rock, believed to be where Jesus met with His disciples after His resurrection where He said to Peter, "Feed My sheep." Eva went to the rock and feeling tired, rested her head on it, thinking that as Christ is the rock, so we can rest on Him. She then spent considerable time in intercessory prayer for the sheep and lambs God had given to her around the world, and for the leaders of The Salvation Army in every country.

She knew them all by name and the image of each face would come to her as she prayed through the territories. "It was a beautiful experience," she recalls, "and I felt a great sense of Christ's presence."

The Holy Land visit provided grist for her homiletical mill. In Africa for a centennial celebration, she related how she looked for a souvenir to take home, something important from Israel, something very old.

> I went to a shop that sold things of the past. The man showed me a little lamp that he said came from about the time of Abraham.
>
> "How much?" I asked. "$500," he replied.
>
> "Too much," I said. "Show me something not so old."
>
> He brought another lamp that he said came from the time when Jesus was on earth. "How much?" He held it up and said, "$250." I told him, "I'll think about it."
>
> Walking along the streets of Jerusalem, I saw a similar lamp in a window. I entered and enquired of its price. "$1 each," the man said. "That's wonderful," I said, "How old is it?"
>
> "It was made yesterday."

Burrows deftly drives home her point to her African audience. "Things that are old are very precious. We must hold on to the good things of the past, the rich African culture, the heritage of the Army for 100 years. Hold on to them." Her telling story beautifully wedded an experience from the streets of Jerusalem to a people in the heart of Africa.

Resilience

Burrows' resilience has been a hallmark of her life and ministry. Commissioner John Clinch, who served with her in Australia and later at IHQ, says, "I have seen her on more than one occasion sitting at her desk following a heavy and demanding period away, grey-faced, bone-weary, head in hands, completely drained. Most people would need a week or two to recover. But one good night's sleep and she is back on the job, full of vitality, and ready for anything. She also draws energy from people. She can be completely exhausted when facing a meeting or gathering, but as soon as she gets among the people, it's as if she draws energy from them and becomes transformed."

Her resilience was especially evident in the two U.S.A. Congresses she conducted in September of 1987. The two-week schedule was grueling, with as many as five messages on a given day and yet she seemed indefatigable. In an interview for *The War Cry,* she was asked, "What is the secret of your resilience?" She replied, "I have been blessed with physical resilience. That's a gift from God. But also, people nourish me. Mind you, I am also blessed by being able to sleep soundly so that each morning I awake refreshed." As she traveled around the world, it was often noted that whenever she encountered people, she seemed uplifted, indeed — "nourished."

Burrows was further queried, "How do you nourish your spirit?" Once again her answer was revealing, "God is nobody's debtor. When I give out for Him, He Himself replenishes my spirit. And I must say that I live very much with a consciousness of the presence of Christ. I can be driving along in the car and talk to the Lord in prayer. That nourishes my spirit. I am replenished by prayer, the Word, and devotional books. I receive refreshing thoughts from writers, often stimulated by a seed thought that helps me develop my messages."

Colonel Arthur Thompson, a longtime associate, observes, "Surviving a major heart attack, and then recovering well enough to go on to fulfill the most demanding responsibilities in a worldwide movement, is nothing short of miraculous."

Distaff Complaints

There is no doubt that overall, Eva Burrows prefers the company of men to women. This is evident in gatherings as well as in day to day involvement.

The most common criticism of Burrows is that she tends to be dismissive toward officer wives. The women who themselves have leadership roles and responsibilities have on occasion felt ignored or disregarded in contacts and conversations of the General with their spouses. One international leader echoes a common observation, "At times when she has become absorbed in discussing some matter relating to an officer's appointment, she opts to speak to the husband alone, thus giving the impression that she fails to recognize that the husband and wife are a team and deserve to be consulted together." In conferences it is felt she tends to ignore the participation of the women.

This trait may be due in part to the fact that men officers hold most of the responsibility in positions to which she relates. It should also be recorded that most women officers find her warm and caring and have a profound respect and affection for her.

Another disappointment in the Generalship of Eva Burrows has been her failure to advance more women officers to top leadership positions in the Army. Many married and single women officers had high hopes that the disproportion would be corrected when a woman was elected General, but have not seen the results for which they had hoped. In fielding this question, Burrows points out that the initiative must come from the national and territorial rather than from the international level. Major Ruth Richards, Personal Assistant to the General, recalls Burrows' frustration on more than one occasion when she has exclaimed, "Why aren't they encouraging the women in the territories?" Burrows also emphasizes that she does not believe in promoting married women to positions above their husbands and herself is averse to promotion on the basis of gender rather than on merit.

Vacations

Soon after becoming General she tried to take a holiday in London, but found she could not escape the phone. She spends some vacation time planning and preparing for programs and work, but needs to get completely away in order to be renewed.

One of her favorite getaway places is the Army's vacation lodge in Leysin, Switzerland. There she stays in a room that looks out on range upon range of snowcrowned mountains and Alpine flowers. Once she sat on the mountainside and watched the sun set over beautiful Lake Geneva. Overcome by the beauty of God's handiwork, she quietly started to sing one of her favorite songs, "How Great Thou Art." Her mezzo-soprano voice sang in praise the words of the first verse, "O Lord my God, when I in awesome wonder, consider all the worlds Thy hands have made." Soon others who heard the lilting strains gathered round. She was unaware of their presence until they applauded; then she invited them to join in.

Eva has had a lifelong romance with the sea and often plans her vacations so she can enjoy the beach and swimming. Majorca, an island in the Mediterranean off the coast of Spain, is another place she enjoys where, free from the burdens of her office, she finds renewal in the sun, and the sand and surf of the sea.

On several occasions she has shared holidays with family members.

They well know that behind that ambassadorial coiffure there still lurks a fun-loving Aussie. "Holidays with Eva are fun," observes Bram Southwell. "She has great enthusiasm for exploring the world we live in, whether it be the coast of Cornwall, Welsh castles, cathedrals, or the world of art, music, and drama. She loves a good play or musical. She has been known to take visitors to such events, even though she has been before. A visit to Canterbury may coincide with Evensong, and time will be taken to savor those moments for meaningful worship."

Family Contacts

In 1964 her homeland furlough coincided with another landmark event in the Southwell family. This time Eva assisted Margaret and her husband, Bram, as they were packing to leave for India where they would serve as lay missionaries for three years at the Evangeline Booth Hospital in Ahmednagar. There Dr. Southwell would serve as Acting Chief Medical Officer. Once more Margaret remembers, "Eva gave wonderful support at this time, including advice from her missionary experience in Africa."

With Dr. and Mrs Bramwell Southwell, just prior to their leaving for India, 1964, with Eva, and both sets of parents — Brigadier and Mrs. Southwell and Sr. Major and Mrs. Burrows.

As the Southwells left for service in India none knew what lay ahead. Within ten weeks their nine-month-old son succumbed after a short illness. The experience was devastating, and during that critical time Eva maintained a faithful and comforting correspondence. The Southwells write, "Our experience of loss could be matched by so many other families in that land, and a special bond was felt with many. Our ability to relate to their situations was enhanced. Gradually healing took place and we learned that God can use even the disasters of our lives for the good of His kingdom and His glory."

Eva has felt very close to her sisters and brothers and their children. A bond developed between "Aunt Eva" and her nieces and nephews. She remembers many of them on birthdays and special occasions and is interested in their lives and plans. Stamp collections of family members have prospered from the postcards sent by Burrows from her travels around the world. The bibliophiles in the family also are remembered with books and periodicals that enhance their reading.

The children find Aunt Eva a ready tutor for their homework. Her niece Claire received special tuition in mathematics from the one who had led African girl students to first place in school math standings. Claire made her decision for Christ during a visit of her Aunt Eva and was counselled in that decision by her. In December of 1982 Claire was enrolled as a senior soldier of The Salvation Army by Burrows. The felicitous event of the wedding of the Southwell's second daughter, Jane, also had Aunt Eva's support in an officiating capacity and with words at the reception that were described as "a beautiful affirmation of our family."

Hobbies and Pastimes
An avid reader, Eva Burrows finds relaxation and enrichment in the world of literature. John R.W. Stott is one of her favorite authors, especially his *Issues Facing Christians Today* and *The Cross of Christ*. Other favorites are Richard Foster, Charles Swindoll, and Helmut Thielicke. The writings of Catherine and William Booth and other Army publications are sources of inspiration to her. Tyndale's and William Barclay's Bible commentaries provide resources for her Bible research. She reads up on current issues and management studies, with *In Search of Excellence* high on her list. Besides a fondness for poetry, she admits to occasionally enjoying an Agatha Christie mystery and other spy thrillers.

An inveterate crossword puzzle devotee, she has a passion for word games. Her prowess in Scrabble is renowned in Salvation Army circles. She does not like losing, contests any doubtful words and has been known to demand another round even though it is after midnight.

Eva has an insuppressible fascination for floral arrangements. Indoor plants often stop her in her tracks. In Japan, where flowers and plants seem to effloresce at every turn, her escorts had to keep interrupting her pauses to admire the plants in the station, en route to the bullet train that doesn't wait, even for Generals.

A summary of her interests is expressed in a reflection she wrote, titled *Appreciations:*

I love life itself, and there is always something new to thank God for in every day. But perhaps I should be specific. I appreciate:

The beauty of the world, from the smallest snowdrop to the grandeur of the snow-capped Himalaya mountains.

Music, both classical and devotional, for its enrichment to heart, mind and spirit.

Good literature, for a book which adds new dimension to knowledge and insight, is a friend forever.

But above all else, I appreciate people. They matter most to me. They give me joy, and to contribute to their well-being and happiness is my constant delight. To serve them in need, to comfort them in sorrow, to counsel them in distress, to receive their love in return, to share their gladness — what more could one want!

Writing

As General, Eva Burrows has written many formal agendas, addresses, and published reports. She does not consider herself a writer and eschews any suggestion that she write for publication. Yet her presentations and formal papers are masterpieces of simple and effective communications.

Prior to her Generalship she never kept a diary. Upon becoming General she started to record events but after two years found it too difficult to keep up. She identifies with the statement that "The Salvation Army is too busy making history to write about it."

The official writings and addresses of Eva Burrows as General are replete with arresting anecdotes and definitive statements of the Army's mission. As General, she also maintained the tradition of contributing an inspirational article for the Easter and Christmas editions of the Army's publications around the world. In one Christmas article she tells this story.

> A woman was hectically busy buying Christmas presents and all the food needed for the Christmas celebrations, when she suddenly realized she had forgotten to send Christmas cards to her friends. So she dashed out to a stationery shop and, seeing a Christmas card with a nice picture, she said "I'll have forty of those." She hurried home and soon had them posted off. A couple of days later she was looking at the few cards that still remained. What a shock she received when she actually read the verse in the card which she had not even noticed before. It read,
> > This card comes just to say
> > A little gift is on the way.

Burrows gives her punch line, "So all those disappointed friends are still waiting for that promised gift." She then deftly drives home the truth, "It wasn't like that with God's promised gift to the world."

A Work Ethic

Eva Burrows is endowed with surplus energy. But her strength at times becomes her weakness. She is unsparing of her energies and "burns the candle at both ends." Family and friends remonstrate with her for not taking better care of herself. They believe she drives herself too hard, as well as those around her. Hard work is ingrained in her perfectionist nature. One close observer sums up the impression of many, "The 'failure' most prominent is the General's availability to people, at great personal expense to herself and without thought for her own well-being."

Striving for Christlikeness

"Jesus Christ is the center of my life," says Burrows. "Everything in my life revolves around Him. He is with me always and I'm aware of Him. I know whom I have believed and the foundation of my theology is a personal faith in Jesus Christ."

In her practical brand of Christianity, General Burrows quotes the late General Clarence Wiseman, "A Salvation Army officer is an idealist without illusion." She amplifies that with her own philosophy saying, "You develop your faith in God, and while your head and heart are in heaven, your feet are on the ground."

The Cost of Discipleship by Dietrich Bonhoeffer has contributed to her spiritual life. She identifies with Bonhoeffer's emphasis on conforming to the life of Christ. Referring to Romans 8:29, she says, "We should be conformed to the image of Christ. That is not psyching ourselves up to be like Christ, but allowing the Holy Spirit to conform us to His image, the shaping of our lives by the Holy Spirit, producing in us the fruit of the Spirit which equals the characteristics of Jesus. It's not our self-effort but His work in us."

When asked in an interview by Major Max Ryan, "How has being General changed you?" she said that she came to have a greater awareness of her dependence upon God, learned to set priorities more carefully, and grew even more positive and enthusiastic as she saw so many encouraging signs around the Army world. She said, "I now leave more room for the initiatives of the Holy Spirit in my life, more room for the Spirit to surprise me."

Singleness
She is not inclined to talk about her personal relationships with the opposite sex. But during her student days at the university she worked in a pineapple processing factory in order to earn much needed funds for her schooling. At that time a friendship developed between Eva and a young man at the factory. However her parents indicated to her that the relationship should be terminated and Eva was obedient to this request.

Eva Burrows has always been very much at ease in the company of men. She acknowledges that in 1958 at the university in Sydney, a friendship developed which "could have deflected me in my calling." She recalls, "During my year in Australia, when I did my master's degree, there was one serious friendship with a Salvationist older than myself. We were very fond of each other." But the friendship was outside the ranks of Army officership, and she had already settled on what she knew was God's will for her life and would not allow the relationship to develop beyond the constraints of her calling.

Burrows admits, "I would naturally have very much enjoyed having children and a family. I really think that was something God required me to give up. The single woman who is a leader lacks the companionship of marriage and also the valuable critique of a partner. I would be very appreciative of a partner who, when I came home from preaching, would tell me I'd spoken too long or was irrelevant. A single person has no one to share with in the way that married people do. Therefore they are thrown more on God. On the other hand, they don't have the immediate demands of family, such as the concerns for children and the time that must be given to them. I don't have those kinds of demands on my time and psychic energy. In that sense, as the Apostle Paul says, I am then able to give myself entirely to the flock of God. I look upon singleness as part of my dedication to God."

Those who have studied the psychology of singleness point out its pluses. It forces one to take full responsibility for oneself, helps develop personal strengths, and gives opportunity to try new things that might be difficult with a spouse. Eva Burrows gleaned all these advantages from her singleness, developing a self-reliance, confidence, and strength that ultimately equipped her for her role of world leadership.

Residence
Shortly after becoming General, Burrows moved from her suburban residence to the Barbican—a complex of apartments within the old fortress wall of London, built in the 1960s amid the bombed ruins of London. Her flat is cozily winsome, bright, and cheery, and graced with attractive memorabilia from around the world.

She is not a collector of things and is described as one who "sits rather easy when it comes to material things." Many of the gifts that she receives from around the world are passed on to others. She is fond of art and likes good reproductions, being rather keen on the French impressionists, and also Van Gogh. On her living room wall is a painting of the rugged beauty of the Australian outback, a gift from Salvationists in Melbourne. Along the corridor are original paintings of scenes in nature.

Her tenth-floor balcony of the forty-one-story tower overlooks the Barbican garden park and lake. It gives a superb view of London that embraces St. Giles Church where Shakespeare was married, and historic Aldersgate Street and Wesley Chapel. To the right is the magnificent dome of St. Paul's Cathedral.

At home she often plays her CDs, favoring Beethoven, Mozart, and the light classical works of Strauss. Music is a source of relaxation, especially melodic background music, including Salvation Army recordings.

On a Friday evening she may take in a play or concert in the Barbican, the venue for much of her leisure time activity – the concert hall, theater, restaurants, and library – all at her doorstep. Sometimes on Saturday afternoons she will take a stroll in the London parks, enjoying the scenery and stopping for afternoon tea. Near the end of her tenure as General, she had to limit her walking due to an arthritic problem in her knee.

Those who have spent any time with her know her to have a hearty appetite and a penchant for desserts. She likes her food well seasoned and often opts for salads to help control her weight and cholesterol. She delights to entertain at home when rare opportunities permit and has a reputation for being as competent in the kitchen as she is companionable at the dining room table. She looks forward to good conversation and prefers to have the subjects different from Army matters, finding with some guests that "she really couldn't get them off the Army."

Computer Memory
Burrows is legendary in Army circles for her computer memory. One leader said, "Don't ever tell her anything you want her to forget!" Names of people she has met, and minute details of their lives, are remembered and recalled decades later. Her mental cassettes are crammed with acquired information from her study of people. Her phenomenal memory for names and places is a natural gift that she hones by diligent study and preparation.

At the Lausanne II Conference on World Evangelism in Manila in 1989 where she was a plenary session speaker, Bernard Kuiper greeted her, not expecting she would remember him. It had been almost forty years since he had known her in Australia. But she immediately recognized him saying, "You were in the young peoples' corps in Dulwich Hill Corps in Sydney in 1951."

In 1983 in Melbourne Eva Burrows received a phone call from a man who had seen her on television. He asked if she were the Eva Burrows who went to a certain school in 1946. Eva immediately replied, "Yes, and you are Mr. Adsett, my old teacher." There had been no contact between them in over thirty years, but as soon as she heard his voice she recognized him as her old schoolmaster. Eva says, "I could remember his name because he was a wonderful teacher who enabled some of us to receive small scholarships to high school."

She disclaims having a photographic memory, but acknowledges that knowing and remembering the names of people "is something I learned and practiced all through my officership." It relates to the importance she places on people and to her awareness that nothing is more personal than a name.

When visiting Perth in 1990 to conduct the State Congress, General Burrows was confronted by a man who had been in a chapel service she conducted at the Sunrise Center for Alcoholics some seven years before. The General paused, then calling him by his Christian name, inquired whether he were still sober and a Christian, since his decision seven years earlier. The man was very moved by her personal remembrance.

She is always pleased to be able to pass her "Name the executive officers test." Before visiting an Army territory she will memorize the names of all the executive officers and data of their work and family, using photos to identify the faces with the names. With more than 400 executive officers around the world listed in the Army's *Year Book,* she knows each by name and can picture what most of them look like.

Her hardest test came in Korea, where the names are difficult for Westerners to pronounce. During their visit in 1992, her ADC, Lt. Colonel Issitt, said, "You won't be able to do it this time." That statement seemed only to challenge Burrows to even greater effort. There were eighteen heads of departments and divisional commanders. She resorted to an old schoolteacher technique of writing the name down twenty times to learn its spelling as well as pronunciation. The testing time came when Burrows met with the executive staff for a meal. To the amazement of her hosts, and even to her ADC, she went around the tables and flawlessly called the name of each officer.

Personality Traits
Burrows has great powers of concentration. Her personal assistant and driver, Major Ruth Richards, shares that the General often uses time in transit to work. "She can be so absorbed," says the Major, "that she is oblivious to everything else around her. Once we were motoring through a severe rainstorm with much thunder and lightning. It wasn't until some time later that she looked up and remarked, 'Oh, has it been raining?' "

Many persons have been surprised to discover that meeting Eva Burrows is an experience absent of formality. To her troops, she is a down-to-earth First Lady of the Army. Although she mingles with ease in company of the rich and famous, she is most at home and derives her greatest satisfaction when mingling with the rank and file and the needy of the Army's parish.

Eva has the knack of relating with ease to the unexpected and to what others may find awkward. In Sri Lanka she was having a meal at Captain Lyell Rader's home when their preschool daughter, Evangeline, helped herself to a drumstick from Eva's plate. Always unflappable, the Territorial Commander negotiated the matter, "Vangie, why don't we share? You take a bite and then I'll take a bite!" And so they did throughout the meal.

"She is enthusiastic about everything she does," says Margaret Goffin. "To her life is an adventure. Her cheery, 'Good morning!' is like, 'It's great to be alive. Let's get started!' " Goffin adds, "She is an enthusiast the way she looks out the dining room window and watches the skyline change with the sunrise. When the mornings are dark she will look eagerly for the dawn. She takes great delight in nature. She likes to have flowers in the house and sometimes we buy daffodil buds here in London. She gets excited when they start to blossom and sits looking at these cheerful daffodils while having her breakfast. With her, everything is an adventure.

"At home, she just keeps going, working more often than not. When she arrives home from the office, while tea is being prepared, she often goes into the lounge and reads the daily paper. We have tea before she watches the evening news on TV, and then it is back into her office at home to work, right up to the time she goes to bed. After working late in preparation for an overseas tour she may come out and say, 'I had twenty-seven talks to do, and now I've only got twelve more to go.' "

General Burrows is perceived differently in the various cultures in which she moves. In Europe, some may interpret her confidence and mode of leadership as bordering on the presumptuous, whereas on the American scene she is seen as having a due sense of self-worth and optimism. This dichotomy is noted in letters of appreciation from the States and Australia, and letters from India which border on the worshipful. But such panegyrics are not forthcoming from territories with her more conservative constituencies.

Always the teacher, she habitually slips into the "schoolmarm" mold, giving instructions or asking questions to which she already knows the answers.

The struggle to overcome a prima donna complex has been a lifelong one for her. Some who have observed her closely have found it unbecoming that she would often remind people, "I am the General." But those who perceive this weakness readily admit that her extraordinary strengths and spiritual qualities far outweigh her lapses, and they "wouldn't change her for anyone."

The Short Fuse

Eva Burrows is no plaster saint. Those who know her or work closely with her are quite aware of the chinks in her armor. She is often described as having a "short fuse." She has earned the reputation that she can be difficult because she is very demanding, requiring efficiency and a person's best effort. She tends toward irritation with people who are tentative, and finds it difficult to accept that not everyone is as decisive as she is. However, she is most demanding upon herself, and is intolerant of expediency and mediocrity in the Lord's work in the Army. She acknowledges, "Perhaps my greatest temptation is to explode."

At times she can be imperious with close associates, regarding them as extended family with whom she can ventilate her feelings. The volatile temperament inherited from the Irish sheepshearer flashes out and as quickly subsides. She does not realize that those who are the object of her outbursts are not equally "teflon personalities." On more than one occasion a faithful comrade has come away from "her majesty" with a royal wound.

One Friday afternoon she came down very hard on one of her key staff persons. He took it but went back to his office thinking, "She shouldn't have said that to me. It was unfair." Monday morning, when called to her office on a matter of business, he reminded her of the Friday incident and the way in which she addressed him. She responded by expressing regret. Later that day the General called him on the intercom and said, "You know, I haven't got a spouse in whom I can confide and there are few with whom I can 'let off steam.'" She concluded the conversation by saying, "It is good to have friends like yourself."

Another of her former staff officers received quite a dressing down from her. Her eyes blazing, Eva angrily said, "You let me down." The staff officer stalked out of her office with very unpleasant thoughts toward his leader. Ten minutes later he received a phone call from her, saying, "We can't part that way. It's time to have a prayer." Her associates acknowledge she never holds a grudge.

Lt. Colonel Issitt has been especially adept at coping with the short fuse. Shortly after the General's arrival at IHQ, one of the staff members came to Colonel Issitt and said, "I've just been to the doctor and my blood pressure has suddenly shot up, much higher than it has ever been before." About a week later another of the office staff came to Colonel Issitt and remarked, "My blood pressure has skyrocketed. I never had high blood pressure before. She's the cause of it." A short time later Colonel Issitt went into the General's office and said to her, "You know, these other folks have had their blood pressure shoot up. You're not going to do that to me." The relationship between the General and her ADC forged into one of mutual respect and affection.

Some working with her in the administration section have been heard to say, "The heat's on this week." A code word among Burrows' close associates at IHQ is GFD—"General Free Days," referring to times when she is traveling and the staff can catch up with their work. Sometimes when she leaves for an overseas trip after a very busy time at the office, they may exclaim with relief, "We have fourteen GFD!"

She has never been afraid of hard decisions, even when it has meant strong disagreement. She can be as tough as any business executive when the situation calls for it. It is said that she has two sides—the strong, no holds barred "male type" aggressive executive leader, and also the soft-spoken, warmhearted feminine approach. Both seem to fit her equally. She is viewed as always fair, and building self-esteem in those she has ruled against.

Burrows is well known for not suffering fools gladly "and she's not afraid to tell them that they're fools," says one of her staff members. If in presenting business, the details are not stated with clarity, she will lose patience and tell the persons concerned to come back when they have done their homework. When the occasion warrants, she is quite ready to say, "I don't like the way you're doing this." Her staff quickly get the message that she expects their best. And she doesn't want "yes" people. More than one staff member has been told, "Don't say yes if you don't mean yes."

A former General discovered that Eva Burrows was no respecter of rank when it came to expressing her disagreements. An international

251

leaders conference was scheduled to be held in Toronto with Eva Burrows at that time coming as the Territorial Commander from Sri Lanka. She had made plans to visit with friends en route back. At the conference the leaders were reminded of the ruling that all officers were to return directly to their appointments following the conference. Eva bristled at this decision that would thwart her personal plans. She strode up to the podium and told the General she had made arrangements for personal visits with friends and it was unfair to issue such an edict. The General responded, "I am sorry but the decision has been made." Burrows argued her point and the General responded with greater firmness, "You know the decision has been taken and I do not want to hear any more about it." The irresistible force still pressed against the immovable object, and on that occasion Eva Burrows, undaunted but outranked, had to accept the decision of the General.

Commissioner Ron Cox, her former Chief of the Staff, saw a positive side to her impatience. He says, "I personally rejoice in having someone with a little bit of impatience. That's far better than a lack of urgency, an acceptance of the status quo, and no end of inertia to overcome." An Army book of early history records that Burrows had an interesting predecessor in this regard:

> In certain respects he was exacting. For example, he required that any information I set before him, or for which I was responsible, should be authentic beyond cavil; and if I tripped, as I am afraid occasionally happened, either through my own fault or the inefficiency of others, and circumstances turned out otherwise than he had been led to believe, he could be very angry, and rightly angry. On such occasions he showed his displeasure in a way that was sometimes grievous to bear.

This one who "could be very angry" is none other than the Army Founder, William Booth, as described by his son and Chief of the Staff, Bramwell Booth. [*Echoes and Memories,* 24] It seems Eva Burrows, with her short fuse, is at least in good company!

The Most Embarrassing Moment
On an occasion in Africa as General she had to negotiate around a ticklish diplomatic quandary which she describes as her most embar-

rassing moment as General. She was paying a courtesy call on a tribal king in a large African city and, with a large contingent of local Army leaders and Salvationists, was ushered into an ornate reception room. After they were seated, the king came in and with due ceremony sat upon his throne. He and Burrows then proceeded to converse and at the conclusion the General presented a gift to the king. It became obvious that the king had not prepared a gift and he called a servant over and whispered to him. The man shortly returned with a tray covered with a white cloth. The king then presented his gift — three bottles of whiskey!

Burrows recalls, "This put me in a dilemma. To refuse the gift would be very discourteous. At the same time I had Salvationists present who know our strong position on abstinence. I quickly arrowed a prayer to the Lord for guidance. I knew we were in a Muslim community and I was led to say that I knew as a member of the Islamic faith the king had some very strict rules. Then I explained that we have some very strict rules in The Salvation Army and one of them is we are not allowed to take intoxicating drink.

"The king seemed to understand and had his servant bring another gift. The thought flashed in my mind, 'I hope it's not cigarettes!' But it was a monetary gift, so I accepted and thanked the king for his kindness."

Comparisons with Evangeline Booth

Many tend to compare Eva Burrows with Evangeline Booth, daughter of the Founder and the only other woman General in the history of the Army. They sometimes refer to Burrows as "the second Eva," or "another Eva."

But upon inspection the comparison seems to have more contrasts than similarities. Evangeline Booth was sixty-nine years of age when she became General, almost a decade and a half older than Eva Burrows. Booth came from the Army's most famous family, Burrows from humble and hardworking corps officer parents. Booth had a personal magnetism and eloquence as a dramatic preacher in a style that has long become obsolete. Burrows' preachment is of a conversational, teaching style.

Students of Army history know that Evangeline Booth, although a colorful personality and a peerless national commander for thirty years of The Salvation Army in the United States, did not distinguish herself as General. Frederick Coutts, writing as official historian, gives scant pages for her tenure as General and states that her term was an international coda to her American post. "She was a phenomenon as a woman on her own," says Burrows of Evangeline, "and I have my own way to make."

Friendships

In retirement, Commissioner Ingrid Lindberg writes of General Burrows as a lifelong friend. "One could never say that her position has distanced her from her friends. When we meet she is the same old good friend as she has always been. She has a marvelous way of being able to relax with her friends, leaving work and burdens aside, and be completely herself. I marvel at her way of remembering her friends, their birthdays and events in their lives, and her thoughtfulness of writing postcards from all over the world."

Lt. Colonel Lucille Turfrey, with whom Eva forged a close friendship over the years, says, "I have been enriched in choice fellowship during the years of our association. Eve, as she is known to her family and friends, brings much to a friendship—the strength and veracity of character, her transparent godliness, the warmth and generosity of spirit, her absorbed enjoyment of the beautiful in nature, in art, in music, in literature. She takes delight in exciting escapades, for example, a jet-boat excursion on the Shotover River Rapids in New Zealand, or a hair-raising ride on the Space Mountain roller coaster at Disneyland. Her adventuresome spirit and sparkling humor are the spices of good companionship."

The ability to reduce discomfort in others is one of Eva's trademarks. On one occasion, at the Bicentennial Congress in Sydney, Australia, a certain Sergeant Major was understandably nervous before addressing over 2,000 delegates. But Burrows eased the tension when she presented him as "a very wise man." The reason given was that he had the good sense to marry her sister Margaret!

Salary and Perks

General Burrows, world leader of The Salvation Army, does not command a salary commensurate with the norm for top executives. Salvation Army salaries are considered allowances based on the cost of living in the country and culture in which the officer serves. Burrows' salary is a modest amount, plus provision of furnished quarters and a car.

Officers are required by Army regulations to turn any honoraria over to the Army. Monies Burrows receives from speaking and media engagements are put into a special fund for overseas projects. Once when visiting in Malawi, Africa, she on the spot donated money from this fund for a new building for the training of Army leaders.

An Expressive General

Australians are a reserved people not given to lavish show of public affection. In contrast, Eva Burrows exudes a warmth, believes in the power of touch, and is the first General of The Salvation Army given to hugs and kisses. In her world travels, General Burrows has kissed thousands. Taking hold of their hand she kisses them on the cheek. Her handshake is not the routine type, but a two-handed affair, with the left hand usually gripping the right forearm of the recipient and her right hand warmly clasping their hand.

Eva Burrows adapted the Apostle Paul's mode of becoming all things to all people. When in Africa she has done as the Africans do. She quickly identified with the culture and assimilated many of the customs of the African people. She was captivated by the happy expression of dancing that characterizes the African Salvationist, in their worship experience. When singing a song of praise they often break into a rhythm of a simple, yet joyful dance, accompanied with timbrel, drum, and often hoshos—gourds with dried seeds inside. Seventeen years among the African people endowed Eva Burrows with a spontaneous response of rhythmic movement that, natural in the African setting, would in later years often delight and at times startle some in the Western world.

Her audiences around the world on occasion have been treated to a momentary reversion to this custom from her African days. At the 1990 International Congress, when the Jonkoping Band (Sweden) played the captivating music of "Light Walk," Burrows was unable to resist the urge to dance, African style. The sight of a General dancing was one never before seen at a Salvation Army international gathering. Later, one young woman officer interviewed by an editor said a highlight of the Congress for her was "to see the General dance. She is really with it!"

"She Has It All"

Commissioner John Larsson, who worked very closely with her in the landmark IHQ restructuring project, gives his assessment.

I would describe her as a very gracious, feminine lady, and yet with immense strength. There's no question of the fact that she is the leader. She has a charming and easy way with people. She has a phenomenal memory and can remember people from years before and leave everyone in awe as to how she can recall the details of people's lives. She is exceedingly efficient. If any letter goes to her, you know it's going to come back within a matter of days with a clear answer. She is always looking for ideas from other people and has this ability of picking up ideas. She's always looking for action and wanting to move the thing forward. She's a gifted speaker, a good administrator, a brilliant meeting leader. She has personality, charisma—she has it all. I consider Eva Burrows to be one of our greatest generals.

Brigadier Jean Geddes (R) lived for one year as her housekeeper companion when Burrows was Territorial Commander in Australia. From that observation she writes, "Living close to Eva as I did for twelve months and sharing life daily with her, I saw that she lived very close to the Lord. I have never been with anyone else who impressed me as she did. At times I felt I was on holy ground. God is certainly at the center of her life."

PART FOUR

★ ★ ★ ★ ★ ★ ★ ★ ★ ★ ★ ★ ★

THE WORLD HER PARISH

26

★ ★ ★ ★ ★ ★ ★ ★ ★ ★ ★ ★ ★ ★ ★ ★ ★ ★ ★

THE CROSS REPLACES THE
HAMMER & SICKLE

*"These countries have been living under the
cold, compassionless hand of Marxist communism,
and they're looking for freedom, democracy, and meaning."*

The world of General Burrows was changing with kaleidoscopic
speed. The Cold War had melted, the infamous Berlin Wall came
tumbling down, the monolithic force of communism died an inglori-
ous death and the Soviet Union disintegrated.

"There is a tide," wrote Shakespeare, "in the affairs of men, which
taken at the flood, leads to fortune." Eva Burrows had the vision to
see the high tide of history that was rushing in for the cause of
freedom, and to move God's Army ahead of its crest to new conquests for the kingdom of God. On the international scene, General
Eva Burrows was leading her generation of Salvationists to a rendez-
vous with destiny.

As the thunderclap of freedom resonated across Eastern Europe,
Burrows led a dramatic return to lands where the Army had been
persecuted and disbanded. "These countries," she said, "have been
living under the cold, compassionless hand of Marxist communism,
and they're looking for freedom, democracy, and meaning. I believe
there is great opportunity for the Gospel in Eastern Europe today.
After the cynical disillusionment with communist philosophy, there
is a spiritual vacuum and people have their hearts open to the Gospel."

When communist governments came to power in Central and
Eastern Europe, the Army was proscribed in one place after another.
In Russia this occurred in 1923. Work in Latvia and Estonia was
maintained until 1939 and 1940 respectively, when those nations
were absorbed into the Soviet Union. The Army in Hungary ceased

in 1949 and in Czechoslovakia the following year. The Salvation Army's flourishing work in East Germany disappeared with the partition of the country following the Second World War.

Communism had just been kicked out the back door in Hungary and Czechoslovakia when the Army returned through the front door to resume the ministry that had been disbanded for over forty years. The Berlin Wall had hardly crumbled when General Burrows led her troops back into East Germany. Before the Soviet Union collapsed, she was marching with the Army tricolor on the streets of Leningrad. Her initiatives for The Salvation Army's advance into Central and Eastern Europe go down as epochal events and hallmarks of her Generalship.

In the Army's return to these former communist countries, General Burrows was putting into practice her philosophy to be proactive rather than reactive. She was moving ahead, seizing the opportunity of the moment, with an acute awareness of the changing tide of history. "We want to be careful not to look on our return to Eastern Europe as a public relations exercise," she stated. "I have to see that it is what God wants for The Salvation Army. My concern is to find God's will, because only then will the Spirit give us the power to do what He wants.

"We also must very carefully, as Jesus taught us, to contemplate what it is going to cost and what it is going to mean, so we don't just jump into a new country. We have to consider whether we have the resources of personnel and money and consider all the legal aspects. We don't lack faith, but we need to proceed wisely."

The momentous events leading to its return to these countries galvanized the Army world. "We're all out of breath trying to keep up with her," says Commissioner Peter Hawkins of her IHQ staff. Commissioner Paul A. Rader of the U.S.A. further echoed the outlook of Army world leaders on these events. "For years we have prayed for world peace and open doors in the communist world. We have prayed for Salvationists denied the freedom we enjoy. We have prayed for a chance to proclaim the Gospel behind the Iron Curtain. And now, in one of the most dramatic moments in world history, the answer has come. Great gates have begun to open in the impenetrable wall of what we thought to be the impregnable fortress of world communism. Waves of humanity are bursting forth and the sweet pure fragrance of freedom is rushing in." Commissioner James Osborne, U.S.A. National Commander, whose country would play a major role in financial support, said, "The prospect of reestablishing Salvation Army ministry in Central and Eastern Europe is the most welcome news in decades."

Burrows employed her time-tested strategy in this daunting enterprise—that of getting the right people for the job. She called out of retirement her former Chief of the Staff, Commissioner Caughey Gauntlett, to coordinate the Army's return to Central and Eastern Europe. Gauntlett's grandparents and parents had served in Europe and he himself had been born in Czechoslovakia. He also served in Europe, was fluent in German and French, knew well the countries involved and brought proven leadership to the task. He took this position for one year, reporting directly to the General and maintaining a close consultation with the International Secretary for Europe.

Countries whose doors were opening were assigned to neighboring territories and commanders. Czechoslovakia came under the oversight of the Netherlands, East Germany under West Germany, Hungary under Switzerland, Russia under Norway, Latvia under Sweden, and Estonia under Finland. Careful organization and strategy preceded the Army's return to assure viability for the future.

Return to East Germany

The Army first returned to East Germany before the infamous Berlin Wall had been completely dismantled. The General presided over the inaugural public meeting in Leipzig on June 16, 1990, officially reopening the work in East Germany.

Among the crowd of almost 400 people which filled the public hall were two who had been Salvationists before the Army had been banned, proudly wearing the uniform for the first time in forty years. Government, civic, and church officials joined the Army and the appointed single woman officer and two lay helpers in the first religious meeting held in a public hall since the establishment of the East German Republic.

A poignant moment was the presentation of a flag by General Burrows to Lieutenant Cornelia Vogler, the newly appointed corps officer. The flag, a gift from West German Salvationists, was placed beside the old torn flag which had been preserved throughout the past four decades. At the end of the meeting, Lieutenant Vogler and her two helpers knelt at the mercy seat to dedicate themselves to service in the city, with others joining them in rededication to Christ.

Hungary

The Secretary-General of the Conference of European Churches, Rev. Dr. J. Garfield Williams, inquired, "What about Hungary, General?" He said the time was opportune, the Army was needed, and he would be glad to help with the needed arrangements. Commissioner Gauntlett, with Commissioner Egon Ostergaard, traveled to Hungary where Dr. Williams introduced them to influential persons who could help the Army receive official recognition. Former Salvation Army officers in the country were also contacted and enthusiastically pledged their support.

A cable received by General Burrows' office on May 10, 1990 reported, "As from today, our flag is officially flying in Hungary. Hallelujah! God bless The Salvation Army!" It was sent by eighty-year-old Major Adam Macher, who had recently been appointed by the General as the Army's official pro tem representative in Hungary. The Hungarian government had now recognized the Army as a church equal with the country's other official churches.

Government, church, and civic leaders were united in welcoming the return of the Army to Hungary at the inaugural rally in November 1990 when General Burrows visited Budapest to mark the re-commencement of its service. Burrows' visit revealed a hidden army of well-wishers and resources of goodwill. She offered to make immediately available enough money to purchase 500 sleeping bags to be given to the homeless. Her scriptural message was a call to true freedom which may be found in surrender to Christ, a freedom, she said, that Hungarian Christians never lost, even when religious and political freedoms had been denied them.

Czechoslovakia

While attending as a plenary session speaker the Lausanne II International Conference on World Evangelism in Manila in 1989, General Burrows had been approached by Dr. Pavel Titera, principal of a theological college and president of the Czechoslovakia Baptist Union. He revealed that he was a Salvation Army soldier and candidate for officership at the time the Army had been banned in 1950. He asked, "When is the Army coming back to Czechoslovakia?" Burrows replied, "One day we hope to return and pray the Lord will open the door for us to do so."

They kept in touch through correspondence. When the Army officially reopened in Prague on April 4, 1990, it was Dr. Titera who presented the Army leaders at the press conference and who expressed words of welcome from the religious community in the Army's first meeting. Shortly thereafter, in retirement from the Baptist Church, he became enrolled as a soldier of The Salvation Army and upon the visit of the General to Prague, he was there in full Salvation Army uniform!

The Army's Netherlands Territory, under the enthusiastic leadership of Commissioner Reinder Schurink, was assigned the responsibility for the reopening and oversight of the Army in Czechoslovakia. Brigadier Josef Korbel, Salvation Army hero who as a Czech officer had suffered imprisonment under the communist rule, came from his retirement home in the U.S.A. as one of the first to help spearhead the Army's return to his native land.

As Brigadier Korbel approached the former Army hall in Brno, after an absence of over forty years, he fell silent and then in deep emotion said, "It was here that I was arrested. It was our officers' quarters, and they took me, leaving my wife and children." Commissioner Caughey Gauntlett says of that moment, "We all knew his story, but suddenly this piece of real estate became hallowed ground. It was from this very place, in the living apartment above the corps hall, that he as the corps officer had been summarily arrested, and that his many years of inhumane incarceration began, for no other reason than that he was a Salvation Army officer preaching the Gospel under an atheistic regime."

In her first visit to Czechoslovakia in September 1991, General Burrows discovered that the spirit which had kept the Army alive in the hearts of a dedicated band of retired officers, had been captured by a fine group of young uniformed Czech Salvationists who were making headway in evangelizing their own generation. In the initial meeting with over 200 people present was Major Bohuslav Bures, age ninety-one, a former Salvation Army officer in Czechoslovakia. He produced a corps cadet flag belonging to the Prague corps which he had cherished for forty years, and draped it over the pulpit.

The Army established social services in the country with remarkable speed. Burrows visited one of the three day centers in operation, participated in the daily feeding program, opened a hostel for thirty-six homeless men with plans to add a workshop for industrial training, laid a foundation stone for a center for the elderly, and inspected other properties soon to be brought into service. She was accompanied by Commissioner Schurink and the Amsterdam Staff Band and

With President Vaclav Havel, Prague, Czechoslovakia, 1991.

Songsters, whose open-air ministry made a great impact on the citizens of Prague, with thousands gathering round to hear not only the music, but the words of witness for Christ by the musicians. One venue was the Old Town Square in Prague, dominated by the statue of religious reformer John Huss. There beneath the symbolic statue Burrows preached a Bible message to hundreds of listeners.

The Army has been greatly helped by the cooperation of the government, and the General's first call was to Prague Castle to be received by President Vaclav Havel. A visionary who had suffered imprisonment under communism, Havel was a symbol of freedom to his people. In a warm and lengthy conversation with General Burrows he offered his government's full support to the Army. After leaving the Palace, Burrows went to the mainline railway station where the Army conducts a nightly soup-run, and the hands that had just been grasped so warmly by the country's national leader were now embracing the most needy of its citizens.

Sunday meetings were conducted in Prague in a building that had been the meeting place of the local communist party. Inside the corps hall, General Burrows called attention to the fact that a wooden cross was placed exactly over the spot where the hammer and

General Burrows, through a translator, preaches before the statue of religious reformer John Huss which dominates the Old Town Square in Prague, Czechoslovakia.

sickle had been fixed; the Bible took the place of the Manifesto, and where the activists had been trained in communism there now were enthusiasts for the Gospel of Christ.

Sitting in the front two rows were smartly uniformed young men and women who recently had been sworn in as soldiers. General Burrows presented certificates to several retired officers which confirmed their commissions in view of their faithfulness during the long years of separation from the international Army.

With both the past and future in mind, General Burrows challenged them to remain faithful. Josef Korbel, she reminded them, had been destined for missionary service in Africa; he had found instead his mission field in a prison cell. One of her visits during the weekend had been with a political prisoner converted under Korbel's influence. In her Bible address she recalled seeing television pictures of the crowds in Wenceslus Square only two years before. Their cry was "Freedom." Political and economic freedom were now theirs, but that would not solve every problem; man's true freedom was to be found only in Christ, she said. An invitation to make a public declaration for Christ was met with a prayerful, thoughtful response, one which boded well for the future of the Army in that brave country.

Latvia

The Army's work in Latvia had been proscribed in 1940. General Burrows announced its reopening in that Baltic Republic in October 1991. The Army hall in Riga, long owned by the city council, was turned over to the Army which renovated its foyer for the opening ceremony and regular meetings until further refurbishment would allow use of the main hall. Former Salvationists gathered for the opening, joining new soldiers of the Riga Corps alongside Commissioner Lennart Hedberg of Sweden who gives oversight for the work in Lativa. "Pestisanas Armija" (The Salvation Army in Latvian) replaced the name of a defunct communist youth club on the outside of the building.

Russia

In what by Burrows' penultimate year had become a mountain range of world achievements, Russia now stood out as one of the highest peaks to conquer for God and the Army.

Another Macedonian call to "come over and help us" was heard by Burrows when she spoke at the Lausanne II Conference in Manila. Following her plenary address, Russian delegates besieged her with questions about The Salvation Army and expressed a strong hope to see the Army return. They even sang for her a verse of the Army Founder's song, "O Boundless Salvation," saying it is in their Russian Baptist hymnbook.

In the fifth year of Burrows' Generalship, cataclysmic events brought the mighty Soviet Union to a state of collapse, its economy to the brink of complete implosion, and potential civil war between rival ethnic groups which had been without freedom during seventy-four years of Soviet rule. But before the collapse took place, Burrows already had her troops poised for another kind of conquest.

The Army had been in Russia from 1913 to 1923, before it was banned. The return to Russia was made difficult because no Salvationists from the former days of the Army remained as a link.

At Lausanne II Conference in Manila, 1989, Russian delegates ask General Burrows to have the Army return to Russia.

General Burrows meets Joni Eareckson Tada at Lausanne Conference.

"People in Russia are open to the Gospel," said Burrows, "and I think that when they see a movement which joins together concern for people's social and spiritual needs, that will mean something to the Russian people."

Commissioner Ingrid Lindberg, Territorial Commander in Finland, at the General's request visited Leningrad in early 1990 and she opened an exhibition about The Salvation Army. She was the first Army officer to reenter the Soviet Union officially. Most approaches to the authorities and visits to Russia were initiated by Norway which played the major role in preparing the way for the Army's return to Russia. Commissioner Gauntlett scheduled a visit to Moscow to establish procedures and priorities for the Army's return.

On January 1, 1991 Lt. Colonel John Bjartveit of Norway was appointed as officer in charge for Russia. A chapter of Salvation Army history was reopened in July of that year as General Eva Burrows led her troops in a triumphant march and return through the streets of Leningrad (soon to be renamed St. Petersburg), equipped with funds and personnel to establish a beachhead in Rus-

Leading her Army back into Russia with a march through Leningrad, General Eva Burrows is welcomed by a gypsy child.

sia. It was the Army's first official presence in Russia since 1923 when it had been closed by the Bolshevik government. Crowds visiting in Leningrad were captivated by the sight of the Army tricolor waving against the clear blue sky and the martial strains of the Army's Oslo Temple Band from Norway. Some 80,000 pamphlets announcing the return of the Army had been distributed and posters put up throughout the city. The procession made its way to October Platz where the General preached the message of salvation and Captain Sven Ljungholm of the U.S.A. held the new flag, his grandfather having carried the Army colors in the same square seventy-five years earlier.

The General and the large contingent of Salvationists, including fifty from Finland and Commissioner and Mrs. John Ord from Norway, received an enthusiastic welcome to Russia from government, community, and religious leaders. A meeting was held in a sports stadium with 600 in attendance. When General Burrows invited people to accept Christ, there was a significant response, along with many Christians expressing their willingness to become actively involved in helping reestablish the Army in Leningrad.

One person quite impressed by the band was a member of the Soviet military band who attended the Army meetings to hear more of the Oslo Band. His interest led him to become a "captive" of this new Army of compassion, and within a year he was wearing a Salvation Army uniform, playing in the Army's ensemble, and then became a commissioned bandmaster.

"There is a great deal of poverty in Leningrad," stated Burrows. "Elderly people who can't get out to food areas need help." Officers appointed to Russia reported that people were standing in food lines for hours. Within weeks of its return to Russia, The Salvation Army was distributing massive quantities of food, donated by Canada, Sweden, Norway, and the United States. In keeping with its best tradition, The Salvation Army in Russia was addressing the hunger of the body as well as of the spirit, with financial help and encouragement from around the Army world.

"Much depends on the first team," was Burrows' assessment of the new start in Russia. To the six officers making up the team of pioneers for the reopening, she advised that they identify with the people and communicate through the Russian language. "There is a great need for evangelism," she stressed. "For years, official policy has tried to eradicate the teachings of Christ; yet there is now an openness to the Gospel and a hunger for spiritual meaning. We answer that best by speaking of Christ. Make converts and then bring the converts on to discipleship."

In her travels she reported with obvious pride on the Army's advance in Russia. She took delight in telling of an innovative publicity venture in St. Petersburg that involved a new soldier who is manager of a tram depot. He had two large trams freshly painted in bright colors with one side bearing the Army crest and its slogan, "Heart to God and Hand to Man." The other side bore the Army red shield, announcements of the corps meetings and the words of Jesus, "Come unto Me all you who labor and are heavy laden, and I will give you rest." With a smile, Burrows added, "They are becoming known as the 'Hallelujah Trams.' "

In March 1992, General Eva Burrows returned to Russia to reopen the Army's work in Moscow. She enrolled sixty-five senior soldiers — almost one for each year the Army was banned in Russia — and twenty junior soldiers. In response to her messages, more than 200 persons moved forward in an act of dedication to Christ. Uniformed soldiers from St. Petersburg, sworn in two months earlier and trained in counseling by their Canadian officers Lieutenant and Mrs. Geoffrey Ryan, moved among them to encourage and counsel.

"Why would Russians want to join The Salvation Army?" a French journalist cynically asked the General in a press conference. Burrows did not answer the question herself but invited her translator, eighteen-year-old student Olga Barykina, to answer. "Christ has given so much to me that I want to serve Him and do something for Him and others," Olga said. "When I met The Salvation Army, I immediately loved its spirit and its work. It is a way we Russians can help ourselves." Olga had been enrolled as a soldier the day before.

In meetings in Moscow, new Russian Salvationists proudly wearing the Army uniform gave moving testimonies of their newfound faith in Christ. A psychologist told how through her profession she had spent fifteen years trying to bring healing and harmony to troubled people, and discovered that only in Jesus Christ can salvation and true peace be found. A retired Red Army officer in his late sixties said he used to handle dangerous and destructive weapons, but now had found an Army whose weapons are love and Christian action, and he joined up.

Laurisa Almazov, a schoolteacher, was attracted to the Army, accepted Christ, and took up full-time work in the Army's ministry.

General Eva Burrows on Red Square in Moscow, March 1992.

Dr. Valody Pateosov, a pediatrician and psychoanalyst, became a soldier involved in the Army's prison ministry. Within a few weeks of the reopening of the Army's work in Moscow, Captain and Mrs. Sven Ljungholm reported the soldiership recruitment had grown to 131. These testimonies and scores of others confirmed to Burrows that Russia was indeed a "field white unto harvest," and already yielding rich results.

Burrows' visit coincided with the landmark International Conference on Social Work in Moscow, organized by The Salvation Army and the first of its kind in Russia. The four-day Conference had 250 delegates and featured workshops on alcoholism, social work structure, juvenile delinquency, unemployment, family abuse, and care of the elderly.

General Burrows was greeted with applause when she opened the keynote session in Russian. She stressed that the Army had not come to tell the Russian people what to do, but to share with them so that they could take from it what they could use. The Youth Institute rector told the conference that the word *general* was a rigid one in Russian. "It is connected with stern discipline and hard faces," he

271

said. "But today we have seen another type of general, a most gentle General."

More than fifty tons of food, medical supplies, and clothing were airlifted to Moscow, coinciding with General Burrows' visit. The project, "Operation Provide Hope," was sponsored by the U.S. and Canadian governments, and channeled through the Army.

Russia remained a top priority on Burrows' agenda in her final months in office. She believed there was a window of only two or three years to take advantage of the great vacuum that had followed the demise of communism and she called for an all-out effort to establish the Army's evangelistic and social work there. Burrows made a strong appeal for personnel to help start the work in Russia. "It must be with a readiness to sacrifice," she challenged. "After all, isn't that the kind of discipleship to which Christ calls us?"

In the U.S.A. Southern Territory Congress that same month, Commissioner Kenneth L. Hodder presented a check for $1 million to Burrows under the banner, "To Russia with Love." At that same Congress the clients of the Adult Rehabilitation Centers themselves gave contributions and raised funds to present to Captain and Mrs. Ljungholm a fully equipped emergency canteen and vehicle valued at more than $100,000. Two years earlier Burrows had announced, "Russia, look out, here we come!" Now the Army's work in Russia was exploding with converts to the Christian faith and it had full support from their brothers and sisters in Christ around the Army world.

One woman in North America wrote to General Burrows, saying, "I read that if you had $1 million you would use it for evangelism. Here is a check for $100,000. I will send checks in that amount for the next nine months." Burrows took this as a sign from the Lord to move ahead in the expansion of the Army's evangelistic mission in Russia.

In July 1992 General Burrows' epic exertion in Russia announced an unprecedented and dramatic new strategy for the Army's advance in Russia. A bulletin went out to the Army world stating, "Under the compulsion of the Holy Spirit, I have been made aware that there is a need for a great leap forward in our planning for the growth of our work in Russia." In this "new, audacious strategy," she appointed Commissioner Reinder Schurink of the Netherlands in charge of Russia with his office to be in Moscow, and Colonel Fred Ruth of the U.S.A. as Secretary for Russian Development with his office at IHQ. These appointments gave the work a priority status. A call went to every Territory for a large reinforcement of personnel, funds, and prayer support. A plan was set in motion for the training of Russian soldiers to become Salvation Army officers. Colonel Howard Evans of the U.S.A. responded with his wife, immediately following their retirement, to serve as training principal for the first session of Russian cadets. An invitation was later extended to Burrows to conduct the first commissioning of Russian Cadets in June 1993, one month prior to her retirement.

The Army's return to Russia was a high meridian on the landscape of Burrows' generalship. "Carpe diem" was the order of the day for the open door the Lord had set before the Army. General Burrows was mobilizing resources from around the Army world for its advance in Russia. As her communications officer, Lt. Colonel Cecil Williams said, "When a matter is decided, she has an intolerance for delay."

A Restless Banner

The sun never sets on the Army tricolor. It is a restless banner, proclaiming its Gospel message in nearly 100 countries around the world. It once traveled to the moon, carried by an American astronaut. Banned for four decades in countries oppressed by atheistic communism, it marches forward once again in the triumph of the cross.

The advance and reopening of the Army in these communist bloc countries was a high solstice of General Burrows' term. With vision and vigor she advanced the Army into new frontiers in Liberia, El Salvador, Czechoslovakia, Hungary, East Germany, Latvia, and Russia. Under Burrows, the Army banners were marching forward at a brisk pace and the cross was replacing the hammer and sickle.

27

★ ★ ★ ★ ★ ★ ★ ★ ★ ★ ★ ★ ★ ★ ★ ★ ★ ★ ★ ★

THE WORLD HER PARISH
"I am a citizen of the world."

General Eva Burrows would feel an affinity with Socrates when he said, "I am not an Athenian or a Greek, but a citizen of the world." Although born and bred in the isolated island continent of Australia, and having served seventeen years in the heart of Africa, Eva Burrows has emerged from that geographical insularity to become the consummate internationalist, a "citizen of the world."

In many places of the Army world there is no opportunity for interaction with Salvationists from other countries. But wherever the General visits, she is to her constituency the symbol of the Army's internationalism, the "global parent" for the widely dispersed world-wide family of The Salvation Army.

During her seven years in office, General Burrows has journeyed to sixty-one countries, logging over a million miles in her travels throughout the world. She has journeyed from the remote cities of Australia to the bush villages of Zambia, from Canada to the Congo, from the Bay of Bengal in India to the snow-clad Alps of Switzerland.

She has visited the Emperor in the Imperial Palace in Japan and has mingled among the poverty-stricken in the hovels of Portugal. In her travels she has been the guest of kings and queens and heads of state around the world, and has also clambered over improvised shelters in cardboard cities to offer a bowl of soup and a prayer to the homeless and hungry.

Her visits often included press interviews, commissionings of cadets, enrollments of soldiers, tours of Army centers, and large meetings that featured her preaching and programs geared to different groups. Some visits included an audience with a head of state or the awarding of the *Order of the Founder* and other recognitions.

Her international travels as General are selected on the basis of the significance of an event—such as centennials and territorial congresses, the numerical strength and geography of a territory, and a balance in visiting the overall territories of the Army world. But for Burrows, no Army section is too small or too far, and she often has traveled to remote centers of operation. Weather conditions also dictate seasons for visits, especially in places such as Africa where large meetings are held outdoors.

Although as General she has not been able to visit every country in which The Salvation Army operates, she has visited each of its fifty territories and commands, becoming the first General in the Army's history to do so. Some territories comprise more than one country, with the Caribbean Territory, for example, consisting of sixteen independent entities, and the Latin America North territory with headquarters in Mexico comprising seven countries. On the other hand, some countries have multiple territories—India has six and the U.S.A. four.

In her preachment she has been translated into forty languages, from Korean to Kiswahili, from Swedish to Sinhalese, from Zulu to Russian. Translators often imitate her hand gestures and voice inflection, interpreting with their hearts as well as with their heads and voices.

Zonal Conferences
The international Salvation Army is divided into five zones, with leaders meeting in triennial zonal conferences. In January 1987, just six months after taking office, Burrows conducted a zonal conference in India with leaders from India, Pakistan, Bangladesh. From there she traveled to Hong Kong and met with leaders from the South Pacific and East Asia. Within the same year she met in Paris with leaders of Europe, and soon after traveled to Nairobi to confer with Army leaders from the African continent. These conferences provided her with an invaluable orientation to the people, problems, and programs in these near and far-flung places of the Army world.

An International Family
When General Burrows was asked in a press conference if keeping the Army together in a multicultural world would become increas-

ingly difficult, she replied, "The Army has qualities which transcend cultural differences. A Salvationist from India has more in common with a Salvationist from Australia than two non-Salvationist Australians. We are a family," she emphasizes, "not a federation.

"Salvation Army culture and its values and customs have been transmitted across cultural lines of nations where we exist. The Salvation Army has adapted itself in uniform, music, worship, preaching, evangelism, social programs, and in many other ways to particular cultures.

"The internationalism of The Salvation Army is fostered by international congresses, zonal conferences, the visits of music forces around the world such as the Soweto Songsters from South Africa touring America and Europe. The International College for Officers strengthens our bonds of internationalism. And my own position, the office of the General, is symbolic of the oneness of The Salvation Army family."

The Travail of Travel
The words *travel* and *travail* are linguistic as well as true life cousins. A heavy schedule of travel has its wearisome features. When traveling internationally there are the many forms to file out, the delays, and the long waits for luggage.

In one series of travels, General Burrows computed that on fourteen main flights, they had ten serious delays or "travel sagas." For example, in London upon return from Germany, she had to wait well over an hour in the cold until a suspicious package could be "exploded" in the car park. En route to Washington in 1986 to visit President Reagan, the pilot nonchalantly remarked, "Those on the right side of the plane will see that a piece has fallen off the wing." Forced to return to London, they waited another seven hours before departure. Upon arrival in Washington she was grateful to learn that her visit with the President had been rescheduled to later in the day.

On Burrows' trip to the Congo in 1989, during a changeover in Paris her new camera was stolen from her case. At one hotel in Africa the water was off for several days. A certain hotel arrangement in a Third World country was described in her diary as "ghastly."

Twice when leaving Miami, U.S.A., her luggage was misdirected and delayed until several days later. In Zambia, Burrows and her party experienced the saga of an overbooked plane that required four of their party to delay their takeoff until the next day. Lt. Colonel

Issitt had a seat only through the courtesy of a doctor on board who gave her his seat and traveled in the cockpit with the pilot who was a friend of his.

For the first almost six-and-a-half years she never missed an engagement due to illness, weather, or travel breakdown. That impeccable record was broken in November 1992 when the plane on which she was traveling from Miami to Haiti had to return shortly after takeoff, make an emergency landing, with Burrows missing the first meeting in Haiti.

The one perk Army Generals are allowed is first class travel. This enables Burrows to rest either in preparation for or recovery from the demanding schedules and the adjustment to time zones. She and her party are also accorded V.I.P. status at many airports, which saves waiting in line for luggage and clearance checks.

Not a Tourist

General Burrows has said, "I am not a tourist. I have seen neither the colossal statue of Christ above Rio de Janiero nor the Statue of Liberty in New York. The excitement for me is seeing the Army in action, fulfilling its mission in so many lands and cultures. Every country is special to me for that reason."

When Burrows made her first visit to Portugal there was a short break in the schedule and her hosts offered to take her to see the city of Lisbon and some of the historic sights. She responded, "I am not here as a tourist, I am here as a Salvationist. I would like to see the work you are doing among the poor and the homeless."

Major Barbara Bolton who accompanied the General on this trip describes what then ensued. The General did not see the Castle of St. George which overlooks the ancient city of Lisbon. Instead she saw the shanties where some of the poorest people in Western Europe eke out a precarious existence. The Sergeant Major who regularly visits the people took the General from house to house to meet the inhabitants. The shanties are kept as clean as possible. Many have flowers in jars on tables and some even have plants. The homes are a triumph of the human spirit over adversity. The women's faces are stoical, their days being a constant battle to turn the shanties into homes, to give their children hope, and to feed their families. Some of the people are refugees from former Portuguese colonies.

The poverty Burrows saw on every hand tugged at her compassion. She was especially impressed with the Sergeant Major and said,

"I was amazed and delighted with this new Salvationist who had grasped the concept of what the Founder meant in caring for the poor and homeless. When we went through these hovels she greeted each person by name and took a great interest in them. She did a beautiful work of grace among those people, helping them with food and clothing. Now if I had gone sightseeing instead of making that visit, I would have missed seeing this beautiful ministry and encouraging this wonderful Salvationist in her work. Also when I see the work being done, not only am I better informed, but upon return I can talk about these programs and often help secure needed support."

Later that day, Burrows said, "The little children I met this morning were more beautiful to me than any palace. Among them were junior soldiers who had come to know Jesus through the Army's ministry. Such children are the future of Lisbon and of the Army."

On rare occasions Eva has paid her obeisance to a celebrated place or scene. On a free day in India she went to see the Taj Mahal. She had seen it before, but wanted Lt. Colonel Issitt to have the opportunity also. In Zimbabwe she took a day to travel to Victoria Falls, relaxed with a boat cruise on the Zambesi River and enjoyed a plane ride over the famous Falls. In Japan she made a day trip to see the renowned Mount Fuji, and in Korea toured a traditional village and attended a Korean dance and song theater. Such personal excursions were infrequent, but she entered into them with enjoyment and a keen appreciation for the beauty and history of each place.

An Office on Wings

The office of the General of The Salvation Army is essentially wherever the General happens to be. Communications are maintained with her London office and she is consulted for decisions that have to be made for the Army around the world. In this day of instant communication, fax messages go back and forth with her IHQ office as she is kept apprised of events occurring within the Army.

Often in her messages at Army meetings, she will read a fax message just received, reporting on some significant happening in the Army world. This was especially common during the Army's return to Eastern Europe. When in Japan in early 1992, she was handed a fax message upon leaving the hotel, read it in the car on the way to the meeting, and then shared an hour later with her audience the report on the Army's distribution of food supplies to people in Moscow.

Above: At Mount Fuji, Japan — 1992

"Top Tambourine"

News reporters were continually captivated by this woman who blended the charm of her femininity with a quiet yet ostensible authority. One Canadian reporter, upon attending meetings in Toronto conducted by the General, seemed to have caught something of the measure of the Army's international leader. He headlined his article on the newly elected General: "Top Tambourine — Salvation Army's youngest general leads troops in faith, hope and levity." His article reported:

> She looks as though she could dress down the Almighty Himself in the unlikely event that He stepped out of line. In the meantime, she did not shrink from giving Margaret Thatcher a piece of her very capable mind. "She tried to impose a tax on our hostel residents in Britain," Gen. Burrows said crisply. "We wrote back and forth and got it changed." This is not a woman to be trifled with, and even the Mounties who escort her into Massey Hall to the strains of "The Maple Leaf Forever" look diminished in her presence.
>
> Her orations are down-to-earth and she stresses the good

The General travels, modern style

Left: The General meets some very interesting "people" in her travel.

At an American Congress, the General is greeted by a "friend" from back home.

news of evangelism rather than the bad news of despair. The lighthearted, fun-loving side of The Salvation Army personified by their leader probably comes in handy as comic relief, since they do much of society's dirty work.

The Priority of People

Wherever in the world Burrows travels, individual people are her priority. She became notorious for being among the last to leave a building, often holding up her hosts who waited to usher her out, or sometimes having to be warned to exit as the union workers were about to turn off the lights in a rented building.

Her phenomenal correspondence by postcard, while visiting throughout the world, has provided many with precious remembrances. Sixteen persons receive postcards from her on each overseas trip, in addition to others who are remembered for particular reasons on that journey. Privileged to accompany the General on her second visit to Africa, and again to Japan and Korea, upon return home, I learned that my wife had received gracious cards from the General. Many persons share similar experiences of this type of thoughtful remembrance from General Burrows on her worldwide travels.

Upon return from an overseas journey, she often calls or writes to family members of persons seen on her trip. Commissioner Ron Cox shares an incident that occurred following his retirement, just after Burrows had returned from a two-week campaign in Africa. His son, Captain Andre Cox, had coordinated the Congress programs in Zimbabwe. "After her tour in Africa, on the very first day back at the office she picked up the phone to call and sing the praises of our son Andre. It meant a great deal to us. Numerous times I had seen her take the time and trouble for this kind of personal touch. Perhaps it has something to do with the psychology of her feminine nature. A man would come back and tackle his work and plan that when he had time he would attend to the personal things. But a woman deals more promptly with personal things, notwithstanding the other pressures and demands. She is constantly producing those personal touches. It is natural to her."

A World Outlook

Many administrative benefits accrue from her travels. Her notes are replete with names of people in the various countries for whose leadership and dedication she expresses generous appreciation.

Sometimes she notes personnel needs to be addressed; for example, she observed a very efficient single woman officer who had served for twenty years in two Third World countries. She wondered why the officer had not been given more responsibility equivalent to her years of service and capacity, and made a note to discuss it with the International Secretary for that area. She seeks to assure that national officers are advanced to be able to move into positions of top leadership in their countries. To enhance their development, she has sometimes appointed them for a short time to a Western country before sending them to take up further leadership post in their homeland.

Visits with Heads of State

General Burrows has met with more than twenty heads of state, more than any other General of The Salvation Army. These visits aid understanding of the Army's purpose and program by the nation's leadership, gain publicity and stature for the Army, and often result in better support for the work of the Army in those countries.

When in Africa, her audiences with the Presidents of Malawi and Zimbabwe made front-page headlines and TV news. People in the hotel and on the street were quick to recognize her as "the one who met with the President." In Japan, her audience with the Emperor opened many other doors of opportunity for the Army. In Korea, the 6,000 Salvationists gathered for the 1992 Congress took great pride that their international leader met with their President.

In visits with heads of state, General Burrows usually asks the question, "What is your greatest problem? When the occasion allows, she asks if she may pray for the leader's country and the work of government. She never has been refused this opportunity. I would like to think that those occasions will not just be polite moments for protocol," she said. "I would like to feel that I could speak with government leaders at some depth, and even pray with them."

Diligent Preparation

She diligently prepares herself for overseas visits by reading up on the country to be visited—its history, culture, economy, politics, people, needs, problems, politics, and religious profile. She also requests and receives from Major Jenty Fairbank at the International Heritage Centre valuable data on The Salvation Army in that area. Thus she goes well informed and prepared to discuss with both

Salvationists and public officials the topics pertaining to their country. In South Africa where many Zulus would be in the meetings, her messages were illustrated with stories from the book, *Zulu Crusade* by Commissioner Allister Smith who pioneered the Army's work among the Zulus.

When visiting multilingual South Africa, she responded to the welcome in Afrikaans, English, and Zulu. After practicing throughout the day, she was encouraged when at several points in her Zulu greeting the black Salvationists gave rousing hallelujahs.

She has been keen to note the prayers and testimonies of participants, often expressing appreciation for a moving prayer or thoughtful testimony of lay Salvationists. She prefers testimonies with "up-to-date reference and not the long biographical type." The way people pray, she believes, is a good index of the depth of their spiritual life and relationship to God.

Order of the Founder
In her world travels Burrows has recognized a number of the heroes and heroines of the Army with the highest recognition accorded to Salvationists—the *Order of the Founder*. It marks distinguished or memorable service that would have specially commended itself to the Founder, William Booth. Fewer than 200 soldiers and officers have been admitted since its inception in 1917. Admission to the *Order* must be approved by the General. Most often it is the General who presents the *Order*. During her term as General, Burrows has admitted over twenty-five persons to this illustrious company, the largest addition by any General since Bramwell Booth.

In Canada in June 1988, General Burrows admitted Lt. Colonel Philip Rive (R) posthumously to the *Order of the Founder,* with the announcement made during his funeral service. The citation read that Lt. Colonel Rive devoted thirty-four years of active officership to the education of African youth and the translation of Scripture, Salvation Army songs, and materials into the Ndebele, Shona, and Tonga languages.

Burma's stalwart, Lt. Colonel Saratha Perieswami, was admitted to the *Order of the Founder* by General Burrows in May 1989. The citation reads that the Colonel "has, by courageous endeavor through times of difficulty and isolation, maintained and extended the Army's work in Burma and shown unwavering faithfulness to its practices and principles."

At the 1990 International Congress, a record four admissions were made, including Major Yin and Brigadier Korbel as described earlier. Envoy Kim, Hyun-Sook of Korea was cited, who despite personal suffering and loss, gave sacrificial service in Korea in the interests of homeless women and children, the poor and hungry, and women afflicted by alcohol addiction. Envoy Wilbur Walker of Australia was admitted for his untiring efforts to reestablish links with mainland China and for helping many Chinese students emigrate to Australia.

In March 1992, Major Tora Rasmussen was admitted in recognition of her ministry to the underprivileged in Denmark. General Burrows described how the Major had established a pioneering advice center in Copenhagen twenty-four years earlier and in retirement still runs the center, helping 1,400 people a year with the aid of an all-volunteer team of helpers. "The Founder," said the General, "would rejoice at the Major's sacrificial service."

These are only a few of the heroes and heroines upon whom Burrows has conferred the Army's highest honor. In their selection, their place in the Army's noble history and tradition of compassionate ministry has been ensured.

A Major Test and a Lesson
In the third month of her Generalship, Burrows embarked on an extended overseas campaign that was to be a major test of her international leadership. It was an eighteen-day visit to Canada and the four U.S.A. territories, with engagements in Toronto, Vancouver, Winnipeg, Washington, Atlanta, Chicago, New York, and Los Angeles. Twenty-five percent of her total officers would be represented in these visits. She would be addressing some of the most sophisticated of her worldwide audiences and meeting with an impressive array of male leadership. The schedule of travel and over fifty meetings was described as "torturous."

Salvationists of North America were eager to see their new woman General. What was she like? How was she on the platform? How would she relate to the various types of meetings? How would she handle the media, the Advisory Board, and prominent persons who would be introduced to her? One American officer had even worn a black arm band the day it was announced that a woman had been elected General. Thousands were waiting to take the measure of the first woman General known to most Salvationists. Also a woman General was a novelty and her North American hosts were exploiting the schedule to exact "every pound of flesh and every last farthing" from their new celebrity.

About one-third of the way into the itinerary, after a grueling schedule of meetings and speaking engagements from breakfast until the evening, the new General came to her hotel room in the late evening, totally spent. She had desperately wanted to succeed on this critical North American tour and had given herself unsparingly to the unmerciful schedule. Now she was on the verge of collapse. Tears started to flow, and a very human woman General said, "I can't do it. I just can't do it."

In that moment the Lord spoke reassuringly that she could claim the spiritual resources of His presence and power, and that a good night's sleep would be restorative. Following the night's rest and with a new sense of dependence on the Holy Spirit, the General went into the next day and the remainder of the tour with a renewed strength. On that lonely night in the hotel room, she came to a fresh awareness of the resources of God, and a practical lesson on exercising some control over the schedule. This lesson would serve her well in her worldwide travels and ministry over the next seven years.

The U.S.A. report for those October 1986 plane-hopping visits said, "From the nation's chief executive to the most-recently enrolled Salvationist, there was an openhearted rapport with the General." In this "test campaign," American and Canadian Salvationists showered her with enthusiastic affection. In each city many responded to her preaching ministry. The Lord had proven to be her sufficiency.

A world parish awaited her ministry. The schedules and responsibilities would be demanding, beyond human resources. On this first major overseas series as General, she had found and tapped the divine resources that enabled her to rise up to the rigorous schedules and events.

28

★ ★ ★ ★ ★ ★ ★ ★ ★ ★ ★ ★ ★ ★ ★ ★ ★ ★ ★

THE WORLD CLOSE BY
"The heartbeat of the Army is the corps."

On Sundays when General Burrows is not traveling abroad, she often preaches at corps in the United Kingdom. She believes the corps to be the core of The Salvation Army, where the basic spiritual results occur that give the Army its vitality and the ongoing recruitment of personnel. For the Salvationists, the corps is their church home, their place of spiritual nurture and service. In a visit to a flourishing East London Corps in Romford, she said, "Where the corps is strong, the Army is strong. The heartbeat of the Army is the corps."

Burrows maintains her soldiership—church membership—at the Regent Hall Corps in London, commonly known as "The Rink." When not traveling or speaking elsewhere she attends there to worship, not as the General but as a soldier. She enjoys telling the story of a night when the soldiers went to conduct an open-air meeting just before their evening indoor service. The young Salvationist assigned to lead the street meeting asked her to lead the closing song. She said she would be glad to do so. The open-air meeting progressed well and then when it came time for her participation, the leader announced, "And now one of our *soldiers* will lead us in our closing song."

Whenever Burrows preaches in the United Kingdom, it is to a full and often overflowing attendance. "She can fill any Army hall here in Britain when she does a meeting," says Commissioner Larsson of her visits to the United Kingdom Territory. "People revere her. They will travel miles to see and hear Eva Burrows."

Modulating the Message

Burrows has the skill of modulating her message to her setting and audience. While speaking at the corps in Norwich she drew from Mother Julian of Norwich, describing the fourteenth-century mystic as one of her spiritual heroines. She said that because of Julian's devotion to God and practical concern for people, she would have made a good Salvationist.

In Gloucester, the General conducted anniversary meetings 107 years to the day after the first Army meeting in that city. Having done her homework before the visit, she took delight in reminding the packed hall of Salvationists that the corps had been opened by a woman. She also revealed that the Founder, following his first review of his Gloucester forces, said he anticipated that they would prove to be "thoroughly reliable in the hour of battle." As she enrolled new soldiers, led in worship sessions, and listened to dramatic testimonies by recent "trophies of grace," she said that evaluation was still true.

In her visits to Liverpool and Birmingham, great industrial centers of the United Kingdom, she again tailored her message to the setting, preaching a "holiness for the factory." Speaking to overflow crowds she challenged, "We all accept holiness as a spiritual ideal, but there are many who are not convinced that it is an attainable experience. Holiness is much more than a code of spiritual etiquette. It is more concerned with what you are than with what you do. It is as much for the factory floor as for the monk's cell."

In January 1987 General Burrows took part in a discussion on religious music on the BBC Radio program, *Opinions*. In her remarks she emphasized, "We have music with a message—and the message is more important than the music. Words are very significant in Christian music. Salvation Army bands will be out playing in the streets and when people hear them it is the connection with the words to the melody that stirs their hearts or moves them towards God."

In a visit to Nottingham, the birthplace of William Booth that has become known as "the Founder's City," she shared that wherever she was in the Army world, she had a sense of the Founder looking over her shoulder. "Tonight, he really is!" she quipped, pointing to the painting of William Booth hanging on the wall behind her.

Also in Nottingham, she prayed with an estimated 1 million people when interviewed on BBC Radio. The popular daily live broad-

With the Archbishop
of Canterbury,
Dr. Robert Runcie,
at Lambeth Palace
in September 1987.

cast invited listeners to telephone and ask questions of the General. Her response was "articulate, sometimes humorous, and always concerned, as she spoke easily and informally about her commitment to God and the Army." One listener exclaimed, "It's better than all the film stars!" The presenter took the unprecedented step of asking the General to pray with his listeners, which she gladly did.

In May 1988 General Burrows was among eight guests of Her Majesty Queen Elizabeth of England at an informal luncheon held at Buckingham Palace. In October 1988 General Burrows was a featured speaker in the historic Guildhall of London, the event hosted by the Lord Mayor of London. In her Bible message to the civic leaders, she appealed for justice to be measured with mercy.

Return to Portsmouth

Eva returned in August 1987 to the Portsmouth Corps, her first appointment as a Salvation Army officer. Upon her entrance to the rally, the over 1,000 persons gathered ignored the notices on the doors of the rented education center which read, "Silence, exam in progress," according a deafening applause to their "Lieutenant" who now returned as their General. "Portsmouth 87," a march written for the occasion, includes the Australian melody "Waltzing Matilda."

In the Sunday morning service at the Portsmouth Citadel Corps, Burrows indulged in nostalgia. From that very platform in 1951 she had preached her first sermon as a Salvation Army officer. She recalled with admiration the faithful example of the corps officer at that time, Captain Lilian Glase, now over eighty years of age and in the audience as a retired Colonel. Following her sermon, chairs had to be used to extend the mercy seat for the large number of seekers who responded.

The "Heart of Methodism"

General Burrows was invited as guest preacher at a commemorative service that marked the 200th anniversary of the death of John Wesley, held at Methodist Central Hall in Westminster. At this heart of world Methodism, she urged the 800-strong congregation to rededicate themselves to the purpose of proclaiming Christ. She described John Wesley as "a great evangelist," and in a reference to his journals, quoted his phrase, "I offered them Christ." Stressing the words of the Apostle Paul, she said the Christian message was summed up in the words, "We preach Christ crucified." The Superintendent Minister who led the service remarked at the end of her message, "We have been brought to the heart of the Gospel." A few days before Christmas of 1989, General Burrows preached in Wesley's Chapel, the mother church of world Methodism, where Wesley had often preached. She spoke on the many links between Salvationists and Methodists.

Christmas Cheer

On Christmas of 1989 Burrows visited five Army institutions in and around London. Accompanying her was well-known Army musician, Major Joy Webb. They started with a 10:30 A.M. visit to a children's home, spent the afternoon in the company of homeless men at three of the Army's hostels. At 5:30 P.M. they concluded with reminiscences of Christmas in Africa with a group of retired officers.

On a former Christmas Day, she had visited a women's hostel in Dundee, Scotland, and was told that all the women were lonely, lacking any family or friends, with no one to look after them but the Army. She noticed one woman had a Christmas card on her locker and said to the officer, "There's someone who has a friend who cares for her, surely?" "No," the officer replied. "She sent that Christmas card to herself knowing no one else would be sending any." For Burrows, it was a poignant moment.

In her preachment on an Advent Sunday, she said, "If Christmas began in the heart of God, it finds its completion only in the heart of man. Just as His coming into the world changed the world, so His coming to us in a personal way can change our lives."

Going Forward in the U.K.

"The condition for growth is total surrender to Jesus Christ," challenged General Burrows at the British Territory Congress in June 1988. In response, people queued for places to kneel as seekers streamed forward. Many were accompanied by friends; married couples knelt together, fathers and sons, mothers and daughters, some coming in twos and others alone, all responding to God's revealed will for their lives. Burrows moved among them, encouraging them in their dedications.

"Irrevocably place yourself on God's altar; abandon every other ambition! Put yourself at God's disposal," was the charge made by General Burrows as she commissioned the cadets at the first commissioning for the new United Kingdom Territory in June 1991.

"Don't be a chameleon Christian, changing your color according to the company you keep," challenged General Burrows at the East Midlands Celebration Congress in Northhampton. "Jesus, who moved among the most sordid yet remained pure and attractive, does not want His followers to be crushed or molded by a godless world." The many who indicated their personal commitment to Christ gave evidence of the serious response to the General's message.

9 Million Viewers in the Living Room

Imagine having 9 million people with you in your living room! That is the estimated number of viewers who saw Burrows at home on BBC's "Home on Sunday" telecast in London. Captain Rob Garrad, then director of the Army's information services, describes the scene of chaos that overtook the General's quarters. "The seven-man television crew were up and down the stairs, bringing in endless lengths of cable, lights, monitors, sound recording equipment, and cameras. Within minutes, a home lounge looked like a Hollywood set."

The producer was so delighted with the General's participation that she immediately invited her to be the speaker in one of the program's next series. Captain Garrad summarizes, "The letters which came to me and to the producer give clear indication that such programs are wonderfully used by God to bring encouragement, uplift, inspiration, and challenge to many people."

The Extended Family

More than 400 young Salvationists from thirteen countries crowded into the venue in Cologne, Germany in June 1989 for the Army's first European Youth Congress. The theme was "Vision for a New Generation." The exuberance of youth marked the four-day series of Bible study, interest groups, fellowship, pageantry and praise. General Burrows challenged the young people to ask God, "What do You want me to do? Discover what He wants, because He has a clear answer for you.

In April 1992, during a resurgence of street violence in Northern Ireland, General Burrows told the 1,200 Salvationists present at a rally that their example was a bright light to their comrades throughout the world. She expressed her gratitude that The Salvation Army was still free to march in the streets and proclaim the Gospel in Ireland. "Politicians won't save the world!" she continued. "No political ideology will save us. People need to be saved from sin, from hopelessness, from themselves, from their obsession with things. Only Jesus can do that.

Wherever Eva Burrows has served, the people of that land have claimed her as their own. On her first visit to Scotland as international leader, the people received her as back among "her ain folk." As a citizen of the world, Burrows has found herself in an easy consanguinity with her brothers and sisters in Christ around the world. As the leader of a global movement, the world became her home and its people her extended family.

29

★ ★ ★ ★ ★ ★ ★ ★ ★ ★ ★ ★ ★ ★ ★ ★ ★ ★

RETURN TO AFRICA

*"The spirituality of the African people
is part of their very being, unlike our secular,
materialistic Western culture."*

The unmistakable African drumbeat filled the air at the airport, and beaming faces were everywhere. Zimbabwean Salvationists had come out in September 1987 to welcome back their former teacher, now their General. They considered her a "General made in Zimbabwe," where she had spent the formative years of her officership.

Her delight was just as apparent as throughout her stay she met person after person whom she had trained, now in their forties and fifties. They were especially pleased, when after all those years, she remembered their names. A good number had become teachers and headmasters, and quite a few were in business and politics. She was pleased that her Shona language came back to her, although she had not used it for eighteen years.

Zimbabwe hosts a virile Salvation Army and also the brightest jewel of Africa's natural treasures — the incomparable Victoria Falls. Thousands of Salvationists turned out in force for the Territorial Congress. On Sunday, columns upon columns of marching Salvationists smartly clad in cream uniforms took forty-five minutes to pass by the General on the reviewing stand.

At Howard Institute with its 850 students (650 of them boarders), the headmaster, Robson Kanyepi, was a graduate of the secondary teacher training course under Eva Burrows, as was the headmaster at Usher. "When I stood on the platform at Howard," said Burrows, "and looked at over 800 faces, suddenly a great spirit of joy welled up inside of me. I felt at home again."

On her return to Usher with its 408 girl boarders, where she had served as principal, the students lined up on either side as an honor guard. The General was pleased to see the hall she had built at Usher now "crowded with those marvelous black faces looking up at me. It was a very emotional experience." Usher was maintaining the tradition started years earlier by the young Burrows, of achieving the highest marks in the country.

Four thousand Salvationists in Zimbabwe had been lost through killings and abductions during the unrest of the 1970s. "You suffered from the war. You lost many loved ones," said Burrows, who had known some of the victims personally from her teaching days in that country. "They died for their faith. Yet the Army is advancing. What we need now are soldiers who will live for their faith, with love and holy living." In each meeting streams of people poured forward to the mercy seat even before the invitation, and at the last Congress meeting virtually the entire congregation moved forward in dedication.

The General and her party made a visit to the graves of Sharon Swindells and Lieutenant Diane Thompson, who were murdered when Usher Institute was attacked by terrorists in the unrest of June 1978. Sharing moving moments of prayer, especially for the girls' parents, she laid a wreath to the memory of "two fine young Salvationists."

In April 1991 Burrows again visited Zimbabwe for its Centennial Congress that drew attendances totaling over 95,000 for the week-long series of meetings. The African Army set some records on Easter weekend with its 1,800 massed senior timbrelists, 800 songsters, and 600 hosho players participating in the meetings.

Centennial celebrations were held with pomp and ceremony in the august cathedrals of Harare and Bulawayo, and with exhilaration in Harare's ultra modern Conference Center and National Sports Stadium, the latter accommodating the over 15,000 gathered on Easter Sunday. A stream of over 10,000 Salvationists, with bands and banners, songs and salutes, marched past their international leader in a stirring parade under the warm African sun on a brilliant Easter morning. Smartly uniformed, one would not have known that many of them had traveled far on foot, and had slept the past nights on the ground or a school floor. They were marching into their second century as they proudly saluted their international leader.

Audience with President Mugabe

Burrows' visit to Zimbabwe in 1987 included an audience with Prime Minister Robert Mugabe. The visit was arranged by Mrs.

General Eva Burrows places a wreath and leads in prayer at the grave of the two Salvationist martyrs in Zimbabwe.

Joyce Mujuru, a uniformed Salvationist who is Mr. Mugabe's minister of state for community development and women's affairs. She herself was a student at Howard Institute in the early 1970s and is the wife of the head of Zimbabwe's armed forces.

Mugabe had been elected in 1980 when rule passed from the nation's 220,000 whites to its 7.2 million blacks. Like many other leaders of former colonies, Mugabe graduated from the British penal system—literally having earned two university degrees during his ten years in detention.

The Salvation Army's vital contribution to the life of Zimbabwe was acknowledged by the Prime Minister when he received General Burrows at his Harare home. The two leaders discussed how the Army could best continue to serve the needs of Zimbabwe, with Mr. Mugabe recognizing the General's contribution to the life of his nation. The African people were a spiritual people, he said, acknowledging the importance of spiritual ministry.

On her return visit in 1991, Mugabe was President of the country and granted her a private interview, after which he addressed the Army's Centennial Congress. Some 4,000 exuberant Salvationists in Harare's modern conference complex heard his speech commending

General Eva Burrows with Prime Minister Robert Mugabe of Zimbabwe in 1988.

the Army and its contribution to his country. He expressed profound appreciation for the service Burrows herself had rendered as a missionary.

In a world where freedom of worship should not be taken for granted, he said, "The church must be totally free and independent to cater to the spiritual needs of the society. Our view is, let us hold hands. We do the physical, you do the spiritual, and we together do the intellectual." He contrasted the Army's service in Zimbabwe with the early colonial exploitation and said, "For many years The Salvation Army has rendered a service we can never forget, a service that we hope shall continue to exert its influence on our people. May the 100 years you are celebrating today yield a model we can follow, for your service in Zimbabwe has been truly immaculate."

Her Students Remember
One of Burrows' greatest joys in her return visits to Zimbabwe was meeting former students and seeing how successful they had become in their professions. Many now hold high positions in education and

other professions. Without exception, they paid high tribute to the salutary impact on their lives by their former teacher.

Envoy David Ndoda of Matabeleland, Zimbabwe shares, "Many of the General's former students at Howard are today headmasters in government and private schools. They remember well the General's ability to discipline her class. They all claim they have no discipline problems at their schools because they apply the General's method of dealing with the individual rather than the whole class."

Lezinah Sibanda, former student of Burrows at Usher, is a lecturer at the Hotel School in the Bulawayo Polytechnic in Zimbabwe, with a Master of Science Degree in Hotel and Catering Management from Ulster University in Ireland. She says, "It was because of Eva Burrows' gift in teaching that math was one of my favorite subjects. Outside class she was like a mother to me When I had to stay at school for treatment when I was suffering from T.B., she always called to check on me. She was a disciplinarian, but always with a smile. Although without any children of her own, she has been an exemplary mother to many. To me she is an example of a true Christian—so loving, caring and happy. I am glad she made it to General. She deserved it."

When General Burrows visited Malawi, Ruth Nthubula ran to her and greeted her with an embrace that almost bowled her over. Mrs. Nthubula is the wife and mother of a fine Christian family, and a church leader. As managing director of a large building company and with leadership in national trade associations, she holds one of the top business positions for a woman in Malawi. She recalls, "Eva Burrows used to encourage us that there is nothing a man can do which a woman cannot do. She was a mother who showed her love to each and everyone. In 1968 when my father passed away and it seemed I would have to leave school, she paid my Form 2 school fees. She was a good teacher, as proved by our having the best math results in all of Southern Rhodesia. She gave me a good foundation and that is why I am where I am today."

Elias Marere from Zimbabwe, shares, "My family was so poor that they could not get simple things like clothing and good food." But Elias was a top student in school and earned the opportunity to go to the Teacher Training Course at Howard Institute. He recalls, "Eva Burrows, as my teacher and corps officer, taught me to be smart, quick, hardworking, and to put Jesus first in all I did. She was strict but fair in her dealings with the students. She taught students good table manners by inviting them to her house, a few at a time. She spent much time with African students and in the villages, learned the African Shona language and African customs, and enjoyed the African food.

"At Howard there were many desperately poor students who could not secure enough money to complete the teaching course. Eva Burrows would find some work for them to do, like cleaning her bicycle, washing windows, or watering her small garden. Then she would give them some money from her meager earnings to help with school fees.

"As an evangelist she influenced all her students about the supremacy of Jesus Christ. She set a high standard for Salvation Army leadership. Men and women she taught were not surprised with her election to the highest office in The Salvation Army world."

Elias Marere received his Teacher's Training Certification at Howard Institute in 1956. After a successful term as a Headmaster, he became Schools Manager and is responsible for thirty schools with 930 students and twenty-three teachers in the Mazowe District of Zimbabwe. He is also a corps and divisional Songster Leader, and with the Zimbabwe Songsters attended the Army's 1990 International Congress in London. He says, "In my work as a teacher, I endeavor to influence my teachers, children, and the community to put God first in whatever they do."

At Front Lines in Zambia

Burrows' travels took her to Zambia in November of 1987. In Lusaka she noted that the economy was desperate and that Lusaka, the capital city, looked "rather frayed at the edges." The Army headquarters and other compounds, as well as the leaders' quarters, had to be protected from robbers by a ten-foot wall with broken glass on top. The living quarters of Colonel and Mrs. William Norris, territorial leaders, had been broken into with much personal loss, and now had two watchdogs and a guard stationed overnight. The General was informed that thievery and robbery were the order of the day.

In Lusaka she commissioned a record number of cadets for Zambia. "A commitment to Christ makes for a better person, and better people make a better world," said General Burrows in a TV interview for the Zambian people. A Salvationist rally with 2,000 in attendance resulted in "a tremendous response at the mercy seat." She writes, "A big hit of the meeting was the playing of the hoshos by the twenty-six officers who had come from the Malawi division. The simple movements and the rhythm of the shaking of these seed-filled gourds has a tremendous effect. They are wonderful musical bands, because in the village corps both men and women, old and young, can all be members."

A highlight was her visit to the Army's famous mission station at Chikankata. She was billeted at the home of the Matron, Major Ruth Schoch, who has served there for over twenty years, working with the lepers and more recently with people with AIDS. A U.S.A. *War Cry* feature called Major Schoch "the Mother Teresa of The Salvation Army." General Burrows records, "What a beautiful Christian she is and what a powerful spiritual influence she has, not only in the nurses' school but throughout the hospital itself. Everyone acknowledges her Christlike character and spiritual power."

An evening meal was at the quarters of Lieutenant (Dr.) and Mrs. Ian Campbell with a helpful discussion on the AIDS program at Chikankata, a model throughout the world. The visit was also marked with the dedication of the new leprosy ward.

President Kaunda's Life Saved by SA

With the territorial leaders, General Burrows attended a luncheon given in her honor at the State House in the capital city of Lusaka, by the President of Zambia, Dr. Kenneth Kaunda. She recorded, "At 12 noon we entered this stately home and from the windows looked out on acres of green lawn. We could see deer, impala, and other beautiful animals grazing, with peacocks, guinea fowl and other lovely birds in the garden. Around the walls were magnificent paintings and fine sculptured pieces."

The General and her party were assembled in the State Room when the President came in and greeted them warmly. "I owe The Salvation Army my life," he announced. He went on to explain that when he was a leader of the African people against the colonial government, he was badly injured and his cohorts, because of the dangers to him, would not trust any hospital except the Army's, saying, "We won't take you to any hospital but the Chikankata (Salvation Army) hospital." He described how The Salvation Army had provided medical care at this critical stage of his political career. Colonel (Dr.) Sidney Gauntlett was at Chikankata then and President Kaunda said, "He saved my life and he became my friend."

General Burrows responded with appreciation for his reception and spoke of the Army's rationale and of its work around the world. He obviously warmed to the fact that Burrows herself had spent so many years in Africa. Following the meal and conversation, they were invited to take coffee in the adjoining room with the President pouring the coffee or tea for everyone present, "rather a beautiful gesture," recalls Burrows.

More Than 1,000 Decisions in Nairobi

On her visit to Nairobi in November of 1987, she was especially moved by the blind students at the Army's Thika High School and Primary School. She saw the students in their classroom and was interested to discover that 50 percent of them go on to the university. The General was inspired by the worship service, noting that the organist was blind and all the students were singing from Braille songbooks. She was equally impressed among the visually handicapped at Vision Village and at the Army's Joytown Primary and Secondary School to see hundreds of small children with handicaps and in wheelchairs having the opportunity to learn and find a future.

"The Congress march of over 10,000 Salvationists past the stadium had to be seen to be believed," records the General. From the raised viewing platform on which she stood, thousands of smartly groomed Salvationists in white uniforms marched past. She held her arm up in The Salvation Army salute. The march took a long time and after a period the Territorial Commander, Colonel Angoya, obviously sensed the General's arm was tired. Burrows felt his hand come under her right arm to support her. She has recounted that story many times to illustrate how Salvationists around the world sustain her in the heavy responsibilities she carries.

Following her message there was the movement forward, like the blowing of the wind across a field of wheat, of over 1,000 Salvationists who knelt at the place of dedication. The altar soon was overcrowded, and seekers knelt on the grass and then on the running track as far as one could see. Burrows commented, "No one present at that meeting will ever forget it."

Tricolor Raised in Liberia

A call came from Liberia asking the Army to receive some 2,000 members of a group that called themselves "The Salvation Army Church of Liberia." Major John Amoah was dispatched to survey the situation. Discussions were held on the Army's doctrine, polity, and such matters as its position on the sacraments. Legal, financial, and other matters were carefully assessed and, with all prospects positive, in 1988 Liberia was added to the roster of countries where the Army tricolor was raised.

Ghana's Joyful and Devout Salvationists
Under a peerless blue Ghanaian sky at the Accra airport, 2,000 Salvationists in gleaming white uniforms were on hand to greet their General when she arrived at 6:30 A.M., their welcome festooned with flag-waving, band music, singing, and dancing. There were shouts of jubilation when the General informed the crowd that it was the largest group that had ever met her in any country of the world, as she came for this week-long visit in November 1988.

One meeting venue became a vast sea of dancing Salvationists at various times during the Congress. The receiving of the offering was accompanied by some twenty-five minutes of an exuberant exhibition of thanksgiving to God. Among them was a 103-year-old officer who "danced with as much verve as anyone." The General and her ADC were captured by the spirit of joy and joined in the dance to everyone's delight. Later the television newscast featured not only excerpts of the General's preaching but also some of her dancing with the comrades.

A dramatic moment of the welcome meeting was the presentation of a new flag to the delegation from Liberia for their recently opened work. They received a tumultuous welcome as it was announced that already 400 soldiers had been enrolled and many more recruits were in training.

Burrows recorded, "I have been impressed by the devoutness and strong faith of Salvationists here. They are not just happy dancers before the Lord. They are very reverent in prayer, listen most intently to the messages, adding their resounding 'amen' or 'hallelujah.' The words which received the loudest hallelujah responses were expressions indicating a victory over the devil. No doubt Satan's existence is a reality here. As the days passed, I became more impressed by their fervor and devotion, the sincerity and genuineness of their faith and vibrant salvationism. To say that I enjoyed being with them is a great understatement. I was reminded again of the spirituality of the African people. It is part of their very being, unlike our secular, materialistic Western culture."

At the Officers' Councils she was told by the 103-year-old retired officer that she had bought a new uniform for the Congress. She was impressed with the Army's extensive medical and educational work and overall social program in Ghana.

Multilingual Nigeria

When General Burrows was welcomed to Lagos, Nigeria in November 1988, she was enthusiastically greeted in English and also in the principal tongues of the country — Ibo, Hausa, Yoruba, and Efik. She responded, amid deafening applause, with Yoruba words learned for the occasion. During her visit she presented a substantial sum toward the completion of needed buildings.

"Global Parent" in East Africa

More than 35,000 people attended meetings and seekers numbered over 1,000 during a very busy five-day campaign in three countries of East Africa in September 1989. In eastern Kenya 15,000 Salvationists marched past the General, preceding a series of meetings with many seekers.

On Sunday morning she departed early via a small private aircraft for a village in western Kenya. The journey had an element of drama when the pilot had difficulty in locating his destination. Spotting the thousands of white-uniformed Salvationists on the ground, Burrows helped the pilot find his destination. Eventually on landing, the General was warmly welcomed and took the salute at another large march before ministering to a congregation of 20,000 Salvationists.

Next on the General's itinerary was a lengthy car journey, over rough roads to Uganda, where the Army's work is very much smaller than in neighboring Kenya. Nearly 500 Salvationists greeted her, some having traveled for three days to witness the first visit of a General in office for a quarter of a century. It was also many years since a General had visited Tanzania. Even though she had only a few hours available, Burrows went to encourage the Salvationists there.

In January 1991 General Burrows made her second visit to East Africa where the Army is growing faster than anywhere else in the world, with 126,000 senior soldiers, 131,000 junior soldiers, and 2,500 soldiers in Nairobi at the largest Army corps. The Army's schools and a workshop for the blind in the Territory that cares for 1,100 blind and 700 handicapped persons were visited. She addressed a rally of over 4,000 persons, where 1,500 came forward in dedication.

With President Daniel T. arap Moi of Kenya, September 1989.

A lay leader of the Army introduced her in meticulous English and coined a new phrase to describe the international leader. He called her "the global parent." In response she expressed appreciation for that term and adopted it as an apt description of the General, a global parent of the multiracial and multilingual family, with wide cultural differences, but all bound together in the love of Christ and a commitment to the Army's principles and practice.

In Nairobi both in 1989 and 1991, General Burrows was granted an audience at the State House with the President of Kenya, His Excellency Daniel T. arap Moi. The President shared his personal faith in Christ and expressed his willingness to assist in fund-raising projects for a new training college in Nairobi. They discussed the Christian faith, the Army's work in Nairobi, and General Burrows prayed for the President and his country.

The Congo's Quality and Vitality

General Burrows' first visit to the People's Republic of Congo in September 1989 left strong impressions. Broad smiles greeted the General as she addressed brief words of introduction in French (the official language of the country), and then in English to the 4,000 who had gathered. "The Congolese," commented the General, "have the best smiles in the world. Salvationists in the Congo are quite sophisticated and their French is impeccable."

Music in the meetings was excellent. The territorial band in Brazzaville played the latest Salvation Army music from full score and could play African music with great style and fascinating rhythm without any score at all! The songsters were at times brilliant and the timbrelists can only be described as fantastic. The standard of musicianship everywhere was quite amazing.

"What impressed me about the Salvationists here is their spiritual depth, noted particularly in the quality of their prayers. Similarly, their testimonies were some of the finest I have heard anywhere in the world." Burrows was interested to note the unique position of "Social Sergeant" in the corps—those involved in compassionate work in the community. She opened a new corps at Makelekele, situated right on the Congo River, that has 600 soldiers on the roll and a Lieutenant as a corps officer. "There are a great many corps of this size in Congo," she observes. She discovered that long meetings were enjoyed in the Congo, with some continuing for over four hours. Included in her visit to the Congo was an interview with Prime Minister Alphonse Souchlaty Poaty.

Zaire and Its Generous President
A congregation of an estimated 30,000 Salvationists gathered for their meeting with General Burrows in Zaire in September of 1989. She visited the Army's Center for the Handicapped, an Army secondary school, its new maternity hospital and its Health Center where daily treatment is given to tuberculosis patients, diabetics, and malnourished children. In response to her messages, many moved forward to accept Christ or renew their vows to Him.

She was received by the President of Zaire, Marshal Mobutu Sese Seko, on his boat on the Bateke plateau. During the visit the President made a generous donation to the Army's work of 60 million zaire (over $100,000). At the end of their meeting the General prayed with the President.

Malawi—the "Warm Heart of Africa"
In March of 1991 Burrows made her first visit to Malawi, "the warm heart of Africa." She found that the country's sobriquet refers to

General Eva Burrows at the Mkwayi refugee camp in Malawi, with Colonel Henry Gariepy, Captain Steady Mwanza and Lt. Colonel Jean Issitt.

In 1991 visit to Zimbabwe, General Burrows, with Major John Amoah greets students of Howard Institute.

more than the central geography and tropical climate of this republic. Its Army of Salvationists thrives on smiles, friendliness, and a joyful spirit. This landlocked country of 8 million people, cradled among its towering mountains, sparkling lakes, tropical forests, and emerald green plateaus, takes pride in being a country of peace since its independence in 1964. Her visit to Malawi marked her fifty-first country visited since taking office.

She dedicated a new extension training center, planted a tree, and toured the Army's agricultural and aquacultural projects, which serve as practical ministries in that agrarian economy. At Blantyre, some of the Salvationists had walked sixty-five miles to attend the Congress.

A visit was made to the Mkwayi Refugee Camp in Malawi that hosts 10,069 refugees—2,000-plus families who live in this otherwise barren wasteland. She met with government relief workers, medical staff, and Salvationists where the Army has responsibility for 500 refugees, a feeding program, training in making sun-dried bricks and building homes (huts), growing food, and helping with the training of children. She visited a class among the 682 children three to six years old, in a simple school building provided by the Army, with no desks or chairs. Known for her lack of interest for shopping, she nevertheless went "on a shopping spree" as she moved among the tables of handcrafts and simple articles the refugees had made.

From the stark setting of the refugee camp, her journey next led to the presidential palace of Malawi, with its manicured lawns, exotic landscapes, and breathtaking vistas. Ushered into the presidential conference room, General Burrows awaited the formal entrance of the Life-President of Malawi, Ngwazi Dr. H. Kamuzu Banda. Dressed in white uniform—the Army's color for that warm country, and with white shoes, gloves, and purse, Burrows herself made a regal appearance. Spread out on the table at which they sat was a large leopard skin, the symbol of speed and strength adopted by Dr. Banda in his early years.

President Banda, age eighty-five, one of the longest-serving heads of state in the world, had been the sole leader of this former British protectorate since it gained independence in 1964. "I believe in partnership between the church and state," said the President. He added, "The church takes care of the religious side of our people while the state takes care of the political, social, and economic side." In a warm and friendly exchange, General Burrows commended the country's unity and freedom of worship. She cited the Army's involvement in

General Burrows reviews her notes with translator prior to a meeting in Africa.

Saluting Salvationists on the march through a cornfield in Malawi.

that country in such practical projects as tree planting, pig rearing, and assisting Mozambican refugees fleeing to Malawi. She also reported on the Army's help to people recently afflicted by a devastating flood. Malawi, a country without television, devoted half of the front page of the country's widely read newspaper to a photo of the President with the General and a report of the visit.

Dr. Banda readily consented to Burrows' offer to pray with him. She prayed for the President, his ministers, and the people of Malawi, and for continued political, social, economic, and spiritual stability. One official reporter, who had covered many audiences with the Life-President, shared with me, "This visit was unique." When I asked why, he replied, "It is the first time anyone has ever prayed with the Life-President."

South Africa

Burrows describes her meetings in South Africa in January 1988 with superlatives. Meeting halls had "wall to wall people" with multiracial congregations and Congress chorus, and the internationally acclaimed Soweto Songsters. The magnificent music and the spirit of

General Eva Burrows with Life-President of Malawi, Dr. H. Kamuzu Banda, March 1991.

the people and their movement to the mercy seat were a great blessing to her.

Her visit included the commissioning and ordination of the first multiracial session of cadets — blacks, coloureds, and whites — at the Army's integrated training college.

She was deeply impressed by the beauty of the country, including Cape Town, with a "peerless blue sky as the cloud nicknamed 'The Tablecloth' hung over the flat edge of Table Mountain." But she also saw the squalor in her visit to the notorious Crossroads shanty town. "It is unbelievable," she describes, "to see these thousands of shacks made from corrugated iron and bits of tin and wood, and thousands of tents where the homeless are being housed. I felt tremendous compassion for the people living in such squalor." At the end of that day she wrote, "It has been a very full, interesting and deeply satisfying day, though the sight of Crossroads Squatter Camp will never cease to disturb my mind and heart."

She recorded, "The all too plausible rationalization about the racial situation in South Africa is never convincing for me." She told of a public rally at Port Elizabeth with a multiracial band and mixed congregation. "Most memorable was the singing of the black Youth Chorus from Ciskei, smart in their uniforms. Before my message they sang a melody by Beethoven with the most beautiful words, concluding with, 'Wind of God, blow on me, even me.' It was most moving, and I could only pray in my heart that the white Christians and Salvationists present would join in that prayer, that the Holy Spirit would blow away their prejudice and preconceived ideas about their black brothers and sisters. At a meeting like this the different races are together in worship, but the situation in daily life is so different. At the conclusion of the meeting there were a good number kneeling at the altar — whites kneeling alongside black Salvationists. A beautiful sight, for at the foot of the cross the ground is always level.

"It is amazing to think that black professional people like doctors, university professors, lawyers, cannot live where they please, even though now salary scales are nondiscriminatory. One can imagine the resentment at having their professional skills acknowledged but not their value as human beings — with no vote and no say in the country in which they live."

On her return visit in the summer of 1991, more than 2,000 exuberant Salvationists, young and old, black and white, packed the historic Hall in Pietermaritzburg, South Africa, for the Congress celebrating the Centenary of the Army in Zululand. King Goodwill Zwelithini and his queen and entourage attended the event as they, with General Burrows, were greeted in traditional shield-and-spear fashion. Over 300 people reconsecrated their lives at the mercy seat and 110 new soldiers were enrolled.

Homecoming
Throughout her African journeys, Eva Burrows had come home – to the land and to the hearts of the people that had cast their spell upon her as a young Lieutenant.

30

★ ★ ★ ★ ★ ★ ★ ★ ★ ★ ★ ★ ★ ★ ★ ★ ★ ★ ★

CAMPAIGNING IN THE
AMERICAS AND CANADA
"The Salvation Army's hallmark
is evangelism with compassion."

General Burrows gave generously of her time to the U.S.A., its four territories comprising almost 20 percent of the officers in the world and giving over 60 percent of the critical support for world services.

Congresses and meetings with the General in the U.S.A. are characterized by use of modern technology and multimedia, precision planning with "briefs" that turn out to be books. In Chicago, Burrows noted, "I have never seen a Congress more thoroughly scripted. It took me four hours to review the 'brief.' "

The General is exploited somewhat mercilessly at American Congresses, with programs planned from breakfast to late evening, including annual meetings, officers councils, commissioning of cadets, presentations, service clubs, musicals, and special meetings with women, men, youth, retired officers, and other groups. Almost every meal is tied in with a program, including at one Congress official breakfasts on the three mornings that led her to request that no breakfast meetings be scheduled for Sundays.

In June of 1987, General Burrows led the U.S.A. Southern Territory's sixtieth-year celebration in Atlanta with over 5,000 delegates. She delighted her audience with her response in "Southernese"— "How y'all?"

In her enrollment of sixty-eight new soldiers, she charged, "In our *Articles of War* there is no credibility gap between belief and behavior. Our great need is for more holy-living, soul-saving soldiers." On Pentecost Sunday she commissioned forty-nine cadets and preached on our need for the Holy Spirit to indwell the Christian life. Sacramental moments at the altar culminated with 151 young men and women coming forward in response for full-time service.

Ed Turner had been a chronic alcoholic, living for his next drink. While in prison he discovered his artistic talent and took lessons. He was released as a client at the Army's Adult Rehabilitation Center and there retained sobriety. When his talent became known he was asked to paint a biblical scene of Christ. While painting he pondered for the first time what Christ must have been like. He thought of His manhood, His power, and most of all His compassion and love for the lost, and realized that Ed Turner was included in that company. His painting of the face of Christ led him to turn his life over to Him.

Later when he saw a photo of General Burrows he did a charcoal sketch of her. His leaders were impressed and arranged for him to attend the Congress in Atlanta and present it to the General. Burrows was moved by his story and art and bestowed a "royal kiss" on Ed. He said to his peers after that, "Imagine, she kissed the likes of me. The General is the sweetest, most lovely lady I have met. She shows the light of Christ."

General Burrows' storied compassion became a part of the legend of her visits. After a long day during the 1987 Western Territorial Congress, she asked to be taken to 'cardboard city,' the street abode of the homeless in Los Angeles, so she could meet the people and see the Army's ministry among the destitute. There she mingled with and encouraged the homeless and hungry. Her visit was also a reminder to the Army in America that its parish must always embrace the hurting and lost of society. Later she preached with an unquestioned authority, "Stand up and be counted for Christ. Don't be an anonymous Christian. Don't watch hurting people from a distance. Get involved."

In October 1987, General Burrows attended a two-day working session of the triennial meeting of the Commissioners' Conference at U.S.A. National Headquarters. It was the first time a General shared in the full working agenda of this conference, its ten-person membership comprising the national and policy-making leadership of The Salvation Army in the U.S.A. Commissioner Andrew S. Miller, then National Commander said, "General Burrows manifested an astute grasp and insight into the complex and substantive agenda items. Her active participation was very helpful to her knowledge of our conference — its process, personnel and concerns. We are profoundly

The General digs in for a groundbreaking of new Army facilities.

grateful for her investment of time and thought to share meaningfully with us in this way."

"To accompany General Burrows," said one American Commissioner, "is akin to being caught in the eye of a hurricane, in a whirlwind of activity." In June 1988 General Burrows had thirty-two speaking engagements through two unsparing schedules of the U.S.A. Central and Eastern Congresses. Having come from three other recent congresses, her daunting itinerary had her speaking sixty-four times in five and-one-half weeks. Yet she rose to each occasion with spiritual energy, pulpit eloquence, remarkable rapport, and a Spirit-anointed ministry. When asked how she does it, she acknowledges the grace received from prayer on her behalf around the world, saying, "Prayer sustains me and people nourish me."

At the 1988 U.S.A. Central Territory's Congress in Chicago with 5,200 delegates, Burrows was impressed with the testimony at the Women's Rally of a Salvationist in her early forties who had been in prison for attempted murder. A Salvationist who visits the prison had helped her to find salvation in Christ. From that time she became a significant influence in the prison, and following her release came to work for the Army and began a special ministry to prisoners and their wives. "She is an outstanding example," recorded the General, "of a 'miracle of grace.' "

In a surprise presentation, she admitted Envoy Walter McClintock to the *Order of the Founder*. A former alcoholic, the envoy was cited by Burrows for his extraordinary soul-winning ministry for the past fourteen years as director at the Chicago Harbor Light Center.

She was impressed by the Bible Bowl competitions for young people involving corps teams with study of specific books of Scripture with finalists competing at the Territorial Congress. "I was astounded," she records, "at the depth of knowledge of the Scriptures which the teams showed." Meeting with members of a Future Officer's Fellowship program that involves young people committed to full-time service, she noted that it is a program that "could be copied elsewhere."

More than 500 seekers were recorded in June 1988 when she conducted the U.S.A. Eastern Territorial "Blood and Fire" Congress at Ocean Grove, New Jersey, with delegates overflowing the cavernous 6,500-seat Great Auditorium that was festooned with flags and balloons. A dancing "kangaroo" sang "Welcome to the General!" to the tune of "Waltzing Matilda."

Delegates from the Adult Rehabilitation Centers (ARC), 646 strong, expressed what God had done for them, as they chanted in unison, "Redeemed! Redeemed! Redeemed by the Blood of the Lamb." Burrows often referred in her world travels to the blessing she received from the men in red blazers chanting that refrain. She considered it symbolic of the soul-saving work of the Army. At a breakfast meeting with over 700 ARC clients, she enrolled 103 as adherents, those who had been stabilized as converts and taken the preparation course.

At a Men's Rally she was presented as "a winsome woman with personality plus, as a witty woman, and as a wise woman." The somewhat boisterous crowd of 1,000 men greeted her with vigorous applause and whistling. "Thank you very much," she said in response. "It's a long time since I've been whistled at."

Following the Eastern Territorial Congress with 7,000 persons at Ocean Grove, the highly esteemed retired Lt. Colonel Lyell Rader, O.F., said to the General that he had not witnessed such an outpouring of the Holy Spirit on a territorial gathering since the time of General Albert Orsborn, over forty years earlier. Following these

Congresses in sequence, she said, "I could only rejoice at the hand of God's blessing upon us. Elation overflows within us."

Dr. Eva Burrows
In September 1988, General Eva Burrows arrived at Asbury College with its Georgian Colonial architecture, set in the rolling bluegrass hills of Kentucky, U.S.A. As her car pulled up on the campus at 10 P.M., she was enthusiastically greeted by members of the largest Salvation Army Student Fellowship (SASF) in the world. The eighty-one SASF members welcomed their world leader by waving miniature Army flags as its band played the strains of "O Boundless Salvation." Dr. Dennis Kinlaw, college president, was on hand to welcome Burrows, accompanied by the National Commander, Commissioner Andrew S. Miller who serves on Asbury's Board of Trustees.

The college auditorium was filled for the academic convocation that began the college's centennial celebrations. Attired in academic regalia with gown and hood with its signifying colors and chevrons, General Burrows was presented with an honorary doctor of laws degree. Dr. Kinlaw invited the General's family to stand and be recognized. The 500 Salvationists present stood in proud acclaim of their international leader. In her address she described the reciprocal strengths and traditions of Asbury College and The Salvation Army.

In a reception at The Salvation Army Student Center, she mingled with the students. Addressing them, she recalled her own early university days when she had rejected the Army and Christian teaching. "But," she said, "it was as a university student I came to make my total commitment to Jesus Christ." Speaking on Christ's words, "Learn of Me," she shared that from Christ we can learn head knowledge—intellectual development, hand knowledge—practical learning, and heart knowledge—love for Christ and others.

Two other honorary degrees were awarded to General Burrows in the U.S.—from Houghton College in New York, and Olivet Nazarene University in Illinois.

Ecumenical Gathering
In July 1989 General Burrows addressed *Congress 88* in Chicago, a national festival of evangelism attended by 2,000 delegates from over seventy denominations, including a delegation of evangelical Roman Catholics. The meeting in which she spoke was augmented with 900

*Dr. Eva Burrows —
recipient of four honorary
doctoral degrees.*

Salvationists and a large Army band that blended its brilliant brass with the hundreds of voices in the ecumenical choir.

"The Salvation Army's hallmark is evangelism with compassion, 'a Christianity with its sleeves rolled up,' " said Burrows in addressing the convocation. She graphically described global tragedies from firsthand observation—the carnage of the innocent, the millions dying of starvation, drug addicts flaked out on park benches, despairing victims of AIDS, and the plight of refugees. "Evangelicals do care," she affirmed, "and we must all work together to fulfill Christ's mission to the total needs of mankind."

Speaking with a prophetic voice to church leaders, she echoed the command of Jesus from the Parable of the Good Samaritan, "Go and do likewise," stating "It is costly to love like that." Burrows was one of many eminent speakers. At the end of her address, the assembly accorded the only standing ovation given at the Congress.

Capturing the Capital
In November 1990, it was reported that General Eva Burrows captured the capital city of the U.S.A. Speaking at the Army's annual

civic meeting in Washington, she quoted from President Bush's inaugural address, "This is the age of the offered hand." She said, "It is also the age of the offered hand for The Salvation Army—our hand being extended to wherever people are in need." She went on to describe scenes around the world where the Army's hand is offered to refugees, the homeless, AIDS patients, the alcoholic, drug offenders, the poor, and the unemployed.

In a press interview she was asked to comment on the recent dispute between the Army and the U.S. Labor Department with its demand for Army clients working in a rehabilitation program to be given minimum wage. She said, "I have never heard of anything so ridiculous, that men housed, fed, clothed, given medical, dental, and physical help, should be paid the minimum wage." She quipped, "It took a woman, (Elizabeth Dole, Secretary of Labor) to mediate the dispute."

A strong spiritual tone characterized General Burrows' meeting with President Ronald Reagan in the Oval Office at the White House in October 1986. At one point President Reagan noted that Abraham Lincoln once said, "There are many times when I went to my knees in prayer because there was no other place to go. And," added the President, "I often do the same thing."

With President Ronald Reagan at the White House in Washington, D.C., 1986.

Burrows concluded her visit by praying with President Reagan. In that moment the business of the Oval Office was hushed and the Chief Executive of the world's most powerful nation paused, while the General of God's Army prayed for a power greater than all the amassed weaponry, and for a wisdom higher than all the world's technology. Other generals who come to the White House may discuss war and conflict, but she came to pray for peace. It was just before Reagan's summit meeting with Soviet President Gorbachev in Reykjavik, and Burrows said, "I thought he needed some more prayer at that time." Reagan was said to have been visibly moved by her words. As the Salvationist leaders left the Oval Office, several White House staff commented on the lift the President had gained from the visit, one saying, "You made his day!"

It was a busy morning in November 1990 for President George Bush in Washington, D.C. On his agenda was a visit with a group of Russian diplomats at the time when the Persian Gulf crisis was smoldering. But the President took time to visit with General Burrows, along with the U.S.A. National Commander Commissioner James Osborne and Colonel Walter C. French, the Army's National Consultant who arranged the visit. The President spoke encouragingly of his appreciation for the Army and in a hushed moment in the Oval Office, they bowed their heads as Burrows prayed for the President to be granted wisdom in those days of crisis, and that peace and justice might be forged in the Middle East.

The time with President Bush was preceded by a visit with Mrs. Barbara Bush and the General's presentation to her of the Army's *Others* award. General Burrows expressed appreciation for her spontaneous support at Christmas for the Army's kettles in shopping malls. Some malls were prohibiting the use of the traditional kettle to raise funds for the Army's Christmas services to the poor. Mrs. Bush replied, "I wanted to do it, for I have always appreciated and admired The Salvation Army and its concern for those in need. Yours is the best kind of Army." They had a delightful visit in the beautiful sitting room. General Burrows found Mrs. Bush to be "warmhearted, natural, and people-centered."

Following coffee, Mrs Bush took the Army visitors for a tour of the private apartments, including the room where President Lincoln signed the Emancipation Proclamation that freed 4 million slaves. Burrows noted with special interest the desk at which he wrote the Gettysburg Address and the copy of this short but powerful message

Right: General Eva Burrows presents Others Award to Barbara Bush, at the White House, Washington, D.C., U.S.A., November 1990.

Below: General Burrows at the White House with President George Bush, U.S.A., accompanied by Commissioner James Osborne and Colonel Walter C. French, November 1990.

displayed in President Lincoln's own handwriting. "I was quite moved," said Burrows, "to read it again."

She reflected, "The private apartments of the President and his wife are quite magnificent—superbly decorated with breathtaking paintings, antique furniture, and glorious floral arrangements. Yet I was interested to see in the corner of one room a large box of children's toys—no doubt for the Bush grandchildren. I didn't find that incongruous."

Whirlwind Tour

In February 1991 General Burrows conducted a four-day whirlwind tour of five divisions of the U.S.A. Central Territory, speaking to 17,000 persons in a series of rallies and programs. During her tour she dedicated several new service facilities, shook hands with thousands of persons, met soldiers, officers, board members, talked one-on-one with homeless individuals on the street and in family shelters, hugged an abused child, and had instant rapport with all she met.

A highlight of her visit took place in the inner city of Detroit. An outdoor event launching a major new offensive against homelessness attracted an estimated 4,000 persons who jammed into and spilled over the grounds where a large tent was set up for the meeting. Homeless persons and low-income residents came, along with leaders of government, business, social service, and religious organizations. General Burrows was very much at home with the crowd that was revved up by the expression of the community's care for them. They voiced a spirited response to Burrows who stressed, "We hate homelessness, poverty, and unemployment. Every human being deserves a decent standard of living, accommodations, and work." Her talk elicited contrapuntal accompaniment of, "That's right! That's telling it like it is! Right on!" Burrows later observed, "These are our people. This is how the Army started and where we belong today."

In St. Louis she addressed 1,000 leading citizens and friends of the Army at an annual civic luncheon. She expressed her appreciation for the strong volunteerism that is a hallmark in America and gave an inspiring perspective on the worldwide mission of the Army. She declared, "We are an Army with no guns, but with an arsenal of love. We are fighting on the front lines of despair, the front lines of homelessness, the front lines of human tragedy." She spent an afternoon at the Army's home for abused and neglected children, and visiting and praying with one of the families in a transitional housing program.

General Burrows visits a family in the Army's Transitional Housing program in St. Louis, U.S.A.

She challenged her hearers at the various rallies to live out the excitement of life in Christ. Her visits were crowned by people making dedications to Christ.

The whirlwind tour concluded with addressing delegates to the Christian Management Association's convention in Chicago, on the topic, "Managing an International Organization in Turbulent Times." Commissioner James Osborne summed up her impact, "Neither the delights nor the demands of her high office have deterred her from the fundamental goals of The Salvation Army. It is an unusual individual who can remain close to people and yet possess more than adequate business acumen to effectively manage an international organization. We have such a leader in The Salvation Army today."

In June 1991 General Burrows commissioned forty-seven Cadets in the U.S.A. Western Territory, which has the only degree-granting accreditation for cadets in the Army world. In October 1992 she returned to that Territory for what she termed "a mini international Congress" as she looked out at the kaleidoscope of uniformed Laotians, Chinese, Hispanics, Marshalese, Indians, Koreans, Black Americans, and Anglos. The record-setting 6,000 persons came from the vast 15,000 mile span of the territory. Burrows' messages were translated in five languages, indicative of the cultural explosion and growth of the territory, which had just received sixty cadets in the present session.

Preceding the Congress Burrows became the first woman speaker in the twenty-five-year lectureship series of the School of World Mission of Fuller Theological Seminary which hosts 450 staff and 3,700 students representing 130 denominations and 78 countries. Burrows in four lectures set forth The Salvation Army's principles and strategies for Church Growth in the setting that has become the international training center on Church Growth. "The response from the students and staff was electric," stated Commissioner Paul A. Rader. "They were mesmerized by her remarkable grasp of the literature and her capacity to make principles practical in the context of the Army's experience in effective evangelism." Dr. J. Dudley Woodberry, dean of the school, said, "General Burrows effectively presented the principles of Church Growth, challenging us all with the need to blend these two mandates of the Gospel." A student said, "This was one speaker I wanted to hear and I was not disappointed." The lectures were taped and offered to the seminary's mailing list of 4,000 persons around the world.

"American giving for World Services is really phenomenal," observed Burrows. "We could not undertake the work we do in the Third World without them." The most recent report by Commissioner James Osborne, U.S.A. National Commander, was for the annual contribution to the Army's World Services of over $18 million, in addition to special projects.

Canada

A Thanksgiving Congress brought together 5,000 Salvationists and friends to Toronto from Eastern Canada and Bermuda in October of 1988, as hundreds publicly declared their allegiance to Christ and thousands were renewed in spirit.

It was a history-making occasion as three Salvationists were admitted to the *Order of the Founder,* two being the first married couple to be so honored at the same time. Corps Sergeant Major Don McBride and his wife, Joan, were honored for their thirteen years of service in Central and South America, where they had built houses for disaster victims with the help of teams of young Canadian Salvationists. Also admitted to the Order was Major Jean Brown (R), a Canadian officer, for her service among the destitute of Calcutta.

From Toronto General Burrows went on to Newfoundland, home of the greatest concentration of Salvationists in the vast Canada and Bermuda Territory. There she conducted fervent and full-to-overflowing meetings in the island province's three major cities.

In Bermuda's semitropical islands a deep awareness of God's presence was in evidence during the Congress conducted by General Burrows in October 1990, with glory dances, exuberant and rhythmic singing, and many life-changing decisions for Christ.

The Caribbean Territory

The Caribbean Territory, with its islands strung out like a pearl on a necklace, hosts sixteen of the countries and territories of the Army world. General Burrows came to this multinational and multicultural territory, and met in Jamaica with 2,000 delegates for their Centennial Congress in October 1987, described as a virtual hurricane of song and hallelujah praise.

As she walked through the streets and toured its poverty-stricken areas, she felt the destitution of people living in such squalor. Her itinerary took her to the Army's school for the blind and to the Army's hostel in Kingston where she helped serve dinner to the needy. She acutely feels the Army's great need for more personnel and money to address the critical conditions that she sees.

When in Jamaica for a zonal conference in 1990, Burrows visited and spoke in the church where her great-great-grandfather, a young Baptist missionary from England, had preached the Gospel more than 150 years earlier. In his honor she unveiled a plaque which marks the place where he is buried under the vestry of the church. Burrows challenged her listeners to look to the past to find encouragement for the present.

In November 1992 Burrows made her first journey to Cuba. She was greeted at the airport by the Minister of Religious Affairs, with their interview receiving generous coverage on television. Over 300 Salvationists and friends came to the meetings. Burrows was deeply impressed with the quality of spirit of the Cuban Salvationists who live and work in isolation from the rest of the Army world. Thirty-four young men and women attending a Future Officers' Fellowship program and five cadets committed for the next session greatly encouraged the General.

A request had been made for an interview with president Fidel Castro. No response was received until 9:20 P.M. on Sunday, follow-

General Burrows meets with President Fidel Castro in Havana, Cuba.

ing the day's meetings. Word then came that President Castro would see the General and her party at 10:20 P.M. President Castro asked many questions, showing keen interest in the Army and its theology, and its recent return to Russia. At the conclusion of the interview General Burrows requested permission to pray with the President. Castro consented and General Burrows prayed for him and his country. As the interview ended at 12:10 A.M., the President said, "Why are you leaving so early? You just came!"

Mexico and South America

General Burrows greeted the people in Spanish and won their hearts in a joyous Congress held in Mexico City in late 1989. Salvationists marched amid a colorful pageant of flags from the countries of the Territory—Mexico, Guatemala, El Salvador, Costa Rica, Panama, Venezuela, and Colombia. The Congress drew 925 delegates, and during the weekend 229 people made public decisions for Christ.

A reporter for General Burrows' visit to Santiago, Chile for the Territorial Congress recorded, "The General's presence, her pleasant smile and sense of humor, her personal contacts with the people, and her clear and profound Bible messages, made this a very special Congress." Commissioner Carl Eliasen, who had been a cadet with Burrows in what was designated "The Ambassadors" session, welcomed Burrows as "an ambassador of God for the world."

Salvationists in La Paz, Bolivia, the highest capital city in the world, responded enthusiastically to the visit of their General with the opening of a new corps, a communal meal, and a response of many seekers. On one trek in La Paz, at an altitude of 12,000 feet, oxygen and an officer trained in mouth-to-mouth resuscitation were kept readily available.

One new country to the Army's international roster began with an earthquake. The Army had "opened fire" in El Salvador following a major earthquake in October 1986. Salvationists from Guatemala immediately responded with shelter, food, clothing, medical help, and counseling. After the physical needs had been met, Salvationists stayed to minister to the spiritual needs of the people. The result was an active corps and social service outreach. General Burrows announced the official opening of the Army in El Salvador on April 1, 1989.

In the Americas, General Eva Burrows found and felt a strong and vibrant heartbeat of her worldwide Army.

31

★ ★ ★ ★ ★ ★ ★ ★ ★ ★ ★ ★ ★ ★ ★ ★ ★ ★ ★ ★

TO THE UTTERMOST
PARTS OF THE EARTH

"It is our business to be among the deepest hurts of our world."

Before Eva Burrows would finish her seven-year term, she would visit each of the movement's far-flung territories around the world. Her over 1 million miles of travel to sixty-one countries literally took her "to the uttermost parts of the earth."

Garlanded in India

Salvationists in the ageless land of India, where Christianity claims only 3 percent of the population, exuberantly greeted Eva Burrows as she came to proclaim Christ. Upon arrival in India in March 1987 she rode in an open jeep in a colorful procession through the streets of Bapatla for the start of her campaign in the India Madras and Andhra Territory. Preaching at a crowded public rally, she found her Indian hearers receptive to the Gospel with hundreds of seekers responding to her invitation to dedicate themselves to Christ.

Four thousand Salvationists gathered in January 1991 for the great welcome meeting of General Burrows to the South Eastern India Territory, under a most lavish, exquisite pandal (a marquee of thatched coconut leaves), with decorations and flags and lights galore. During the welcome song, in traditional South India style, dozens of people queued up to put garlands around her neck and present her with apples and limes, the last a sign of a long life. Indian Salvationists greatly enjoyed the fact that the General and her ADC wore the Indian uniform of a red-bordered sari. They also wore a special shawl around the neck to protect the uniform from the stains that could come from the flowers.

Always alert to using illustrations from the locale, she responded with the reminder that a servant of God should produce fruit for the kingdom and the hope that her visit would be productive for God. The Army, she said, was like the huge banyan tree of India—ever spreading, sheltering, and loving. In another meeting, referring to the deep waters of Cape Comorin, where three seas meet at the southernmost tip of India, she quoted the words of the Founder, "O boundless salvation, deep ocean of love." Christians should let God's ocean of love flow out, she said, to know God's forgiveness and cleansing in their lives.

The General and Lt. Colonel Issitt were billeted in the Army's well-known Nagercoil Catherine Booth Hospital. Burrows was impressed with the size and scope of the hospital and the long-term dedication of its staff. She witnessed the practical compassion of the Army's ministries in India as she visited the Vocational Training College for handicapped girls, the Tucker Girls Hostel for orphans, and some of the Army's many schools in India that train thousands of students.

Her itinerary included a visit to the Aramboly Vocational Training Centre which has a curriculum ranging from farming to technology. Burrows records, "I had looked forward to this visit because I wanted to meet Sundar Egbert, the director for over twenty years. Sundar, who has been handicapped by polio since the age of eleven, has received international awards for his work among the physically handicapped. Aramboly was truly amazing. The quality of work done from the workshops is of the highest standard. The men use precision tooling to make all kinds of objects, including fine wheelchairs, bicycles for the handicapped, beds, filing cabinets. They cannot keep pace with the orders, and Aramboly supports itself as well as making a profit."

Traveling on to Trivandrum in the India Southwestern Territory, she was greeted by 7,000 marching Salvationists with flags and flutes, bands and drums on India Republic Day. Once again she was bedecked with garlands and expressed gratitude to God for the faithful work of the pioneers who had raised up the Army in Kerala. A massive, beautifully decorated pandal was erected for the expected 6,000-strong congregation.

The sounds of bands and the tumultuous beating of traditional drums greeted the General when she visited the Army's Leprosarium and Hospital at Puthencruz. An elephant caparisoned in gold added to the jubilant welcome. In opening a new residence for the aged, she noted the deficiency of the water system and was quick to respond by offering a grant toward the hospital's water supply project.

Thousands of seekers knelt at the mercy seat during her campaign in the India Northern Territory in January 1990. In Mizoram, where a very high percentage of the population are Salvationists, with two being ministers of the government, Burrows addressed a mammoth open-air rally. In her response, she said the Mizoram Salvationists who live in high mountainous areas are "close to heaven." She led a dedication for a newly built corps and laid the foundation stone for a memorial community hall. A contingent of Salvationists from Myanmar had traveled for three days to join with their comrades in Mizoram for the General's visit.

Her itinerary included an active list of engagements in New Delhi, and later she traveled to Punjab where she was again showered with garlands and praised for her courage in visiting this terror-infested province which had a 5 P.M. curfew.

In Calcutta she was greeted with affection by Mother Teresa, world-renowned champion of the poor. Burrows was greatly impressed with Mother Teresa who stressed she did not give much importance to her fame but sought to make the world aware of the plight of poor people. "The work of our mission is not social work, but demonstrating the love of Jesus Christ in action," she told the General. The Nobel Peace Prize missionary nun and the General of God's Army discussed ways in which The Sisters of Charity and The Salvation Army could cooperate. Mother Teresa summed up the situation by saying, "When you need us, we come; when we need you, you come." At the end of their meeting, the two women knelt together in the chapel of the Mother House and each prayed for the work of the other.

Her India journey concluded with a successful campaign in the Army's India Western Territory.

Pakistan and the Army's Largest Project
In Pakistan in January 1989, Burrows wore the national grey uniform of shalwar chemise which had been made for her in Pakistan. It consists of loose harem type trousers and a long tunic—complete with draped scarf and a warm red cashmere shawl—in keeping with the Muslim tradition that women do not show their legs in public.

In the Muslim state of Pakistan, at Karachi and Lahore, she visited

General Eva Burrows and Mother Teresa pray together in Calcutta in January 1990.

the Army's social service projects, officer staff, and Advisory Board. In Karachi she was festooned with twenty-five garlands, weighing her down and reaching to her feet, and was showered with red rose petals, customary signs of welcome. Because Pakistan Salvationists are too poor to travel to one distant congress, her visit included three stops. During her campaign she enrolled new soldiers, saw scores make public decisions for Christ, and dedicated a training center to help young technicians return to rural village areas to work among the handicapped.

On a cold winter morning in northern Pakistan, General Burrows visited a camp which is home to refugees from neighboring Afghanistan. Afghans comprised the greatest number of refugees in the world, over 3½ million living in Pakistan, waiting for the Soviet occupation to end so they could return. In a visit to the Afghan Refugee camp, she saw the largest single project ever undertaken by the Army—caring for over 90,000 refugees. The scheme, supported by Canadian and U.S.A. government funding, had been in operation since 1982.

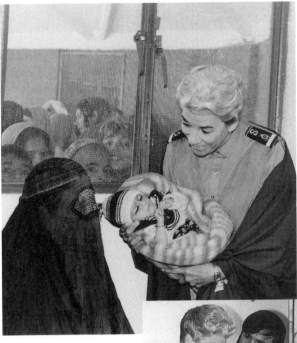

General Eva Burrows at Afghan refugee camp in Haripur, Pakistan, tenderly holds baby receiving treatment at the Army's health clinic.

General Burrows admires craft work done by Afghans in the refugee camp.

Burrows toured a health clinic and a tannery and leatherwork center where goods are made for export. She noted that the Afghans, living in huts of mud-dried brick, were very industrious, not wanting handouts but working to support themselves. Mingling among these people who fiercely sought to hold on to their freedom, she cradled a baby in her arms, and brought smiles to mothers and children who live in harsh isolation from their homeland.

In Pakistan she was granted an audience with the President, Mr. Ghulam Ishaq Khan. But she was disappointed not to see Prime Minister Benazir Bhutto who set quite a precedent in the rise of a woman to power in an Islamic state.

Commitment in Singapore

In Singapore General Burrows opened a new corps and noticed that funds had not been available to finish the floor. She announced that she would donate the money which she had recently received for doing a TV interview in the United Kingdom for the needed flooring materials.

In her preachment she pointed out that holiness is the unfolding

Standing on the deck of the boat named after her in Australia.

of the character of Christ in the believer's life, made possible when the Holy Spirit is allowed to take control of our lives.

Australia's Daughter Welcomed Home

A rather unusual venue marked a moment of the May 1988 Congress in Australia. When the Sydney Harbour Authority launched a new fire fighting ship in 1988, they chose to name the vessel *EVA BURROWS*. Its namesake was allowed to take the wheel and guide it through Darling Harbour for her entry to Sydney. Upon disembarking she was surrounded by press and television reporters covering the return of the Army's Australian-born leader coming ashore from a ship named in her honor.

In Sydney she addressed 1,800 officers, the largest such group up to the time of the 1990 International Congress. She was especially encouraged by the "amens" from the hundreds of retired officers, many who had been friends of her parents. At a missionary luncheon, she commented that she still considered herself as "an Australian serving overseas."

Spectacular pageantry with laser beams, fireworks, bands and banners, drums, drama, and cheers from the 10,000 persons gathered gave a rousing welcome to their Aussie General. She expressed her delight at being "home" and seeing again the Southern Cross. "But," she said, "we see the cross not just as a starry symbol but as the reason for our existence."

Sacred scenes of people queuing up to kneel at the cross crowned the jubilant Congress. During the prayer period it seemed all present at some time queued around the cross to kneel and sign covenant cards, including married couples and families coming to pray together. Burrows records, "I moved among the crowds and the wonderful music from the chorus and band echoed through the building. I was so pleased to meet my own family in the queuing crowd and we were able to pray together." The Congress climaxed with a great Hallelujah Windup with hundreds marching around the cross and banners waving throughout.

One of her acts at the Territorial Congress in Melbourne was the reinstatement to officer rank of Dr. and Mrs. Stephen Dale. He was giving up his surgical practice to take an appointment to the Army's mission station in Zambia and then to direct the Army's hospital in Zimbabwe.

When she had been Territorial Commander in Australia, Burrows

331

With Prime Minister Robert Hawke, Canberra, Australia, 1988.

had taken on Parliament in a number of issues. She was back in her
element as she participated in a Saturday morning march by the
Army on the Parliament House. It was not a protest march but one
with a proclamation. General Burrows on the steps of Parliament
House read the Army's proclamation and then handed it to the
Victoria state premier. The proclamation (which had been published
in daily newspapers, and 5,500 copies of which were handed out
during the march) called on the government and the people of Victoria "to recognize the values and standards of Christian principles as
a model for living."

In 1988, General Burrows had visited with Prime Minister Bob
Hawke of Australia. Her first meeting with him in Canberra had
been just prior to her departure for London to take up the office of
the General. Now the Prime Minister greeted her with a kiss and an
informal, "Hello, Eva. So nice to see you again." He called for tea
and they had an animated conversation. They spoke of the needs of
the people and of the Christian faith in meeting those needs.

When the visit ended, General Burrows placed her hand on the
arm of the Prime Minister and said she was going to pray for him.

With Queen Beatrix of the Netherlands, and Commissioner Reinder Schurink, the Territorial Commander, 1987.

Bob Hawke, son of a clergyman but now an acknowledged agnostic, was deeply moved as they bowed their heads and General Burrows prayed for the nation, the government, the Prime Minister and his family. It was a hallowed moment. With tears glistening in his eyes, Prime Minister Hawke thanked the General and then gave her a good-bye peck on the cheek.

Upbeat in the Netherlands
Queen Beatrix joined with General Burrows and more than 2,000 Salvationists in Amsterdam to celebrate the Army's Centenary Congress for the Netherlands in May 1987. Burrows delighted her audience by responding to their welcome with a greeting in Dutch. She challenged Salvationists at the historic event to "bring the qualities of the past alive in new and contemporary ways." By the close of the Congress, many of the territory's 10,000 Salvationists had pledged again their allegiance to Christ the King of kings.

The opening of three Army centers in one day in October 1991 was a "first" even for the well-traveled General Burrows. She dedicated the new Territorial Headquarters, a training complex, and a shelter for sixty homeless people in the red-light district in Amsterdam.

At the outset of her Generalship, Burrows had expressed concern for the malaise and declension that had come to The Salvation Army in Europe. Now she was seeing new life and vitality that augured well for the Army on the continent where it had first burst upon the scene. Its aging muscles were being flexed with a new strength and its heartbeat with a new passion to take on the challenges of a destiny within its grasp.

Sweden's Unique Theme Music

"Here in Sweden people need to rediscover who Jesus is," Burrows told the large crowd that gathered to welcome her. "We must be people who communicate our love for Jesus." In Stockholm, where women's rights are an issue, public interest was generated by a woman General and a woman Territorial Commander—Commissioner Anna Hannevik—leading the Army Congress. But it was said that the image that would remain with the Congress delegates would be that of people streaming to the mercy seat and of their General kneeling with them in prayer. It was reported that the theme music of the congress in Stockholm was the sound of footsteps of seekers making their way to the mercy seat.

A Date in Denmark and Finland

In September 1990 General Burrows made her first visit to Copenhagen for the annual Congress in Denmark. She won applause for giving her greeting in Danish. She was received by Prime Minister Paul Schluter at the Houses of Parliament; he had known Salvationists since his boyhood and discussed Army matters for half an hour.

During her second visit to Finland in June 1989, General Burrows was received in an audience with President Mauno Koivisto at his palace. He was generous in his praise for the Army's social work in in that country.

"On Top of the World" in Norway

General Burrows led Norway's Centennial Celebration in January 1988 with meetings attended by royal guests and civic leaders. King Olav V, Crown Prince Harald and Crown Princess Sonja, the Lord Mayor of Oslo and other distinguished citizens were among those who paid tribute to the Army in the Oslo City Hall meeting.

Arriving at the palace of King Olav in Oslo, she observed for the first time in a visit to a head of state that the palace was virtually unguarded, and "amazingly open and vulnerable." She concluded that perhaps it was because Norway does not have the same fear of terrorist activities as some other countries. Their visit entailed very little protocol.

The king, eighty-five years of age, spoke of his pleasure in planning to attend the forthcoming centenary celebration of the Army. General Burrows expressed her gratitude for the generosity of the Norwegian government through its support of overseas projects by its charity arm—NORAD, mentioning in particular the Army's leprosy and AIDS program in Zambia and its hospital in Indonesia. Later, when the King and the royal family attended the Army's Music Festival, Burrows noted they joined heartily in the singing of the songs.

In the summer of 1991 General Burrows revisited Norway, presiding at its Commissioning, and opening in Oslo a new Army industrial enterprise with a recycling plant for used paper and clothing. One of the most advanced of its kind in the world, it will provide employment to more than 100 people. During her visit Burrows met with Norwegian Prime Minister Gro Harlem Brundtland. She expressed appreciation to her for Norway's contributions to development aid and also to the Norwegian government for having nominated The Salvation Army for the Nobel Peace Prize. Her visit concluded with a prayer for the Prime Minister and Norway.

In the summer of 1992 in Norway, General Burrows said, "I'm on top of the world," as she became the first General to visit Finnmark and Honningsvag, the latter the Army's northernmost corps in the world.

To Lands beyond the Sea

In March 1989 in Wellington for New Zealand's Congress, TV viewers across the nation shared in the live broadcast of the Sunday morning holiness service with General Burrows. In Fiji and Tonga she enrolled twenty-nine soldiers in what was described as a "grand Gospel meeting."

To the beat of Kundu drums, Salvationists from the villages in full traditional dress greeted their General in Papua, New Guinea with a special welcome dance. Later she was received by Mr. Ted Diro, the acting prime minister, who expressed his appreciation for the Army's work in New Guinea.

General Burrows' return to Sri Lanka in January 1987 was reported as "a rapturous homecoming" for the former territorial leader, featuring elephants, firecrackers, and Kandy dancers in "thrilling scenes of welcome and triumph." An audiovisual presentation of her years in Sri Lanka preceded her addressing the Congress meetings during which she enrolled soldiers, commissioned cadets, and addressed an ecumenical service in the local cathedral.

The internationalism of the Army was much in evidence at the fiftieth Anniversary Philippine Territorial Congress in April 1987, with Salvationists and musical groups from Southeast Asia, Australasia, and America present. Following General Burrows' commissioning of cadets and her Bible message, many of the 2,000 present responded to her invitation to make public dedications with the large hotel ballroom on Sunday evening becoming a sanctuary of dedication and praise.

General Burrows visited the Hong Kong and Taiwan Command in 1990 to celebrate Easter and the sixtieth anniversary of the Army's work. The 2,000-seat hall had been booked "in faith" since such a large building had never before been used for an Army meeting. Faith was rewarded with large attendances and many responding to the General's preachment on the claims of the risen Christ.

The ninety-fifth anniversary of the Army in Indonesia was celebrated with the visit of General Burrows. A highlight was her commissioning and dedication of a brass band from the Army's Medan Boys' Home in North Sumatra, a forty-eight-hour journey by bus. The youth were thrilled when the General dubbed them "the General's band." Later, in her visit to Jakarta the General conducted "her band" in a short march.

With the Troops in Europe

"This centenary is a challenge," declared General Burrows at the Italian Centenary Congress held in Rome in April 1987, during her first Easter weekend as General. The Italian Salvationists were not allowed to bask in past glories, but were urged to "Make the present Italy's finest hour." On Easter Sunday General Burrows preached on the power of Christ's resurrection, available to all to live a victorious Christian life.

The General's visit to Belgium for its centenary climaxed on Pentecost Sunday in May 1989. She called attention to the remarkable difference made in the lives of the apostles and today's disciples when filled with the Holy Spirit. Many responded to the challenge of the General and went forth from their personal Pentecosts to face the future in the power of God. In a private audience, Belgium's King

Baudouin showed keen interest in the Army's work and witnessed to his own deep personal faith.

Revolution in France

"Revolution was in the air in Paris," read the headline reporting on General Burrows' visit to France in April 1989. France was celebrating the bicentenary of the birth of the republic, and the General was in the city to conduct the Territorial Congress and to lead her troops in a spiritual revolution which would bring the kingdom of God in the lives of many men and women.

General Burrows began her first address of the weekend with a quotation from President François Mitterrand, who had received her at the Elysée Palace earlier in the day. The French Revolution, he said, had one revolutionary concept which had sent a resounding challenge round the world—liberty. And true liberty, Burrows emphasized, was to be found only in Christ.

Before the Congress ended, a revolution of love had swept through the ranks as many surrendered to the claims of Christ. "The spirit of 1789 pervaded Paris," recorded the report, "but the Spirit of

With President François Mitterrand of France, Paris, 1989.

God—ever contemporary, ever revolutionary—will pervade The Salvation Army in France in the months ahead."

An Intimidating Conference in Switzerland

On the day before Ascension Day, one of the most sacred days on the calendar in Switzerland, Burrows preached in the great cathedral at Lausanne, celebrating Christ's continuing presence with His people. Some 1,400 people jammed the cathedral for this May 1988 observance. Her message appropriately was based on Christ's Ascension promises, "Lo, I am with you always"—the promise of His presence, and "You shall receive power when the Holy Spirit comes upon you"—the promise of His power. She later said. "Never having been involved in Ascension Day services before, I had to prepare several addresses on this particular event in Christ's life The preparation was a benediction to me and I think I was able to share that spiritual blessing, even through translation."

In Bern she had what she described as "quite an intimidating confrontation." It had been arranged for her to meet with all the church representatives of the Swiss Evangelical Alliance. "Knowing something of the serious way that they take their theology in the land of Calvin, Zwingli, and other great men of the Reformation, I was anxious to present The Salvation Army's position with clarity and on a scriptural basis."

About thirty church leaders were present, including a Bishop of the Roman Catholic Church. She recorded of her meeting with this pride of ecclesiastical lions, "They all introduced themselves and when I discovered their prestigious church positions, I was even more concerned. However, I gave my presentation with a confidence borne of the Spirit, and with an assurance of the rightness of our nonsacramental position; also in the belief that The Salvation Army is part of the church, the body of Christ, and was brought into being by the will of God and in the power of the Holy Spirit. God answered my prayer and there was a warm reception to the talk and an interesting discussion period followed." As the swirl of discussion eddied around her, she discoursed fluently on such topics as the Army's ordination of women and its role in the World Council of Churches.

"One church leader spoke most sympathetically about The Salvation Army's position on nonobservance of the sacraments, saying we need never be defensive, because the whole life of The Salvation

Army is sacramental. The Roman Catholic Bishop was interested in the international structure of The Salvation Army, and made a comparison between His Holiness the Pope and the General. He wondered if I should be called Her Holiness the General."

In May of 1991 General Burrows revisited Switzerland to address the national youth councils and to commission cadets. The European training school for cadets is situated in Basel, on Switzerland's borders with France and Germany, and serves these three countries, as well as Belgium, Portugal, Italy, and Spain. The international delegates joined heartily in the multilingual expression of praise, worship, and dedication.

The Growth and Pain in Korea

"Amazing scenes in Seoul" was the headline of the *Salvationist* report on General Burrows' April 1988 visit to Korea. She went with high expectations, knowing that the church, including The Salvation Army, is experiencing phenomenal growth in that land that hosts the largest Christian church in the world—over 700,000 members, and the largest Christian service ever held—over 1 million for a Billy Graham crusade meeting. She recorded that her visit there turned out to be "far more thrilling and exciting" than she could have anticipated.

General Burrows was granted an honorary doctorate by Ehwa Woman's University, the largest women's university in the world, with 16,000 female students. The degree was awarded for her "devotion to the betterment of women's higher education and her contribution to world mission and development of services to humanity." The 4,000 students and faculty heard her speak on the subject of Christ's advanced views on the position of women. She said, "The wisest advice ever given to anyone was that given by a woman— Mary, the mother of Jesus, when she said, 'Whatever Jesus tells you to do, do it.' "

Burrows concentrated her message to the Korean Salvationists on a celebration of the past, with its rich and heroic history, and a challenge for the future. She commended them for their strategy for growth and their goals set for the next twenty years. Their officer strength alone had almost doubled in the last ten years and there was a current enrollment of seventy-one cadets.

At the Sunday morning holiness meeting 4,000 people crowded into the 3,000-seat auditorium. "And what a meeting it was," recorded General Burrows, "with great congregational singing, beautiful renditions by the songsters, moving testimonies, a great spirit of worship and prayer, and following the message a tremendous response to the mercy seat appeal. The Koreans are so intent in their prayers, often beating on their breasts or hammering their fists on the floor as they struggle for victory at the mercy seat. The whole experience was one of deep emotion and sincerity. The prayer meetings are not long because the response is immediate."

Her translator, Corps Sergeant Major Young, Ung-chul, took her on a walking tour through the red light district of Seoul where the Army hall is located. General Burrows observed, "Some of the girls on display in the windows were very young." The Salvation Army has three homes for women in Korea. Many of the residents are young former prostitutes.

In her presentations she commended the Koreans for having sent missionaries abroad to Canada, U.S.A., and Singapore. A total of over 5,000 rededications, 162 new converts, and 56 responses for officership took place during the General's visit. She summarized, "It had been a God-glorifying visit. I see the Korean Salvationists as people of evangelistic fervor, vision, and a sense of mission. They are people of the Word and prayer—groups meet every morning at 5:30 A.M. for prayer. They also have a deep social concern and compassion."

The harsh reality of living at the point of confrontation was seen by Burrows when she toured the demilitarized zone between North and South Korea and visited Panmunjom truce village. As she stood looking across the demarcation line she felt "a real sense of sadness at the division of this beautiful country. The situation is worse than the Berlin Wall, for there is no contact at all allowed. When the communists overran Seoul, several officers were taken away and never seen again. The lovely Seoul Boys' Home Band was marched away by the communists and has never been heard of since. There is just silence in this atmosphere of aggression and real life tug-of-war."

In February 1992, General Burrows visited Korea for a second Congress. More than 6,000 delegates gathered for what was a Pentecostal experience. A total of 976 seekers responded to the General's appeals, and 205 men and women offered themselves for service as Salvation Army officers. Fervent prayer once again was a hallmark of the Korean Salvationists. At the conclusion the Territorial Commander, Commissioner Peter Chang, said, "Under the leadership of

With President Roh, Tae-Woo of South Korea, February 1992.

our General, this largest and greatest Congress ever held in Korea has refreshed and rejuvenated us and led us to reaffirm our commitment to growth and disciple-making in this territory."

Burrows was impressed with the full day of Growth Seminars that drew 800 delegates. She recorded, "I was moved to discover that one of the seminar topics was 'The Reunion of North and South Korea and our Mission to North Korea.' "

At the Blue House

On April 13, 1988, General Burrows was granted a forty-minute audience at the Blue House with President Roh, Tae-Woo of South Korea. The President warmly thanked Burrows for the Army's work and agreed with her that the nation needed to maintain a strong moral stance. The General spoke of her prayer for the reunification of the land of Korea and, as the interview closed, asked if Commissioner Kim, the Territorial Commander, could pray. "It was a very ardent prayer," the General recalls, "for the President and the country."

In her second visit to Korea, Burrows again met with President

Roh, Tae-Woo. It was an historic moment for the Republic, with President Roh having announced the day before the acceptance of the Inter-Korean Accords for nonaggression and reconciliation between North and South Korea. Burrows expressed her prayer for the reconciliation and reaffirmed the Army's commitment to the people of Korea. The President commended the Army's exemplary service to the hungry and homeless, quoting from the Army's own motto, "You are a good example by giving your heart to God and hand to man."

Japan—Land of Tradition and Technology

General Burrows journeyed to Japan for their Congress, March 28–April 6, 1988. Less than 1 percent of Japan's population is Christian and religious belief is a mixture of Buddhism and Shintoism. It is also the country where Commissioner Gunpei Yamamuro's Common People's Gospel has gone into its phenomenal 561st edition.

She was impressed by the young Salvationists. "In a country like this, to wear the uniform and proclaim yourself to be a Christian cannot be an easy thing. Yet their faces glowed with the joy of the Lord." The exchange of business cards is a cultural tradition in Japan. At one dinner General Burrows, who had been forewarned, exchanged forty cards.

On Easter Sunday morning she conducted the swearing-in of forty-five new soldiers, representing varied age groups and walks of life. "The mercy seat was filled to overflowing time and time again as the marvelous miracle of God reaching the human heart resulted in people claiming His cleansing and a closer walk with the risen Christ."

On her second visit to Japan in February 1992, she said, "The Salvation Army in Japan has become a noble and illustrious movement, well known for its caring work and faithful witness to the Gospel." Burrows came to have a deep respect for the Salvationists in Japan, land of ancient tradition and modern technology, of turbocharged cities and the serenity of sculptured gardens.

During this second visit a reception was scheduled with the Governor of Tokyo, a highly venerated octogenarian. In a briefing in the elevator, Burrows found her cue for openers with her distinguished host. The governor greeted her cordially as they sat down over a formal serving of tea. Then he fell silent, leaving the conversational shuttlecock in her court. She scored well when she told him she had heard two things about him—that he had a social mind, achieving

342

great social schemes for Japan, and that he had a financial mind to assure the bills were paid. That discerning comment established an instant rapport and opened the way for a very pleasant tete-a-tete over their tea. Burrows once again had the savoir-faire for the situation at hand!

With the Emperor of Japan

In General Burrows' first visit to Japan, the aging Emperor Hirohito was ill and receiving no visitors, but an audience was granted with the Crown Prince Akihito and Princess Michiko. The Prince was already beginning to take over the Emperor's responsibilities. The interview was conducted in fluent English by the Crown Prince and Princess, both of whom were well versed in the General's biographical material. The Princess, who was educated at a Christian university, spoke with a spiritual sensitivity which the General found moving. She was distressed that in the material prosperity of her homeland, spiritual values were lost. On her second visit to Japan, Burrows was again granted an audience in the Imperial Palace, this time with His Majesty Emperor Akihito and the Empress. Such an audience is the highest honor accorded to a person in Japan.

The Greatest Challenge

As she looks out on the worldwide Army entrusted to her by God, what does General Burrows consider to be its greatest challenge? "It depends on which part of the world you consider, because the challenges differ. In the Western world it is the materialistic, humanistic philosophy that has made so many people push God to the fringe of their lives. In other parts of the world, it may be the challenge to present the Christian faith in an environment of non-Christian cultures and religions.

"There also comes to us the challenge to truly care for people—the refugees, the handicapped, the outcasts, the hurting. Our social and evangelistic work are inextricably bound together. It is our business to be among the deepest hurts of our world.

"But if you take the overall blanket challenge, it would be to draw people to Christ. And with that is the ministry of reconciliation—whether it be reconciliation of broken homes, broken marriages, or conflicts between races. We must work all the time for redemption and reconciliation."

"Every land is my fatherland for all lands are my Father's lands," declared the Army's second General, Bramwell Booth. In her world travels, General Eva Burrows has given up-to-date credence and application to that philosophy of The Salvation Army. Her life and ministry resonate with the commitment in the words of an earlier Eva, General Evangeline Booth —

> *The world for God, The world for God,*
> *I give my heart, I will do my part.*

32

★ ★ ★ ★ ★ ★ ★ ★ ★ ★ ★ ★ ★ ★ ★ ★ ★ ★ ★

THE LEGACY

"I hope I will be remembered as a General for the people."

On July 8, 1993, Eva Burrows will retire as General of The Salvation Army. A fanfare of Farewell Salutes for General Eva Burrows will be launched beginning with a U.S.A. Celebration in April 1993, led by Commissioner James Osborne, the National Commander. Preceding the public Salute in New York, a banquet will be held in her honor at the United Nations with ambassadors invited from all the countries in which The Salvation Army serves. On July 3, 1993 her official retirement program will be held in London, led by the Chief of the Staff and attended by Salvationists from around the world. A grand welcome home will be held in Melbourne, Australia as she returns to her homeland to take up residence in retirement.

Burrows aspires to realize her lifelong ambition to learn to paint in oils and to return to the University to take theological studies. She also hopes to be able to give some service in Africa or Asia "in a practical way, at the ground level. I was a missionary for so many years, and never happier than when I lived in Africa."

Long before her retirement she already is accepting invitations to speak and preach throughout the world. As she comes toward the end of her marathon mission, she obviously has no intention of slowing down. God willing, she will no doubt cross the finish line with an impressively strong kick.

The Legacy

Major Jenty Fairbank, Director of the Army's International Heritage Centre in London, has a keen insight and sense of history. She makes the discerning observation, "When we don't have her anymore, then we'll see that we had someone very special."

When it's all over, and the General's office and all its duties are left behind, how would Eva Burrows like to be remembered? What would she want as her legacy to The Salvation Army? "I would like to feel that The Salvation Army is known more as a church and not just a social service agency. I would not mind so much if I'm forgotten, as long as the Army has grown. I hope I will be remembered as a General for the people, and especially a General for youth, because I believe in giving youth their place. They challenge us, shake us up, and help us to move forward.

"There are many things I hope for, but if you ask me my ambition, I would say very simply and humbly, my ambition is just to please God."

The Salvation Army has had its Generals, several with a special quality that stood out. Among them Albert Orsborn the poet, Erik Wickberg the statesman, Arnold Brown the orator, Clarence Wiseman the evangelist, Frederick Coutts the writer. But Eva Burrows eludes any such narrow categorizing or stereotype. She is both an ideologue and a pragmatist. She is a woman for all seasons.

Touching the Future

Normally the office of the General does not allow for great action. "But," observes an associate, "she has somehow pulled the rabbits out of the hats. She has managed to make an impact in several vital areas." Retired General Arnold Brown, who considers Burrows his protege, sums up with emphasis, "She has done it. She really has done it."

Commissioner Paul A. Rader shares, "In my judgment one of the most significant parts of the legacy of General Eva Burrows is her repositioning of the Army as an essential part of the Evangelical movement. She has done this by taking the risk of exposing herself to some rather daunting and demanding speaking opportunities." Indeed Burrows has proved her mettle in various theological forums such as *Lausanne II, Congress 88,* the *Swiss Evangelical Alliance,* the Annual Ministers' Conference at Asbury Theological Seminary, and a series of lectures at Fuller Theological Seminary. Rader summarizes, "It was she who called us to join in prayer with other Evangelicals all over the world, praying for world evangelization on Pentecost Sunday. In so many ways she has contributed to a whole new perception of the Army in the Evangelical community."

Eva Burrows will no doubt be treated kindly by history and will be remembered as the General who "got things done." But for those who will know her only from the historical records, the archives, a book, or a photo, they should know that above all, during her tenure she was "the people's General." She loved and cared for people and made a tremendous impact on innumerable lives around the world.

The one who has moved so easily through all the executive suites and chandeliered chambers of power has remained first and foremost a woman of deep compassion and commitment for the people God called the Army into being to serve. Her greatest legacy will be the immeasurable enrichment and spiritual impact on the many lives she touched for God.

Lt. Colonel Lucille Turfrey, speaking from a long friendship and official relationship, states, "There is the mark of greatness upon the General. In a sense she is as the years have made her. Yet, over and beyond that, the touch of God upon her life has enhanced her capacity for leadership. The potential for world leadership of our movement was always there; yet it is as though a mantle had fallen about her shoulders.

"In every way she is the same Eva. Here is no new person, suddenly made so by a High Council's decision. It is still the young Captain who joyously strode the ground of Africa, the Colonel who so inspired her ICO delegates, the competent Commissioner who accepted confidently and triumphed in the immense administrative responsibilities of three territories, loved her people, took up the cudgels against injustice, and shared her faith so effectively in the proclamation of the Word."

It was said of Charles de Gaulle that his greatness was not because de Gaulle was in France, but because France was in de Gaulle. The greatness of Eva Burrows is that she carries within her a compelling and shining vision of The Salvation Army and its mission under God and her own calling of God to that mission.

Valedictory

Since that day in August 1948 when Eva Burrows as a teenager committed her life totally to Jesus Christ, her entire life and work has been an eloquent expression of that dedication. Her favorite Bible verse and life theme has been "that Christ may have the preeminence" (Colossians 1:18). Eva Burrows has emphasized to me that above all she desires for this volume to bring honor and glory not to herself but to her Lord, that her devotion to Him may be interwoven through all the pages. May it be so.

APPENDIX I

CHRONOLOGY OF EVA BURROWS

September 15, 1929	Born in Tighes Hill, Australia
December 1946	Graduation from Brisbane High School
March 1947	Entered Queensland University
August 1948	Dedication of total life to Christ
May 1950	Bachelor of Arts degree from Queensland University
August 1950	Attended International Youth Congress, London
September 1950	Entered International Training School in London as a Cadet
May 1951	Commissioned as an officer of The Salvation Army, with the rank of Lieutenant, and appointed to assist at Portsmouth Citadel Corps
October 1951	Appointed to study at London University Institute of Education in preparation for service in Africa
June 1952	Earned postgraduate certificate in education at London University
November 1952	Appointment to education staff at Howard Institute in Rhodesia
May 1960	Earned Master of Education degree from Sydney University
May 1960	Appointed head of Teacher Training School, Howard Institute in Rhodesia
June 1965	Appointed vice-principal at Howard Institute in Rhodesia
January 1967	Appointed principal at Usher Institute in Rhodesia
July 8, 1967	Promotion to Glory of Eva Burrows' mother
July 1967	Appointed a delegate to the International College for Officers in London
January 1970	Promotion to Glory of Eva Burrows' father

June 1970	Appointed vice-principal of International College in London and promoted to rank of Lt. Colonel
January 1974	Appointed principal of International College For Officers, London, with promotion to rank of Colonel
November 1975	Appointed leader of Women's Social Services in Great Britain and Ireland
January 1977	Appointed Territorial Commander for Sri Lanka
May 1977	Attended her first High Council
June 1979	Appointed to rank of Commissioner
December 1979	Appointed Territorial Commander for Scotland
January 12, 1980	Heart attack
April 1981	Attended her second High Council
October 1982	Appointed Australian Southern Territorial Commander
April 1986	Attended her third High Council
May 2, 1986	Elected 13th General of The Salvation Army
May 30, 1986	Appointed *Officer of the Order of Australia*
July 9, 1986	Took office as General
May 18, 1990	Extended term for two years as General
June 16, 1990	Officially reopened the work in Leipzig, in then East Germany
November 1, 1990	Establishment of United Kingdom Territory
November 1990	Recommenced Army's work in Hungary
February 1, 1991	Inauguration of new IHQ structure
July 1991	In St. Petersburg, reopened Army's work in Russia
September 1991	Visit to Prague, confirming Army's work in Czechoslovakia
October 1991	Spoke to an estimated 30 million people on BBC World Service Phone-in program
March 1992	Reopened Army's work in Moscow
November 1992	Visit to Cuba
February 1993	Visit to China
June 1993	In Moscow, commissioned first Russian Cadets
July 9, 1993	Enters retirement

APPENDIX II

VISITS WITH HEADS OF STATE AND ROYALTY

June 1986	Prime Minister Bob Hawke, Canberra, Australia
October 1986	President Ronald Reagan, Washington, D.C., U.S.A.
May 1987	Queen Beatrix, Amsterdam, Netherlands
September 1987	Prime Minister Robert Mugabe, Harare, Zimbabwe
November 1987	President Dr. Kenneth Kaunda, Lusaka, Zambia
January 1988	King Olav V, Oslo, Norway
April 1988	President Roh, Tae-woo, Seoul, South Korea
May 1988	Queen Elizabeth, London, England
May 1988	Prime Minister Bob Hawke, Canberra, Australia
January 1989	President Ghulam Ishaq Khan, Karachi, Pakistan
March 1989	Prime Minister Ted Diro, Papua, New Guinea
April 1989	President Francois Mitterand, Paris, France
May 1989	King Baudouin, Brussels, Belgium
June 1989	President Mauno Koivisto, Helsinki, Finland
September 1989	President Daniel T. arap Moi, Nairobi, Kenya
September 1989	Prime Minister Alphonse Souchlaty Poaty, People's Republic of Congo
September 1989	President Marshal Mobutu Sese Seko, Zaire
September 1990	Prime Minister Paul Schluter, Copenhagen, Denmark
October 1990	President George Bush, Washington, D.C., U.S.A.
March 1991	Life-President Dr. H. Kamuzu Banda, Blantyre, Malawi

April 1991	President Robert Mugabe, Harare, Zimbabwe
June 1991	Prime Minister Gro Harlem Brundtland, Oslo, Norway
September 1991	President Vaclav Havel, Prague, Czechoslovakia
February 1992	Emperor Akihito and Empress Michiko, Tokyo, Japan
February 1992	President Roh, Tae-woo, Seoul, South Korea
November 1992	President Fidel Castro, Havana, Cuba

ACKNOWLEDGMENTS

It is with deep gratitude that I acknowledge those who contributed to the contents of this book. Without them it could not have been written.

Commissioners' Conference of Salvation Army leaders in the U.S.A. for their sponsorship: Commissioners Kenneth L. Hodder, Kenneth Hood, James Osborne, Paul A. Rader, Harold Shoults, Robert E. Thomson, and Colonels Harold Hinson, Ronald Irwin, Edward Johnson, Robert Watson.

Correspondents: Lt. Colonel Ian Begley, Major Barbara Bolton, Joy Bugler, Hilda Bulle, Marie Chalk, Major Emma Chimusaru, Mrs. General Olive Coutts (R), Major Graeme F. Crowden, Moses Dube, Major H. Ella, Colonel Gordon H. Fischer, Brigadier Jean Geddes (R), Alan Gill, Major Mrs. Margaret Goffin, Wendy Green, Brigadier Beth Groves (R), Colonel John Hounsell, Commissioner Jillapego Israel, Major Judith Johansen, Lt. Colonel Stan Kingston (R), Lt. Colonel Ernest Lamotte, Commissioner Ingrid Lindberg (R), Commissioner Roy Lovatt (R), Elias Marere, Jonah Blessing Matswetu, Commissioner Earle Maxwell, Mrs. Brigadier Jean Milley (R), Commissioner Albert Mingay (R), Lt. Colonel K. Brian Morgan, Commissioner David Moyo (R), Florence Muchanyuka, Benjamin Ncube, Absalom Nevanji, R. Nthubula, Major Lyell M. Rader, Jr., Commissioner Edward Read, Lt. Colonel Peter Rigley, Commissioner William Roberts (R), Commissioner Reinder Schurink, L. Sibanda, Colonel Ronald L. Sketcher (R), Dr. Bramwell Southwell, Margaret Southwell, Brigadier Catherine Stephen, Commissioner Robert Thomson, Colonel Arthur Thompson, Major Frances Tomlinson (R), Brigadier Margaret L. Trefz (R), Lt. Colonel Lucille Turfrey, Mrs. Commissioner Marion E. Westcott (R), Lt. Colonel W.J. Wickramage, Lt. Colonel Ruth Wilkins (R), Mallory Wijesinghe.

Interviewees: Colonel Malcolm Bale, General Arnold Brown (R), Robin Bryant, Captain Sylvia Burt, Commissioner John Clinch, Commissioner W. Stan Cottrill (R), Commissioner Ron Cox (R),

Lt. Colonel Leah Davids (R), Major Jenty Fairbank, Commissioner Caughey Gauntlett (R), Colonel Lilian Glase (R), Commissioner Peter Hawkins, Lt. Colonel Jean Issitt, Captain P. Jayaratnasingham, Robson Kanyepi, Captain Charles King, Commissioner John Larsson, Colonel Frank Linsell, Commissioner Andrew S. Miller (R), Lt. Colonel Almey Morris (R), L.L. Mutowemba, Envoy David Ndoda, Commissioner James Osborne, Major Ruth Richards, Commissioner William Rivers, Major Janice Sapsford, Major Robert Street, Colonel Lyndon Taylor (R).

Readers of the manuscript: Priscilla Burgmayer, Major Marlene Chase, Major Jenty Fairbank, Lt. Colonel Miriam Frederiksen, Mrs. Colonel Marjorie Gariepy, Stephen Gariepy, Elisabeth Garrett, Lt. Colonel Jean Issitt, Commissioner John Larsson, Commissioner Ingrid Lindberg (R), Jeff McDonald, Commissioner Andrew S. Miller (R), Commissioner James Osborne, Commissioner Paul A. Rader, Commissioner William Rivers, Dr. and Mrs. Bramwell Southwell.

Victor Books for their professional service and dedication to the quality and ministry of this book: Myrna Hasse — production manager, Joe DeLeon — cover and text design, Carole Streeter and Barbara Williams — editors, Mark Sweeney — vice-president.

Prayer partners for this daunting project are owed a special debt of thanks — Colonel Lilian Glase (R), Commissioner Ingrid Lindberg (R), Lt. Colonel Lyell Rader, O.F. (R), Major Ruth Schoch, Dr. Bramwell Southwell, Margaret Southwell, Ung-chul Young.

My computer, for its wizardry that made possible the accomplishment of this project within our stringent time frame.

INDEX

361

Prostitution   135, 142

Queen Beatrix   333
Queen Elizabeth   93, 288
Queensland University   35–36, 38, 40, 42–43

Racism   83–84, 203–4, 308
Rader, Evangeline   249
Rader, Lyell (R)   313
Rader, Lyell M., Jr.   115–16, 249
Rader, Paul A.   260, 321, 347
Rasmussen, Tora   284
Read, Edward   229
Read, Harry   151, 229
Reading   67–68
Reagan, Ronald   170, 214, 276, 316–17
Refugees   13, 305, 328–30, 343
Regent Hall Corps   48, 52, 286
Regional College for Officers   114–15
Resilience   238–39
Restructuring of IHQ   217–23
Retirement   345
Richards, Ruth   248
Ridley, Giles   229
Riga   266
Risden, Bob   136
Rive, Philip   70, 91, 109, 283
Rivers, William   121, 149, 166, 175, 194–95, 222
Roberts, William   161–62
Roh, Tae-Woo   341–42
Romance   37, 40, 245–46
Royal Albert Hall   46, 51, 201
Russia   259, 261, 266–73
Ruth, Fred   272
Ryan, Geoffrey   270
Ryan, Max   245

Sacraments   179, 338–39
Salvationist   13, 227–28
Samuel, Mannam   151
Samuel, N.J.   156

THE AUTHOR

Henry Gariepy, is a Colonel and Editor-in-chief of The Salvation Army National Publications for the U.S.A. with headquarters in Alexandria, Virginia. He is a prolific author of books and articles. Two of his nine books have exceeded 150,000 copies with some going into multiple editions and translations abroad. The author maintains an active schedule of speaking engagements, including Bible conferences and national writers conferences. He is an outdoor enthusiast, including being a three-time twenty-six-mile marathon finisher. He earned his Bachelor of Arts and Master of Science degrees at Cleveland State University. He, and his wife, Marjorie, take great delight in their four children and twelve grandchildren.